Whole
Language

Emily Beesh

Whole Language
Theory in Use

edited by

Judith M. Newman

Heinemann

Portsmouth
New Hampshire

#12552601

Heinemann Educational Books Inc.
70 Court Street, Portsmouth, New Hampshire 03801
Offices and agents throughout the world

10   9   8   7

Library of Congress Cataloging-in-Publication Data
Main entry under title:

Whole language.

   Bibliography: p.
   1. Language arts (Elementary)—Addresses, essays,
lectures.   2. Language arts (Elementary)—Curricula—
Addresses, essays, lectures.   3. Language acquisition—
Addresses, essays, lectures.   I. Newman, Judith,
1943–
LB1576.W487   1985   372.6   85-17636
ISBN 0-435-08244-2

Designed by Wladislaw Finne
Printed in the United States of America

Reta Boyd has been teaching elementary school children in the city of Halifax for twenty-eight years. She has been interested in the relationship between language and learning. During the past few years she has become involved in writing with her students. She has also been exploring the role that language plays in science.

James Boyer is currently teaching an experimental resource class for elementary students aged seven to twelve. A graduate of Trent and Acadia universities, he has been a resource teacher for the Halifax County–Bedford School Board for five years. He is particularly interested in how teachers' expectations affect what students actually learn.

Susan Church, formerly a resource teacher, is now a curriculum supervisor with the Halifax County–Bedford School Board. She holds an M.Ed. from Boston University, an M.A. from Acadia University, and has taken graduate classes at Dalhousie and Mount Saint Vincent universities. Her interests include developing whole language curriculum for older students in junior and senior high school.

Meredith Hutchings received her B.A./B.Ed. degree from York University. She is presently developing a handbook for adult literacy tutors as part of her M.Ed. work at Dalhousie University. As a teacher of five- to ten-year-olds at the Dalhousie University School, she is interested in the development of children's reading and writing through the use of thematic curriculum.

Winniefred Kwak is a classroom teacher of seven- to ten-year-old children at the Dalhousie University School. In addition to an M.A. in Sociology, she has recently completed an M.Ed. degree from Dalhousie University. For the last several years she has been most concerned with the development of whole language curriculum in classrooms with vertical grouping of children.

Judy Mossip, now a teaching vice-principal, has taught both third- and fifth-grade children for the Halifax County–Bedford School Board. She obtained her B.A. degree from University of Western Ontario, her B.Ed. from Dalhousie University. Her efforts to make language learning functional have led her to explore learning opportunities that arise from real-world situations.

Dr. Judith M. Newman is an independent scholar, currently half time in the Department of Education, Mount Saint Vincent University in Halifax. She teaches both undergraduate and graduate classes in the role of computers for language development. Her current research interests include exploring ways of helping teachers see themselves as learners.

Olga Scibior is with the Department of Education, Mount Saint Vincent University in Halifax. Her doctoral studies at Indiana University have focused on children's spelling development. Her interest in how children learn to spell developed out of her classroom experiences with third- and first-grade children.

Wayne Serebrin is a fifth-grade teacher with the Halifax Grammar School. His earlier experiences with four-, five- and six-year-old children led him to explore children's writing. In particular, he has become interested in children's need to be real authors. He is also interested in using computers for helping children develop as readers and writers.

Sumitra Unia is a fifth-grade teacher with the Halifax District School Board. She holds a B.A. from Manchester University and an M.A. from Dalhousie University. For the last several years she has been using journal writing as a vehicle for exploring whole language theory in her classroom.

Contents

Most readers expect, I suppose, to encounter some sort of framing of the topic at the start of a book. Generally, authors outline how they will proceed, provide indices, titles, forewords, etc., to prepare readers for what is to come. To set a frame is the intention of this opening chapter. Yet, I find myself in the uncomfortable position of being unable to tell you succinctly what "whole language" is. One reviewer, for example, suggested I define that term in my opening paragraph. But I can't, because there is no simple definition of "whole language." For me, "whole language" is a shorthand way of referring to a set of beliefs about curriculum, not just language arts curriculum, but about everything that goes on in classrooms. I subtitled this book "Theory in Use" in an attempt to allude to the complexity of the problem.

I frequently hear teachers mention an interest in "the whole language approach" as if "whole language" were some kind of published program which can be purchased. But "whole language" isn't an instructional approach in the sense in which we usually use such terms. "Whole language" is a philosophical stance; it's a description of how some teachers and researchers have been exploring the practical applications of recent theoretical arguments which have arisen from research in linguistics, psycholinguistics, sociology, anthropology, philosophy, child development, curriculum, composition, literary theory, semiotics, and other fields of study. And, as with all theoretical arguments, each of us is obliged to explore the practical ramifications in our own way. In lieu of a definition I offer to share what I have learned about "whole language" over the last several years, from my own learning and teaching, from my sharing with classroom teachers, and from my observations of children as a way of explaining what I currently understand by that term.

The ideas for this book, as with most publications, began to develop a couple of years before anything was written. I had been meeting regularly with several teachers. In our study sessions we discussed current theories of reading and writing and we explored classroom application of those theories. Our primary intention was to support one another as we tried out what we hoped were theoretically sound curricular ideas. As we explored whole language curriculum in the classroom our understanding of theory grew. As we learned from our students we were better able to talk about our theoretical beliefs.

Several summers ago we decided to share our ideas with other teachers interested in knowing more about whole language theory and curriculum. We organized a week-long workshop, using that forum to share what we were trying in our classrooms. The following year we repeated the workshop. We realized at that point, however, that we needed to begin writing about what we were doing, both to clarify our ideas for ourselves as well as to share our thinking with others. We recognized that other teachers were beginning to explore the same theoretical ideas and were looking for assistance and support translating those ideas into curriculum.

So we began to write about our explorations. We approached this language task in a "whole language" manner. We brainstormed; we met to discuss which aspects of our experiences we should highlight, and how we should explain them. We wrote rough outlines and shared those with one another. We continually returned to the research literature to enrich our understanding of the issues. We wrote, we shared our texts, then we argued about whether we were saying what we wanted to say. The more we talked, wrote, and read, the clearer our ideas became and the easier it was to capture what we wanted to say.

We had many insights about learning and about curriculum along the way. First of all we discovered our teacher role was changing. Instead of disseminating or transmitting information we found ourselves shifting to what Douglas Barnes (1976) calls "interpretive" teaching. That is, we began to see writing and reading (in fact, all aspects of language) as a means by which students "can take an active part in their own learning." We came to realize that knowledge isn't something which exists separate from people; people are actively engaged in creating what they know or understand. We recognized that as students write and read they reshape their view of the world and extend their ability to think about it. To this end we explored how various experiences and invitations encouraged students to play an active role in the shaping of their own knowledge.

We started watching our students more closely. We had to learn to use our growing understanding of language and literacy development to help us make sense of what the students were showing us. We needed to learn to observe how they engaged in learning—to "kid-watch," as Yetta Goodman (1980) calls it—so that we would be better able to offer experiences which supported those learning efforts. And as we learned to kid-watch we discovered two things. First, we discovered that the information we were seeking was there right before our eyes and under our noses all of the time. We began to see how each student was conducting his or her own experiments, one testing out ideas about punctuation, another exploring the use of dialogue, a third trying a new reading strategy. Because the students were exploring various aspects of literacy we learned that activities had to be broad enough to accommodate many different experiments simultaneously. Second, we began to understand that our observations in turn helped consolidate what we understood about reading, writing, and learning. We came to believe that activities had to be based on the strengths of students. We came to realize that mistakes are an inevitable part of language use; that students can and will take responsibility for their own learning when that learning is perceived as interesting and valuable.

In fact, we were learning that the "what" of curriculum was inseparable from the "how." We were learning that each activity we offered students carries with it both intended as well as inadvertent messages—what Frank Smith (1981) refers to as "demonstrations." Smith argues that demonstrations "are continually and inevitably provided by people and products, by acts and artifacts." Learning, he maintains, "occurs in the presence of demonstrations, and what is learned is whatever happens to be demonstrated at the time" or rather, it depends on the learner's interpretation of the situation, the way the learner makes sense of what is going on. As Elliot Eisner (1982) has expressed it, "what pupils learn is not only a function of the formal and explicit content that is selected; it is also a function of the manner in which it is taught. The characteristics of the tasks and the tacit expectations that are a part of the structured program become themselves a part of the content." In other words, we began to see that what our students learned had a great deal to do with what we ourselves believed about learning and the way in which those beliefs were reflected in the learning activities we offered.

We came to understand curriculum in a different way; to see it not as a prescribed course of study or a particular set of instructional materials but as the mental trip taken by each learner (Harste & Stevers, 1984). The activities we were offering students represented a potential for learning, but learning occurred only when they engaged with some of the demonstrations possible. The problem, of course, was that we couldn't predict which aspects of any particular learning event would draw the attention of which learners. Consequently, we needed to provide as complete and as complex a learning environment as we could so that students could engage with the activities in whatever way was useful to them.

As our understanding of what was meant by demonstration expanded we could see that while we needed to create activities for the students we couldn't expect all students to approach an activity in the same way with the same outcome. We discovered that activities had to be open-ended and had to be shaped by student input. The notion of "invitations" as opposed to assignments began to take shape. And here was where the kid-watching came in. We had to be willing to be informed by our students (Harste & Burke, 1980). We had to learn from what they were trying to do, to accept their efforts, and to extend the next "invitation" based on our understanding of the language learning process as a whole.

We also came to appreciate the social nature of learning. Contrary to common belief, learning, we discovered, isn't something one struggles to do on one's own. One of the most important insights gained from the research on child language development has been the significant role that other individuals play in a child's becoming an oral-language user. Gordon Wells (1981) showed how language learning must involve collaboration in the negotiating of meaning, where talk is a form of social action, where contexts are actually produced by the language participants in the process of producing language. Similarly, the work on writing development emphasizes the necessity for feedback from other individuals during the writing of a piece and afterwards. Frank Smith (1981) counters the myth that writing is a solitary activity by asserting that writing "often requires other people to stimulate discussion, to provide spellings, to listen to choice phrases, and even just for companionship in an activity which can be so personal and unpredictable that it creates considerable stress." Reading, too, is a social activity. Social in the sense that the meanings of words and sentences are not abstract and autonomous but rather embedded within a structure that is dependent on the situation in which they occur with its assumed background of practices, purposes, and goals. Meaning of both written and oral texts is constrained and modified by the interpretive community (Fish, 1980).

As we came to understand that meaning is socially constructed and context-dependent, we realized that learning must involve collaboration—collaboration between students and teachers, between students and published authors, between writers and readers, and among students themselves. This meant that we had to structure the learning environment in such a way that students had ample opportunity for sharing with one another, for exchanging information, for reading and discussing their own writing as well as that of published authors, for sharing ideas as they solved the problems with which they were engaged. We had to learn to make it legitimate for students to seek out others for feedback and help when the going was difficult or for celebrating a piece of work with which they were satisfied.

We could see that for too long we had been laboring under the illusion that we were in control of students' learning. The extent to which this was untrue became evident as we saw students surmount some of the negative demonstrations embodied in our activities. We watched them disregard what they felt was misguided or useless. They continued to trust their own sense of what was useful for accomplishing what they wanted to. The interesting students were the less proficient, less confident ones, who accepted that we had the answers, who bought into our limited strategies for learning, for reading and writing, rather than trusting their own. Our challenge was to discover ways of helping them come to value their own strategies.

Only gradually did we learn to create activities which encouraged students to risk using their own strategies. While basal readers and other textbooks were often reasonable sources for reading material, the activity suggestions offered in the accompanying teachers' manuals were usually not very helpful; they presented a simplistic, fragmented view of language and learning to our students. We, on the other hand, were wanting our activities to say to our students that, while language and learning were complex, they had strategies which would work for them. We borrowed heavily from the efforts of many people both past and present. Along the way we encountered Russell Stauffer, Roach van Allen, Jeanette Veatch, Doris Lee, Robert and Marlene McCracken, James Moffett, and many others in whose writing we recognized some of the principles we were wanting to incorporate into our own teaching. Suggestions for activities in the work of Yetta Goodman and Carolyn Burke, Virginia Woodward, Jerry Harste, Dorothy Watson, Donald Graves, Donald Murray, Lucy Calkins, Donald Holdaway, Marie Clay, Douglas Barnes, Andrew Wilkinson, Peter Elbow, and many others featured prominently in what we tried.

The chapters which follow represent our attempts at making sense of the research and illustrate some of the ways we tried to create a learning context in which reading and writing became tools for finding out about the world. We tried incorporating into these activities what we'd learned about language and language learning:

- Language and language learning are social activities; they occur best in a situation which encourages discussion and a sharing of knowledge and ideas.
- Language learning necessarily involves the risk of trying new strategies; error is inherent in the process.
- Reading and writing are context-specific; what is learned about reading and writing is a reflection of the particular situation in which the learning is occurring.
- Choice is an essential element for learning; there must be opportunities for students to choose what to read and what to write about.
- "Whole language" activities are those which support students in their use of all aspects of language; students learn about reading and writing while listening; they learn about writing from reading and gain insights about reading from writing.
- Our role as teachers is best seen as "leading from behind" by supporting the language learning capabilities of students indirectly through the activities we offer them.

We discovered that the clearer we are concerning our beliefs about language and language learning, the sharper our focus on what is happening in front of our eyes. The more we know about how language operates and how students learn, the easier it is to recognize materials which on the surface look like whole language, but actually fall short. We've realized that for instruction to be coherent, it must be based on a conceptual framework. We learned to ask ourselves:

- What do I believe about language and language learning?
- What do I want this activity to demonstrate about reading, writing, and learning?
- Why is this a useful activity for some particular student or group of students?

Why do we think "whole language" is such a useful idea? Because it offers us a perspective which allows us to observe students. Because curriculum based on whole language insights offers both students and teachers continuous demonstrations about how meaning is constructed by an interpretive community, about how reading and writing aren't solitary activities, about how oral and written language are tools for learning. Because it offers us all, students and teachers, criteria for judging our own performances. Because it lets teachers and students be learners together.

This book, then, reflects our current development as "language users." During the process of writing it, we learned a great deal about reading and writing and about the relationship between theory and practice. Our understanding about how students learn and about activities which can support their learning efforts changed quite dramatically and not without considerable anxiety and conflict. We hope our exploration will be of use to other teachers on the same journey. As Tolkien's Bilbo Baggins so aptly put it:

The Road goes ever on and on
   Down from the door where it began.
Now far ahead the Road has gone,
   And I must follow, if I can,
Pursuing it with weary feet,
   Until it meets some larger way,
Where many paths and errands meet.
   And whither then? I cannot say.*

There are many people to thank for their help. First, we must thank the students for letting us explore our ideas with them, for the enthusiastic way in which they learned, and for their willingness to share their learning with us. Without the students none of us would have grown.

I want to thank the teachers whose writing has made this book a reality. I could have struggled to communicate what's involved in creating and sustaining a whole language classroom. It has, however, been important for the teachers to tell about it themselves. They have been able to capture the sense of open-endedness necessary in a whole language classroom far better than I ever could, because they were writing about their own experiences.

And thanks to all of those interested teachers who wanted to know more about whole language. Their constant requests for "How do you . . ." provided the stimulus which helped us decide to share our experiences.

* From *The Fellowship of the Ring* by J. R. R. Tolkien. Copyright © 1965 by J. R. R. Tolkien. Reprinted by permission of Houghton Mifflin Company and George Allen & Unwin (Publishers) Ltd.

1

Insights from Recent Reading and Writing Research and Their Implications for Developing Whole Language Curriculum

Judith M. Newman

We have come a considerable distance over the last two decades in our understanding of the complexity and sophistication of young children's oral and written language development. Recent research has made it abundantly clear that children have a complex repertoire of strategies which serve them well when it comes to making sense of either oral or written language. As more and more pieces of the puzzle have fallen into place we have come to appreciate the extent to which learners themselves create meaning out of their experiences with language, both oral and written. We've learned to recognize the importance of the social nature of learning, the role which language plays in creating the learning environment, and the extent to which language is itself determined by the social situation. We've learned that young children are aware of the print world and are able to make sense, in ways we've never before suspected, of the writing which surrounds them. Equally impressed, we've learned they are able to create meaning themselves with pencil and paper long before their writing looks representational to our conventional eyes. We've also discovered that readers, young children as well as adults, engage in transactions with print by orchestrating a complex of cues of which the marks on the page are but one source of information. We've learned that readers need to supply knowledge about how language works, knowledge about the world, knowledge of what strategies to try in order to create meaning as they read. We've also begun to have some notion of how a written text is created; to understand the intricate interplay between the writers' intentions and the emerging text; we've begun to appreciate the essential interdependence of all aspects of language, but particularly of reading and writing.

As our theoretical understanding of what's involved in language development (oral as well as written) has grown, however, it has become evident that much of what we have traditionally thought to be important in terms of language instruction, particularly instruction in reading and writing, needs to be questioned. In light of what we now understand about how children learn and use language, many of our classroom practices seem to rest on inadequate or, worse, inappropriate assumptions. As teachers, then, we need to know what current research has demonstrated about many aspects of language learning in order to build curricula which can support children's language development. The discussion which follows presents the findings of four areas of research and considers some instructional implications for language instruction which derive from them. First we will explore children's oral language development. Next, we will investigate how very young children both become aware of and use written language. We will also look at the reading process to gain some insight into what transpires when people read text. Then we'll examine what has been learned about writing. Finally, we will consider the implications of what we have learned for the development of curriculum.

Learning Oral Language

One uncomfortably warm summer evening, about half an hour after she'd been put to bed, three-year-old Jane was up once again calling from the top of the stairs. I went to see what she wanted.
"I'm rather tired of water, you know," she said rather assertively.
"What would you like instead?" I asked her.
"Some apple juice," she replied.

Let's look at the intricacy of this brief language exchange. The circumstances help explain why Jane was up. The evening was still very warm, her bed uncomfortable, and she was having some difficulty falling asleep. She knows, however, that I expect her to stay in bed, so when she does finally decide she wants a drink she does it in a way that gives her control of the conversation. She doesn't ask directly, which would give me the option of refusing her. Instead she makes an indirect assertion which informs me she's probably already drunk the water I left by her bed and at the same time forces me to continue the conversation by returning an open-ended question. That then allows her to tell me what she really wants. Both her tone and her topic organization tell me this isn't just another "get me a drink of water" request. Tone and content as well as context direct me to infer she's really thirsty and increase the likelihood I will comply with her intention—to get a drink of juice. Through this example we can get a sense of the sophisticated orchestration of semantic/syntactic structure, contextual constraints, and conversational moves of which a young child is capable.

However, such an appreciation of the linguistic sophistication of young children is relatively recent. Not long ago we used to believe that children were passive receptors of language, that they developed speech by imitating first the sounds and later the words in their environment. We thought parents and other individuals directed this imitative behavior through some form of "positive reinforcement." We first began to move away from this simplistic explanation of oral language development when Noam Chomsky (1957) demonstrated

9

**Insights from Recent
Reading and Writing
Research and Their
Implications for
Developing Whole
Language Curriculum**

that language is based on a complex set of syntactic, or grammatical, rules for relating the sounds of language and meaning. Chomsky's view of language had an important impact on our understanding of language learning because it led us to see children as actively engaged in generating language. Their oral language development was seen to be rule-governed, and researchers began to investigate how children created such rules.

Following Chomsky's work on syntactic structure a number of linguists (Chafe, 1970; Fillmore, 1973) began to explore the semantic, or meaning, aspects of language. Similarly, research on children's language development shifted its attention to the semantic dimensions of children's oral language. At this point several things became apparent. We realized that children use what appear to be the same utterance to express quite different meanings (Bloom, 1970). For example, a child's statement "Twuck!" might be a comment about a vehicle passing in the street, it might be a request for a particular toy, or it might be the identification of an object in a picture, the child's particular meaning being determined by the situation. This research helped us see the intimate connection between language and context. It became clear that parents use situational cues to help them understand what their children mean. We also came to appreciate how highly skilled children themselves are at using contextual information to understand what adults are saying to them (Clark, 1973; Macnamara, 1972). In other words, children become language users by mapping language onto experience: the situation provides clues to the meaning of words; words, in turn, lead to an elaboration of concepts. The situation provides the support for negotiating the relationship between the two.

At about the same time, Michael Halliday (1975) began exploring the functional aspects of language. He argued that the beginnings of language are identifiable when infants begin offering stable vocalizations which their parents interpret as meaningful communication. Such vocalizations, while having little of adult form and usually intelligible only to family members, function as language; they initiate and maintain social interaction and they help children make sense of their world. With Halliday's work we began to understand how children create language through a process of social engagement with other language users.

Halliday's work (1978) also allowed us to appreciate the complexity of language in use. It let us perceive that every utterance serves several different functions simultaneously. For example, with every utterance speakers have some intention. They are trying to involve the listener in some way: they may be trying to direct the listener to act; they may be trying to add to or modify what the listener knows; they may be trying to express feelings. At the same time, in order to communicate, speakers have to identify, select, and organize the elements of their present, past, or imagined experience in ways that are relevant for their current intentions and then translate these elements into meaning represented by the semantic and syntactic structures of language. In addition, speakers may wish to reveal an affective response to what is being talked about, to show some degree of involvement or distance with the topic, to indicate the formality or informality of their relationship to the listener. And all of the above are affected by the particular situation in which the conversation is taking place. The context determines the speaker's purpose and the sequence of conversational moves, what information is included, and its organization (based in part on how much prior knowledge the speaker thinks the listener already shares). The context also influences how something is said with the speaker taking into account the social situation and anticipating the needs of the listener.

Take four-year-old Matthew, for example: He was enjoying himself at a birthday party when his mother arrived to retrieve him. Noticing her in the doorway with his coat in hand, he turned to her without any hesitation and asked, "Wouldn't you like to talk to Donna [the adult hostess] for a few hours?"

His question engages his mother and attempts to divert her from her intention—going home. It reflects the fact that he's been enjoying himself and that he is a sufficiently skilled language user to be able to concoct a reason for his mother's wanting to stay rather than directly express his unwillingness to depart at that moment. He has identified, selected, and organized the elements of the situation. He has anticipated the response of his listener and offered an alternative which he hopes will appeal to her.

Children come to understand how language works by participating in conversation, by using whatever linguistic resources they have available, and in the process building both their knowledge of the world—of meaning itself—and the semantic/syntactic forms through which that meaning is expressed. The child requires a partner in order to become proficient at listening and speaking. Gordon Wells and his coworkers (1980) discovered that the relatively "smooth" flow of conversation with a young child owes a great deal to the adult's skill in tracking the child's utterances. Their research has shown that parents' overriding concern is with making communication work rather than with trying to "teach" their children to talk. In order to arrive at the child's probable intended meaning parents must interpret the situation as well as draw upon their knowledge of their child's interests, wants, needs, and past linguistic abilities. They use what- ever language cues the child provides and supply the remaining information necessary for understanding from these other sources. Having made an interpretation, parents then comment on the object or activity which is the focus of the shared attention, then expand and elaborate on the meaning they think the child is expressing. By doing so, they provide the child with information about which aspects of a particular experience are important. These adult contributions are the means by which children enlarge their communication resources as well as their understanding of the world and how it operates. In other words, the parent role is, according to Wells, to "lead from behind" by letting children take the initiative, then supporting and extending their efforts.

Children, on the other hand, receive feedback on what they have said. They discover whether their meaning (both interpersonal and conceptual) has been understood. They discover the interactive effect of an utterance through any confirmation and/or extension given. By means of conversation they also receive demonstrations of language

11
**Insights from Recent
Reading and Writing
Research and Their
Implications for
Developing Whole
Language Curriculum**

in action (Smith, 1981)—they encounter the range of meanings in their variety of forms which correspond to and help define whatever meaning has been created from the children's interpretation of the situation.

The following conversation between Christopher (age two and a half) and his mother illustrates the complex interplay between adult and child that facilitates language development. Christopher is playing with some puzzles on the kitchen floor while his mother is washing the supper dishes.

M: You practice over there.
C: You practice right here.
M: All right. Well, I have to finish clearing up the supper right now. So practice by yourself.
C: Practice myself?
M: Mmmmm . . .
C: Look, the basket, the basket is, the basket is broke these things. Me want help. You want help. I give you help. You want . . .
M: I don't need any help.
C: Well, I better . . .
M: Looks to me like you're the one who needs the help, not me.
C: (grunt)
M: Do you need help?
C: YES! I DO HELP!
M: What do you need help doing?
C: These, these, these won't let me pick them up.
M: I'll let you pick them up.
C: No. Oh, don't know. Got pick one. No!
M: If you're finished with them you can pick them up, but if you want to play with them, don't.
C: DON'T! (pause) Don't dare let you any. Oh forget the block. Got all my . . . and yours. Them, they're mine. That way that one.
M: That one's kind of hard. Are you going to use that puzzle or another one?
C: Unh. Unh. Watch me. Both one. Think. . . . Want any help? Don't want any help. It's to me puzzle. Got one puzzle, got two puzzle.

Two important aspects of language development are evident in this conversation. First, we see the importance of parental tracking. Christopher's mother, usually able to interpret his intentions, responds meaningfully to what he says. Notice she doesn't correct his "mistakes." This is most obvious when Christopher has trouble asking for help with his puzzle. His mother first interprets his "You want help, I give you help" literally. Then she offers her understanding of the situation. Finally, she assists by asking him a direct question. All three of Mother's strategies are instances of "leading from behind." She is supporting and extending Christopher's language attempts.

We also see the role which feedback plays in language development. By participating in conversation Christopher learns which utterances work and which don't, and he is able to select from his mother's demonstration of adult language those elements which help him say what he wants to say. We see this happening when his mother offers him the choice of either putting his puzzles away or continuing to play with them. She says, "If you're finished with them you can pick them up, but if you want to play with them, don't." Christopher's "DON'T" tells her which choice he makes. We also see this occurring in his direct question to himself at the end of the conversation. His final "Think. . . . Want any help? Don't want any help" (compare Mother's direct question "Do you need any help?" earlier) is his way of handling, for the time being, the I/you reference problem which caused confusion earlier in the conversation.

But let's look at how language is often experienced in school settings. In the following example of teacher/student language (Lindfors, 1980) the teacher is trying to explain the relationship between the sun and earth:

> **T:** Now here we have the earth revolving around . . . (pregnant pause) . . . What does the earth revolve around?
> **C-1:** The sun.
> **T:** The sun. Right, Marie. But as it moves around the sun, it also keeps turning, like this (turns ball) on its own . . .
> **C-2:** Center.
> **T:** Well, it's kind of . . .
> **C-3:** *AXIS!*
> **T:** Its own *axis.* Right. And do you know what we call that? (pause) When it goes around on its own axis? We say the earth ro . . . (hopeful pause)
> **C-2:** Revolves?
> **T:** No, not revolves. We say it ro . . .
> **C-3:** Rotates!
> **T:** Rotates! That's right. It rotates on its own axis. And that makes day and night. Now if we live right here on this side of the earth where my finger is, are we having day or night when the earth is like this? (T indicates spot away from sun.)
> **Cs:** Night.
> **T:** We're having night. And when we've turned like this so that the side we're on is facing the sun . . . ?
> **Cs:** Day.
> **T:** Day. We're having *day.* Very good.

This example illustrates three common features of school language. First, we see the teacher repeating the children's answers. This repetition effectively closes the exchange. The discussion moves from teacher to child back to teacher, instead of the other way around. We also see this teacher fishing for specific answers. The teacher pauses at strategic places waiting for the children to offer the word she wants rather than giving them either the information or the opportunity to discuss the concepts she wants them to consider. The teacher engages in what amounts to a guessing game—"Guess what word I'm thinking of." This teacher is also asking questions which can be answered by a single word. These questions with expected answers limit rather than expand children's language and learning.

There seem, then, to be several contradictions between what we have learned from research about children's oral language

13
**Insights from Recent
Reading and Writing
Research and Their
Implications for
Developing Whole
Language Curriculum**

development and the way language is often experienced in school. First of all, in many classrooms, children are no longer treated as partners in conversation. Teachers, instead, generally decide what is going to be talked about and how. Leading from behind becomes control from in front. Children are less free to ask questions; that is now largely the teacher's prerogative. Nor are they permitted to engage in discussion among themselves. During periods of instruction, then, children are often faced with a kind of conversational exchange which allows them little opportunity to expand their use of language.

A second potential problem with some school language environments arises because whereas most talk, and consequently most learning, at home develops out of common, practical everyday activity, most of the talk in school centers around tasks involving contexts which are relatively abstract and about which the children have little prior knowledge. Many children, therefore, discover that their language learning strategies, which have served them effectively at home, are less effective and sometimes even counterproductive in the classroom.

What do our observations of children's oral language development advise for creating an effective language learning environment in school? They suggest that we need to learn from the example parents offer us. Parents spontaneously create an environment in which children are invited to be conversational partners. Children are able to question and comment freely about whatever is going on. As teachers, we must make it possible for children to learn through talk. We must invite the children into conversation both with us and with one another. The conversation between parents and children deals with practical, everyday activity; it uses the familiar to extend the child's understanding of the world. Most of this conversation occurs in the midst of ongoing activity, while dressing, shopping, or preparing meals, and capitalizes on the children's own language learning strategies. As teachers, we must let children discover meaning through activities which simultaneously extend their facility with language as well as their understanding of the world. Parents respond meaningfully to their children's language efforts. They sustain their children's involvement and participation in ongoing conversation. Intuitively aware that children learn to listen and talk by listening and talking, parents track children's meaning, interpreting and filling in as required by the situation. As teachers, we must learn to read meaning into children's talk; we must learn to interpret their intentions and help them find ways of saying what they want to say. And parents quickly discover how much children learn both about language and the world in general by eavesdropping on the conversation of others. As teachers, we must create situations in which children are able to learn from exchanges in which they are only peripheral participants.

These insights into oral language learning have relevance for children's literacy development as well. How might we offer children the contextual and interactional support they need in order to figure out how print works? What sort of an environment might we create so that six-year-old Steven doesn't answer the question "When you're reading and you come to something you don't know, what do you do about it?" by asking in return, "Do you mean at home or at school?" The differences between functioning as a written language user at home and at school is something of which Becka, aged eight, is also aware.

One day Becka was listening to her five-year-old sister, Abigail, reading a favorite story aloud. At one point Abigail came to the word "fetch" in the text. Without pause she said "get" and continued reading. Becka interrupted her, however. "That word was *fetch*," she informed Abigail. To which Abigail retorted, "It makes sense, doesn't it?" "Well," replied Becka, "that's OK to do at home, but at school you have to read what's on the page just like it is." Becka has learned that at home it's OK to read for meaning but at school what matters is getting the words right.

The excerpt (Figure 1–1) from a six-year-old's news journal demonstrates how a teacher can encourage a child's exploration of written language through her willingness to "read" meaning into his writing.

Figure 1–1
Translation:
My father caught a partridge
he found it in the greenhouse

This teacher has made it legitimate for Shawn to write about what really interests him rather than forcing him to limit his writing to what he can spell conventionally. His father's catching a partridge in the greenhouse was important to Shawn. The teacher, understanding that, responds to the meaning he's attempting to share, and at the same time demonstrates adult written language in use. She is also trying to extend Shawn's engagement with written language with her question. It succeeds. Shawn reads what she's written, then continues the "conversation."

Learning to read and write would be much easier if we would take the time to understand how children become language users in the first place and then created classroom environments which supported both oral and written language development. Learning to become a proficient language user requires that children have lots of opportunities to experiment with both oral and written language. Using language from the outset in a whole range of literacy contexts enables children to create the knowledge and strategies necessary for fluent reading and writing in the same way as they have with oral language.

First Encounters with Written Language

Not until we were able to appreciate the complexity of children's oral language development did it become possible for us to consider young children's awareness of and interactions with written language. What have we actually learned about young children's ability to use written language? The research I want to examine next has explored very young children's knowledge about how print works. This research, much of it done within the last decade, has startling implications for literacy instruction.

Two early studies (Durkin, 1966; Clark, 1976), concerned with the correlation between home and school environments and the reading proficiency of young readers, showed that these children came from situations where there was a wealth of opportunity to see people reading and to be read to, to see others writing and to use paper and pencil themselves. These studies strongly suggested that children's literacy development depended on the literacy experiences available in the home.

The first studies dealing with young children's use of written language appeared in the mid-1970s. Clay (1975), for example, demonstrated that children's early writing begins well before the children have received any formal reading and writing instruction. Her exploration of children's first writing helped us accept their nonconventional approximations as important for writing development. Read's investigation (1971) of children's development of speech sounds opened windows on children's understanding of spelling. He was able to describe some rules which served as the basis for children's spelling inventions. Children's misspellings now took on new significance.

Bissex (1980) and King (1982) each presented a case study of a young child's reading and writing development. Both case studies revealed the functional and communicative nature of children's early literacy efforts, highlighting the importance of experimentation in what the children were doing. Other researchers such as Ylisto (1977) and Doake (1981), interested in how young children learned about reading, were able to show that young children approach written language expecting it to make sense and to have predictable structure. They argued that young children's ability to re-create favorite stories was important for reading development. Ferriero's research (1981) made us aware of the universality of young children's developing awareness of print. Her Mexican preschool children of illiterate parents engaged in the same kinds of experiments, they interacted with print in the same rule-governed ways, as children from more advantaged circumstances.

The most exciting insights, so far, have been offered by Harste, Burke, and Woodward (1981, 1983). As a result of their investigations of the reading and writing of three-, four-, five-, and six-year-olds they began to see literacy development not in terms of stages, but in terms of four specific language strategies—*text intent, negotiability, risk-*

taking, and *fine-tuning language with language.* These four strategies, which characterize the literacy expectations of adult language users, were used by even the youngest children as they wrote and read.

First, Harste *et al.* found all of the children expected written language to make sense. They responded to books and environmental print in ways that were meaningful both for the children and for the researchers. When asked to write their names, a letter, or a story, they did so and were able to re-create their messages. Harste, Burke, and Woodward called this first strategy *text intent.*

The following illustration may help clarify this notion of text intent.

This past Christmas I was waiting in line to have dinner at a family restaurant. In the corner of the waiting area stood a Christmas tree with a stack of wrapped presents beneath it. At the head of the line was a sign "Please wait to be seated." A two-year-old was waiting in line. Having surveyed the Christmas tree for a few moments, she walked over to the sign, which she was hardly able to reach, and pointing to the words, read aloud, "Do not touch. Do not touch."

This two-year-old expects written language to be meaningful, to be related in some way to the situation. While the situation which was salient for her differed from the one intended by the sign, her expectations of functionality are clearly evident in her response. Not only does she expect the sign to be related to the context, her reading shows expectations of form as well. "Do not touch" is an imperative, structurally similar to "Please wait to be seated." Text intent—expectations about functionality and form of written language—is obviously developed far earlier than we have previously suspected.

Harste, Burke, and Woodward also showed that children use freely what they know about language and the world in general to make sense of their encounters with print. They demonstrated the cognitive flexibility and ingenuity which young children display when dealing with written language. Because children expect print to be meaningful, they are compelled to use whatever knowledge they possess to create a meaningful message. This strategy of *negotiability* is seen in the following example.

Three-year-old Jane and I were leafing through a collection of package labels, wrappers, and signs. She was telling me what she thought they said, how she knew that, and anything else she could share. We came to the following symbol:*

"That's gas," she told me. I asked her how she knew. "Well, my mommy gets her gas there, and I've seen it lots of times." I asked her if she could tell me anything else. "Is that a three?" she asked, pointing to the **Ɛ**. "It looks like one," I replied. "Well, it's an E, then," she informed me emphatically.

* The "ESSO" trademark is used with the permission of Exxon Corporation.

17
**Insights from Recent
Reading and Writing
Research and Their
Implications for
Developing Whole
Language Curriculum**

Jane is using all of what she knows about what signs can say, where she's seen them before, what elements they consist of, in orchestrating her response. Like most other young children confronted with that particular sign, Jane responds with the generic label. That's not really surprising. We don't usually say we're going to get Esso, or Shell, or Texaco as we head toward the gas station; we usually answer children's queries (if they're raised at all) with "We're going to get gas." More likely, we simply drive into the service station and "fill 'er up." The ESSO sign signifies gasoline to Canadians. In addition, Jane knows something about the marks which are used in the sign. She tries out this knowledge in response to my question. Her "Is that a three?" allows us insight into what she considers to be the range of possibilities. Notice her reaction to my intended neutral reply. Because I didn't confirm her hypothesis she assumes she is incorrect, considers other features of the display, decides what she sees must be an Ξ, and, instead of asking me about it, informs me of her conclusion.

Through Jane's brief exchange we see a three-year-old engaging with print, using all the knowledge she possesses which she judges to be relevant in order to create a meaningful message. This is one sort of negotiability. Negotiability, however, sometimes involves an altering of the contract in order to make sense. I encountered an instance of this sort of negotiability in the local newspaper's daily smile not long ago:

Motorist parked beside a sign which reads:
   FINE FOR PARKING.
Policeman to motorist:
   Don't you see the sign?
Motorist to policeman:
   Yes, and I agree with it completely.

The humor in this situation arises out of the motorist's choosing a meaningful but unintended interpretation for the message.

Very young children use this strategy of negotiability readily.

One day a teacher was making cookies with a group of five-year-old children. As they talked about the ingredients she wrote the names of them on the blackboard. One of the items she wrote was *vanilla.* Jeff was heard to comment, "Oh look, there's an eleven in that word!"

In order to produce this response Jeff needed not only to transform the two l's into ones but also to see them as a single unit. He uses all he has learned about print and about the numeral system to make sense of this graphic display. When asked how he knew about the eleven, Jeff explained they had been exploring numbers bigger than ten and "two ones make an eleven." Although the teacher had written a word, Jeff's current interest in numerals allowed him to select from that graphic display those elements which were relevant for his hypothesis. Jeff changed the communication intent to one which made sense to him.

A third strategy used by all language users is *risk-taking*. This strategy involves both the attitude and actions of hypothesis testing.

According to Harste, Burke, and Woodward, it is characterized by experimenting with how language works. Let's compare six-year-old Shawn's first independent writing at school with something he wrote about a month later (Figures 1–2, a and b).

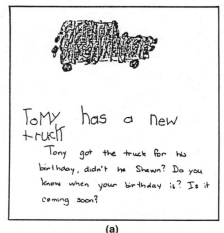

(a)

Figure 1 – 2
Translation:
Tony has a new truck

Translation:
Hallowe'en is soon and witches are coming
and ghosts are coming

In his journal about Tony's truck (Figure 1–2a) Shawn shows us some of the constraints he feels to be operating in the writing situation. On this occasion, early in the school year, Shawn isn't willing to take many risks. He writes very little and he is particularly concerned about spelling; of the five words he's chosen to produce, four are spelled conventionally. Shawn had to decide what it was he wanted to say, then he had to remember it while he found each of the words somewhere in the classroom so he could copy it. Nevertheless, his teacher was well aware of the considerable effort which went into that writing. To support his efforts, she responded to what he had to say and indicated her interest in knowing more. A glance at an entry from his journal a month later (Figure 1–2b) shows Shawn's expectations have changed. Not only is the message longer, but it also reflects a change in his concern about spelling. He's become willing to take some risks in order to make writing a communicating activity. He's decided to choose words which convey the meaning he wants instead of limiting the message to those few words he can copy or knows how to spell. Rather than playing it safe, Shawn has decided to experiment with language. This decision to take risks allows Shawn to grow as a language user.

Fine-tuning language with language is the fourth strategy language users employ. This notion suggests that what we learn from any language encounter becomes a resource for subsequent language situations; oral language provides input for written language and vice versa. The fine-tuning of language with language can be seen to be developed in even very young children. For example, four-year-old Robbie and his dad had gone kite flying. As often happens in such instances, the string broke and the kite took off. To help alleviate

19
Insights from Recent
Reading and Writing
Research and Their
Implications for
Developing Whole
Language Curriculum

Robbie's dismay at having lost his kite, his dad took him to his office. His dad, a radio columnist, had an editorial to compose and while he was working he gave Robbie a tape recorder and suggested he tell a story about what had happened. The following "script" was dictated:

I was flying my kite with my dad, when all of a sudden the string broke and the wind whisked my kite away. Was I ever mad. My kite was black with yellow streamers. We looked for it everywhere, but we couldn't find it at all. We even looked in Dartmouth. Maybe we'll buy another one soon. This is Robbie Thompson reporting.

Robbie's story shows how new language is created out of old. In his story we can see the effect of his previous experiences with books and reading. "I was flying my kite with my dad, when all of a sudden the string broke and the wind whisked my kite away." His choice of words, the syntactic structure, and the story organization clearly reflect his awareness of the formal language of writing. His closing attests to Robbie's recognition of the parallel between his dad's radio commentaries and his own recording of this story. At four Robbie is an extremely sophisticated language user. He has learned to use experiences with written language as the resource for creating new language events.

While each of the language strategies—text intent, negotiability, risk-taking, and fine-tuning language with language—has been discussed separately, it needs to be emphasized that they occur in concert. Two-year-old Daniel allows us to see the complex transaction that takes place between the child as a language user and a particular graphic display.

A synagogue is situated near one exit of the 401 highway running through north Toronto. The building's architecture includes a pair of arches representing the Ten Commandments, which can be seen as you drive by:

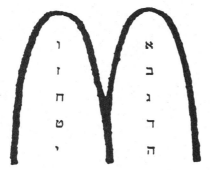

One Sunday, Daniel and his family were out driving. "Look, a Jewish McDonald's!" was Daniel's comment to the rest of the family as they went past that particular exit.

Daniel expects print to make sense. He is familiar with McDonald's signs. He has also learned there are at least two kinds of writing, one of which is called "Jewish." His ability to integrate these two pieces of knowledge produces an original yet understandable meaning for this particular graphic display. He takes a risk by sharing his observation with the family; he uses the language from past experiences to create new language. While the product of Daniel's transaction with this print differs from that of an adult, the strategies he's used for making sense are the same. Daniel, at two and a half, is already an adept user of written language. He is able to make complicated decisions about the meaning of print he encounters.

While many instructional programs treat the development of reading and writing as if it were a uniform linear process, the research on the literacy development of young children makes it clear there is no magic number of words children need to recognize or letters they need to be able to form, or words they have to be able to spell before we can let them read books by themselves and write texts of their own. The following letter (Figure 1–3) written by a five-year-old preschooler is evidence of the sophisticated command of written language possessed by a great many children.

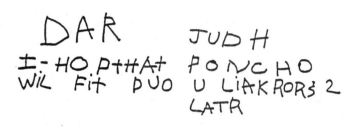

Figure 1 – 3
Translation:
Dear Judith,
I hope that poncho will fit. Do you like Robbie's 2 letters?

This child is already familiar with many of the simple conventions of written language. She knows writing goes from left to right, from top to bottom, with spaces between words. She knows writing makes use of letters of the alphabet, and she can produce them. She's acquainted with apostrophes. She knows she should begin her letter with a salutation. She knows she can choose to use a numeral to represent a number. Her functional spelling of such words as *HOP* (hope), *WiL* (will), *DUO* (do), *U* (you), *LiAK* (like), *ROR'S* (Robbie's), *2* (two), and *LATR* (letters) is very close to convention. She is definitely aware of graphophonic (symbol–sound) relationships. The meaning she wants to convey is easily understood.

This research has shown that although the products may be unconventional by adult standards, even two-year-olds have well-developed strategies for exploring written language through reading and writing. These data suggest we need to provide open-ended classroom activities in which written language functions as it does in the real world. From the very beginning children need to experience reading in a variety of circumstances: for following instruction, for shopping, for finding out what's on TV, for learning more about the world. They need to experience the pleasure of being read to and of reading by themselves. Children also need to use writing for the same purposes adults use it: to keep journals, to leave messages and notices for others, to write letters, to record recipes, to keep track of

21
**Insights from Recent
Reading and Writing
Research and Their
Implications for
Developing Whole
Language Curriculum**

experimental observations, and to explore ideas. Children need to write from their reading and read what they have written. By broadening the opportunities for engaging with literacy we make it possible for children to use the natural strategies they already possess for making sense of written language. Our role is to create situations in which children can discover the predictability of print for themselves.

The Reading Process

Our present understanding of reading as a "psycholinguistic guessing game" is based, in large measure, on the work of Kenneth Goodman (1967, 1973, 1977; Gollasch, 1982). Goodman and his colleagues examined the oral reading of young children as well as older students and adults. Using ordinary stories, in normal reading situations, they demonstrated that all readers make "mistakes." Goodman came to call these mistakes "miscues" because his analyses showed that each deviation from the text made by a reader could be explained on the basis of that reader's use of one or more of the available cue systems; readers' miscues had some syntactic, semantic, and/or graphophonic relationship to what was on the page. Readers were engaged in constructing meaning by coordinating information received from the print with the graphophonic, syntactic, and semantic knowledge they were supplying. By monitoring the sense of what they were reading, they were able to self-correct, or not, as required.

The importance of readers' use of "nonvisual information" has also been emphasized by Frank Smith (1971, 1982, 1983). He, too, describes readers as engaged in anticipating meaning through a process of sampling the print guided by their syntactic, semantic, and graphophonic expectations. Under these circumstances, the more nonvisual information (general knowledge in conjunction with specific knowledge about language) possessed by readers, the less detailed attention they are required to give to what is on the page. Conversely, the less prior knowledge possessed by readers, the more they must depend on print cues.

Let me illustrate this.

Ten-year-old Hugh was handed a copy of "The Fisherman and the Mermaid" and asked to read it orally. It begins:

Once upon a time, an old gray fisherman lived in an old gray hut beside the old gray sea.

Hugh read:

Once upon a time, an old gray . . . gay (No) . . . gray? fisherman? (No, no . . . umm, that's gray) . . . gray fisherman? [giggle] . . . lived in a old gray hut [pause] beside an old gray sea.

Hugh's oral reading offers some important insights into the reading process. We can see from the transcript that Hugh is attending to more than the print. He begins: "Once upon a time, an old gray . . . gay (No) . . . gray? fisherman? (No, no . . . umm, that's gray) . . . gray fisherman? [giggle] . . ." Hugh correctly reads "gray" but abandons it because, as his subsequent comments to himself reveal, he has difficulty with the notion of a gray fisherman; he substitutes "gay," but a closer examination of the word confirms it to be "gray." Hugh rereads "gray? fisherman?," giggles, then reads on: "... lived in a old gray hut beside an old gray sea," substituting "a" for "an" and "an" for "the" without any attempt at correcting them. While "a" and "an" have some visual similarity, "an" and "the" have little. His substitution of one determiner for another reflects Hugh's selective use of the print information, as well as his use of both the semantic and grammatical relationships of language as he's reading. These substitutions indicate his awareness of the author's repetitive use of a descriptive phrase. They also demonstrate that Hugh is more concerned with having the text make sense than with matching every word on the page. He continues as shown in Figure 1–4.

	LINE NO.
... Each day was the	26
same, except that on rainy days he sat on ~~a~~ _The_ bench inside	27
his house ⊙and _mending_ ~~mended~~ his nets ~~and~~ _or_ _smoking_ ~~smoked~~ his pipe.	28
One bright ⊙and rosy morning, the old fisherman found	29
his nets much heavier than they ⟨had ever⟩ been before.	30
My, he thought to himself, what a fine catch I have this	31
morning. I must have four _pole+lock_ pollock, and perhaps some	32
herring, and certainly an extra fine mackerel for my dinner.	33
But, when he pulled ⊙in his nets _up_∧ and emptied them into	34
his boat, he found he had∧ _a_ two _fin_ fine flat pollock, _©and a_ six	35
shivery herring, and a mermaid.] A slim, silvery mermaid	36
with long golden hair that was tangled in the old nets.	37

Figure 1 – 4

Ⓡ — = repeat   _pole+lock_ pollock = substitution

Ⓒ — = self-correction   nets _up_∧ = insertion

⊙and — = omission   had⟨ever = reversal

Throughout this passage Hugh draws upon his sophisticated syntactic and semantic sense. Notice the way in which he alters the grammatical construction of lines 26–28. Because the fisherman's activities were the same "each day," Hugh anticipates the present progressive tense instead of a simple past tense for both verbs. Furthermore, his rendition of the text has the fisherman either mending the nets or smoking his pipe (rather than doing both at the same time, since smoking a pipe usually requires the use of one hand). His omission of "and" (line 29) improves the flow of that particular sentence, his reversal of the words "had ever" (line 30) is grammatically acceptable, and his reading "pulled his nets up" (line 34), with the omission of "in" accompanied by the insertion of "up" positioned after the object, is a complex grammatical manipulation of the text.

Before Hugh began reading, the interviewer asked Hugh what he would do if he came to a word he didn't know. "I'd either sound 'em out, break 'em into syllables, or just take a guess," Hugh answered.

23

**Insights from Recent
Reading and Writing
Research and Their
Implications for
Developing Whole
Language Curriculum**

Hugh's reading of "pollock" (line 32) shows us how he actually deals with something unfamiliar. In this instance (and throughout the text) Hugh adopts a syllabication strategy when he meets something new. We have a sense that "pole lock" signifies something "fishy" for Hugh by the way he reads line 35: "... he found he had a two fin flat pollock. ..."

In this brief passage we can observe a proficient reader at work using his general knowledge of fairy tales, of fishermen, and of fishing in conjunction with a complex sense of the syntactic and semantic constraints of written language. We see him anticipating the author's intentions, predicting certain structures and meanings, confirming his predictions, and self-correcting only when his rendition doesn't seem to make sense to him.

What then, have been the major insights from the research on readers' miscues? First of all, this research has helped us appreciate that reading involves more than the information received from the page. In order to make sense of a graphic display, readers, even very young children, must call into play knowledge they have about how language operates, about how meaning is constructed, about how print relates to language, in order to make sense of what they're reading. This research has also shown us that reading cannot be an exact process, because in the interplay between the various sources of information a reader is coordinating, some misjudgments are bound to occur. The research has shown readers self-correct when what they have read doesn't fit into the meaning they are trying to construct.

The contradictions between what miscue research has shown the reading process to be like and what we frequently do in terms of reading instruction can have serious consequences for lots of children who fail to develop the strategies which allow them to become fluent readers. Because instruction so frequently overemphasizes the graphophonic aspects of reading at the expense of meaning, many readers develop a view of the reading process which makes them more concerned with accurate word identification than with understanding. Many nonfluent readers read the way they do because of the instruction they've received.

The realization that reading is predominantly an in-head phenomenon, that more is brought to the page than is received from it, has important implications for reading instruction. We've seen that readers must rely on prior knowledge, particularly their knowledge of language, in order to make sense of print. Even very young children are equipped with a sophisticated command of language. They've learned how to talk about things that interest them, using the language structures others use. They have considerable knowledge about their world, as well. While, by adult standards, this knowledge may be thought incomplete and sometimes illogical, nevertheless children have constructed complex notions of how the world operates. Even children from so-called deprived backgrounds have a wealth of knowledge gleaned from their own experiences. This knowledge is an essential resource for reading and learning to read. The materials we choose have to be written in the kind of language children have come to expect of books. Children's trade books, both narrative and factual, are an obvious source of material with their uncontrolled vocabularies, complex language, and stories encompassing topics of a wide range of interests. With such materials children are able to use what they know about language, the organization of stories, and the information contained in them to help them figure out how print works.

In this context, reading to children serves several important functions. First, reading to children demonstrates how fluent readers engage in the process. Children see how books are held and pages are turned. Reading to children lets them become familiar with the flow of book language. "Once upon a time" or "All of a sudden the wind whisked my kite away" becomes part of children's expectations of how written language ought to sound. Reading to children also exposes them to the ways in which stories are constructed. How characters are introduced, how events are sequenced, how participants in the story change as a result of what happens to them, all become a natural part of interacting with text. Furthermore, the books we read to children ought not to be limited to storybooks. The reading of factual books is important as well. The more we know, the easier it is to read. One of the important ways we learn about the world is through books. By reading factual material to children we allow them to become familiar with the ways in which information about the world is recorded and communicated. Factual books help children gain access to the wealth of knowledge which surrounds them.

The real value of reading to children is that it allows them to incorporate many of the subtleties of being readers without realizing it. Familiarity with the idiom of books, expectations of how a story might unfold, knowledge about where to look for answers to questions they have about the world, are all part of prior knowledge—that vital input a reader must contribute to every transaction with print.

Another way in which we translate these research findings into classroom practice is by providing opportunities for uninterrupted reading (with an emphasis on "uninterrupted"). Children are independent readers when they themselves are able to orchestrate all of the cues available to them. They can learn to do that only by engaging in reading and making mistakes. The most important thing readers must learn is what to do when what they are reading doesn't make sense. Fluent readers can make several choices at such a point. They can choose to disregard what they don't know for the present and keep on reading to see if something later in the text will help. They can decide to reread to check if they've missed something useful. They may try substituting something that makes sense temporarily, or they can choose to try something else related to what they are reading. Each of these alternatives is intended to maintain the flow of meaning. The ability to decide to use one or more of these strategies develops from the misjudgments a reader makes. Since miscues are an unavoidable part of reading, readers who do a lot of reading get many opportunities to decide whether what they are reading makes sense or not, and what to do about it if it doesn't. It is through uninterrupted reading that children learn how to make the decisions readers need to make. Each time we correct children's miscues for them, we take away the control they need to develop these strategies for themselves.

25

**Insights from Recent
Reading and Writing
Research and Their
Implications for
Developing Whole
Language Curriculum**

The following story perhaps illustrates what I've been talking about.

Six-year-old Steven, a first grader, was busy making an instant pudding for dessert one day. His mother handed him the box. Looking it over, he found the directions on the side and began reading them aloud. "Measure two cups of cold milk into a bowl." He did that. "Next, add the ingredients in the box to the milk." Steven paused for a moment with a very puzzled expression on his face when he came to the word "ingredients." His mother stood silently by, waiting to see what he would do. Suddenly his expression changed, "Oh," he said confidently, "that means the stuff in the box," as he continued reading.

Steven provides us with a demonstration of the reading process in action. He's watched his mother making pudding. He knows there are directions written on packages because he's seen his mother reading them. He also knows what is written in the directions involves the contents of the box. When he comes to something he's never encountered before the information he has available both from his knowledge of the situation and from what he's read so far allows him to understand the writer's meaning without actually identifying the unfamiliar word. He shows us he believes reading is intended to make sense and demonstrates his focus on understanding. His mother's nonintervention was important in this situation. Her waiting allowed Steven the time he needed to orchestrate his knowledge of the situation, his knowledge of the language used in a set of directions, and his understanding of what he'd read to that point. She allowed him control of the situation. By waiting, she learned he had the decision-making capabilities of a fluent reader.

The Development of Writing

There has been considerable interest in writing recently. Both adults and children have been observed while engaging in writing activities in an effort to understand the relationship between the in-head processes and what is appearing on the page. Researchers have become aware of the close parallels between what is involved in understanding written language and what must go on for writing to be produced.

The earliest research on children's use of written language focused primarily on such surface features as the number of words or sentences; the most that could be concluded was that older children wrote longer selections, used longer sentences, knew more words than younger children. Subsequently, Britton and coworkers (1975) became interested in the purpose and the awareness of audience in the writing of eleven- to eighteen-year-olds. They found that school-assigned writing was largely transactional. That is, its function was to transmit information, primarily for the teacher as examiner. They found that students did little expressive or poetic writing, or writing for other audiences (peers, general public, teacher as trusted adult, self) because it wasn't being encouraged. Britton's research raised important questions about the relationship between writing development and the instructional context.

Wilkinson *et al.* (1980) extended Britton's work by examining samples of narrative, autobiographical, explanatory, and persuasive writing done by seven-, ten-, and thirteen-year-olds. They were able to demonstrate increased awareness of audience, greater objectivity, clearer understanding of topic or theme, and less imitation with age. However, they emphasized that development wasn't a uniform progression; the writing of some ten-year-old children was more sophisticated than that of some thirteen-year-olds. Reasons for writing, instructional history, amount of reading, cultural and social background were all seen to influence the complexity of any particular child's writing.

Emig's study of twelfth-grade writers (1971) gave new direction to writing research—it represented an important shift from examining students' written products to observing writing in action. She recorded students as they composed, having them say aloud whatever came to mind as they worked. Her research demonstrated the recursive nature of writing. Her writers made decisions about selecting and orchestrating components of the text; they corrected, revised, and rewrote by adding or deleting elements, reordering parts of what they'd written. Starting, stopping, contemplating the text, and reformulating it were all part of the activity of writing.

Graves (1982) extended Emig's research by exploring writing with elementary school children. He found that children's writing was influenced not only by the teacher, but peer interaction and family response affected what they wrote. When children were able to choose their own topics, the range of topics was exceedingly broad. Graves confirmed the intricate interplay between talking, drawing, reading, and writing. These activities were not confined to a particular time or sequence during composition; talking could lead to drawing, drawing to writing, writing back to talking, drawing, or further writing. From watching children write, Graves concluded that writers discover their meaning while they write. His research demonstrated a continuous transaction between the emerging text and thought.

Graves also found that when children were trying out some new writing dimension they seemed to lose control over other aspects of writing which they had previously been able to handle. Syntax, spelling, punctuation, handwriting, and/or organization could deteriorate when children were experimenting with a new style or were shifting from print to cursive script. However, even while exploring new dimensions of writing, these young writers didn't abandon their focus on meaning; when the going got difficult they continued to maintain the flow of ideas. On the whole, Graves's research confirmed that writing doesn't grow from first mastering a number of individual aspects of the process and then putting them together. Rather, children's writing development involves a gradual refinement of the whole by movement on several fronts at once.

What implications do these research findings have for writing "instruction"? We now understand that learning to be a writer, like learning to become a speaker or reader, involves the refinement of many aspects of the process simultaneously. Development consists not of passing through a series of clearly defined stages, but of using certain well-developed strategies, available even to very young children, for figuring out how written language works as a whole. Instead of

27

**Insights from Recent
Reading and Writing
Research and Their
Implications for
Developing Whole
Language Curriculum**

form preceding function, function—the working out and communicating of ideas to oneself and others—creates the motivation for exploring the conventions used in written language. Reading is an inextricable part of the writing process. Children learn a great deal about reading while writing; they learn about writing while reading. Appraising children's writing development demands an understanding of the complex orchestration each product represents.

If I had an orangutan
I'd take him to The
Park So he can
save me a Swing.
So The big Kids.
won't get it.

Mateo and Tyrone (both first graders) reveal a great deal about their knowledge of written language in their orangutan piece (Figure 1–5).

Figure 1 – 5
Translation:

If I had an orangutan
I'd take him to the
Park so he can
save me a swing.
So the big kids.
Won't get it.

Their writing had been prompted by an invitation to create a scenario of their own following a class reading of Mercer Mayer's book *If I Had*. The boys wrote their piece collaboratively, borrowing when necessary from the couple of pages of Mayer's book conveniently projected on a nearby wall. Their writing demonstrates how learning to use written language is inextricably tied to ongoing experience, involves experimentation, as well as the importance of an interactive social context for learning. The boys use whatever they know about how written language is represented in conjunction with a generalized schema for how Mayer has constructed his text ("If I had a gorilla, I'd take him to school so the big kids wouldn't beat me up") to create this narrative of their own. Their story reveals how easily children are able to find language appropriate for telling about their experiences. Mateo and Tyrone easily share with us difficulties they have obviously had (or had seen other younger children encounter) being able to commandeer their turn on a swing. In this particular situation they experiment with spelling in order to represent their intentions whenever they are unable to scrounge support from Mayer's text. This interplay between Mayer's story and their own helps us see the intimate connection between reading and writing as a composition evolves. The self-corrections which are observable also reflect the transaction between reading and writing. Although not apparent in the writing itself, their story was the product of much close collaboration between the boys. They discussed topic, text organization, spelling, Mayer's piece, specific word choices, correction, and punctuation as they composed.

But what about the conventions of writing? Don't we have to teach spelling and punctuation? The following language story, I think, helps shed light on these concerns. Mark, a "remedial" eighth grader, was asked to correspond with a third grader from whom he'd received a letter. He wrote a few lines, stopped, and reread. Then he crossed out what he'd written and started over. When asked why he'd done that he replied, "What that kid doesn't need from me is writing without punctuation!"

We have here a nice illustration of how the need for conventions arises from a writer's awareness of his audience. On his own, Mark has recognized what this particular reader will require in order to understand his communication. He didn't need a teacher reminding him not to forget punctuation before he began writing. The situation provided the impetus for Mark to consider how his using some conventions would help his reader.

An overemphasis on accurate spelling, punctuation, and neat handwriting can actually produce a situation in which children come to see the conventions of writing as more important than the meaning they are trying to convey.

Eleven-year-old Alysa, for example, had done a homework assignment and had asked her mother to help her edit it. Her mother had circled misspelled words and missing punctuation, then she and Alysa had sat down to discuss the editing. At one circled word Alysa turned to her mother and said "That has to be right—I looked it up in the dictionary!" She had written *PATIENTS* instead of *PATIENCE*. Her concern for correct spelling overrode a concern for meaning.

In contrast, Jillian is intent on working out her ideas. (See Figure 1–6.) Notice her use of functional spelling (*"fanalet"* for "flannelette," *"chits"* for "sheets," *"lik"* for "like," *"be cose"* for "because," *"ther"* for "there," and *"an"* for "and"). Jillian is unafraid of placeholding meaning as she moves to get her ideas down. Toward the end, however, we see Jillian's concern for spelling intruding: she writes *10,* then tries *ten* above it, but scratches that out, electing to leave the numeral instead. She makes three attempts at writing *each.* She finally decides, however, to omit it even though she does actually spell it correctly (her story makes sense without it).

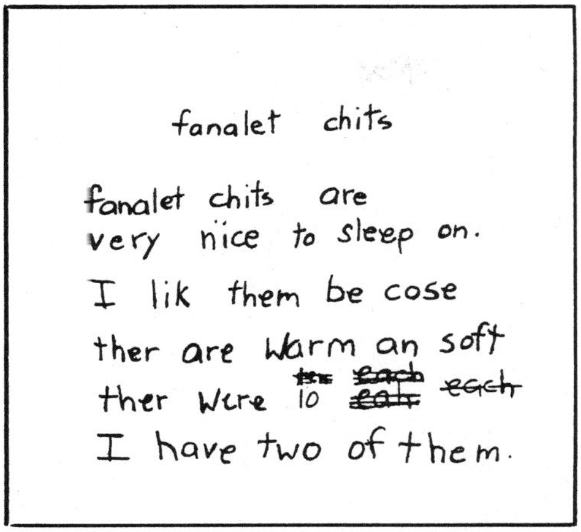

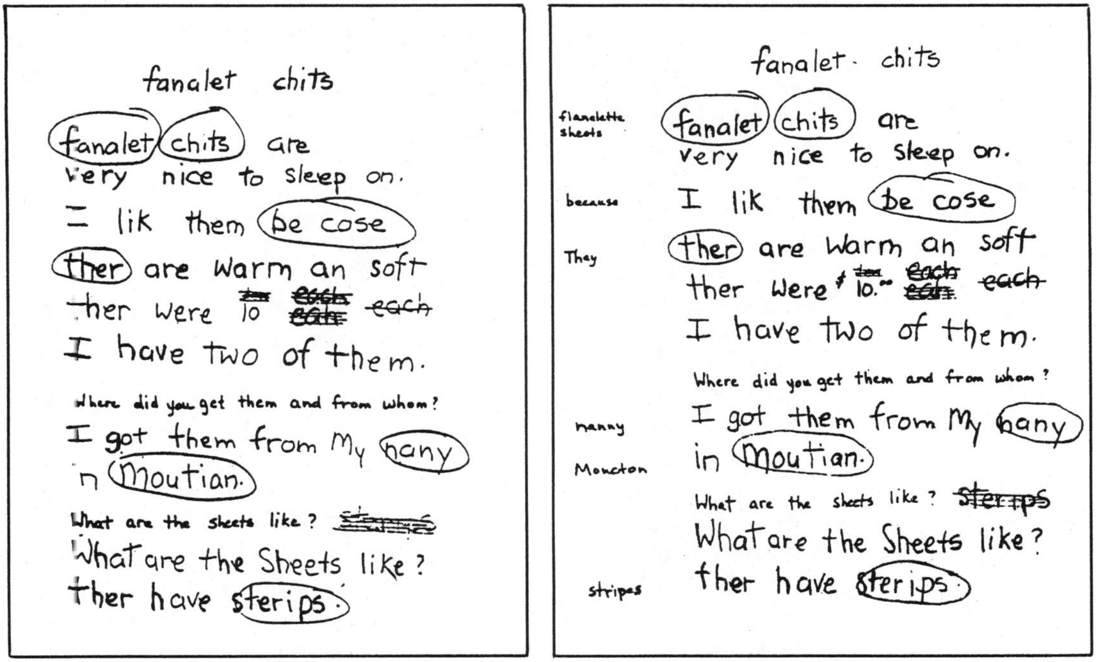

fanalet chits

fanalet chits are
very nice to sleep on.
I lik them be cose
ther are warm an soft
ther were ~~ten~~ 10 ~~each~~ ~~eah~~ ~~each~~
I have two of them.

Figure 1 – 6

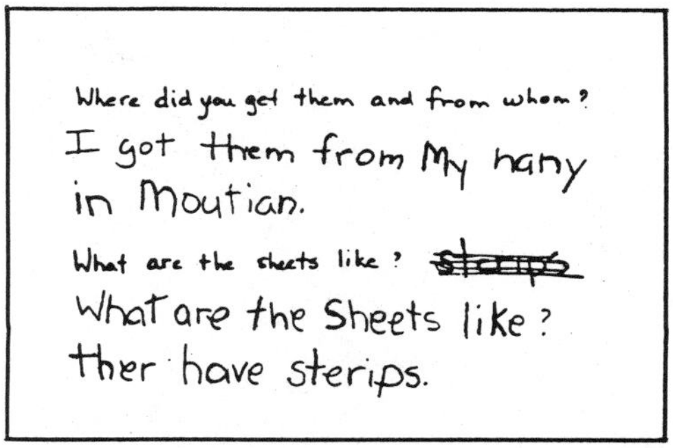

Where did you get them and from whom?
I got them from My nany
in Moutian.
What are the sheets like? ~~sterips~~
What are the Sheets like?
ther have sterips.

Figure 1 – 7

At this point Jillian asked her mother to read her story. Her mother replied by writing a question. (See Figure 1–7.) Jillian answered the question. Mother asked another. Jillian answered this second question with a single word, which she crosses out. She recopies the question (incorporating the conventional spelling for sheets offered to her) then answers what is now a rhetorical question with a complete sentence explanation. At that point, Jillian asked her mother to help correct the words. Her mother suggested that Jillian circle anything she was unsure about. Jillian did. Her mother then wrote what she thought were the conventional spellings in the margin for her (See Figure 1–8, a and b.)

fanalet chits

(fanalet) (chits) are
very nice to sleep on.
I lik them (be cose)
(ther) are warm an soft
ther were ~~ten~~ 10 ~~each~~ ~~eah~~ ~~each~~
I have two of them.
Where did you get them and from whom?
I got them from My (nany)
in (Moutian.)
What are the sheets like? ~~sterips~~
What are the Sheets like?
ther have (sterips.)

(a)

fanalet chits

flanelette sheets — (fanalet) (chits) are
very nice to sleep on.
because — I lik them (be cose)
They — (ther) are warm an soft
ther were ~~ten~~ 10 ~~each~~ ~~eah~~ ~~each~~
I have two of them.
Where did you get them and from whom?
nanny — I got them from My (hany)
Moncton — in (Moutian.)
What are the sheets like? ~~sterips~~
What are the Sheets like?
stripes — ther have (sterips.)

(b)

Figure 1 – 8

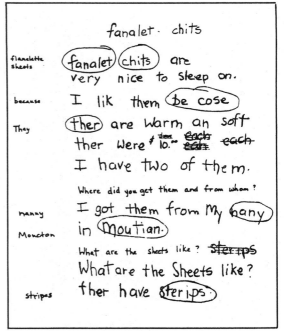

Now Jillian rewrote her story (Figure 1–9).

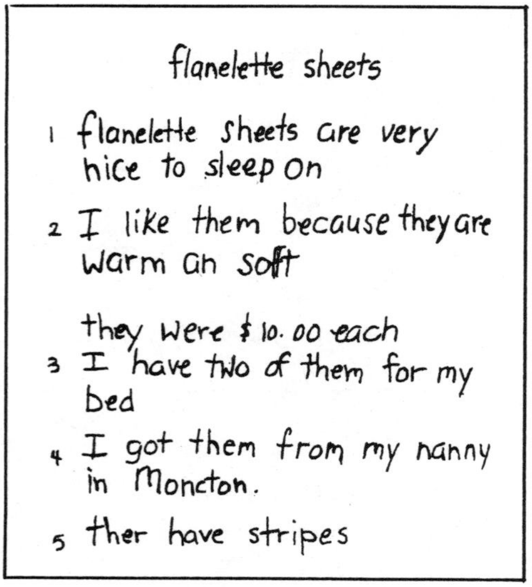

flanelette sheets

1 flanelette sheets are very
nice to sleep on

2 I like them because they are
warm an soft

they were $ 10.00 each
3 I have two of them for my
bed

4 I got them from my nanny
in Moncton.

5 ther have stripes

Figure 1 – 9

In addition to changing the spelling of the circled words, Jillian has made other alterations as well; *"lik"* became *"like,"* *"each"* was reinstated, *"for my bed"* was added, and the question *"What are the Sheets like?"* was deleted. These changes are evidence of the continuous decision-making involved in writing which results from transactions between the text itself, Jillian as reader, and Jillian as writer.

What can we learn about the nature of the literacy learning environment from Jillian's letter-writing experience? The way in which Jillian's mother interacts with her offers us some important insights into the kind of support writers can use. When Jillian handed her the story to read, her mother didn't point out the mistakes automatically; she read it and responded to its meaning. As a reader she wanted more information, so at that point the two of them engaged in a written dialogue. Her mother *wrote* questions; Jillian answered them. After the second exchange Jillian decided her text was reasonably complete and asked her mother to help edit it. Even when Jillian asked her to "fix the words," her mother didn't immediately correct the spelling. Instead, she suggested Jillian make some decisions on her own first. Jillian found all but two (*"an"* for "and," *"ther"* for "they"). Next, her mother wrote in the margin only those words Jillian had circled. Now on her own initiative Jillian redrafted her story. In the process she didn't just recopy the first draft with the spelling corrections; she actually reworked her piece. Her mother is aware that in order for Jillian to develop as a writer she needs to retain what Jerome Harste calls text ownership (Harste, Woodward, and Burke, 1984). What will be talked about, how it is said, how much attention will be paid to conventions are all decisions Jillian must make for herself. The fact that Jillian was writing her story to send to a grownup made her aware of the need for some conventions. Her

31
**Insights from Recent
Reading and Writing
Research and Their
Implications for
Developing Whole
Language Curriculum**

mother waited for Jillian to decide that she needed help and let her specify what particular help was required.

We can draw several important implications for classroom practice from this example. As Frank Smith (1982) argues, teachers must provide an environment in which a child will want to write and in which a child can learn about writing. This means, first and foremost, allowing children to be owners of their own work. They need to decide what they will write about, what they will say about it, and how much attention to pay to conventions at any particular time. Every time we set the topic, ask for a particular rhetorical form, expect accurate spelling and punctuation, and correct "errors" we take away text ownership. Children can only become writers by learning to make these decisions for themselves.

We also need to create a setting which encourages lots of reading and writing. Children need to read a lot of different kinds of writing in order to learn the diverse forms writers use for communicating their ideas. They need access to books (both factual and fiction), magazines, newspapers, pamphlets, notices, letters. They need to write for real audiences. They need to write for themselves, for both younger and older children, for adults they know, for some general unknown audience as well. We need to share in the writing process by being writers ourselves. Children don't need to be told how to write; they need to be shown. By providing demonstrations of writing in action, by being partners in the creating process, we do more to help children figure out how to be writers themselves than all of our correcting of their "mistakes" can ever hope to do.

We've seen that children from their earliest encounters with language, both written and spoken, expect it to be meaningful. They use what they know about the world to make sense of their interactions with print. They take risks in their intent to mean and they use what they know about language in one form to refine language in another. These four strategies must be allowed to operate in the classroom. Children must feel comfortable exploring written language in whatever way interests them. Learning to become writers involves a constant sharing with others, talking and writing about ideas, and getting feedback on whether they have worked or not. A silent, orderly classroom with children working each in his or her own workbook is not such an environment. That children do become writers (and many do) is evidence of their wonderful capacity for ignoring instruction. They know that much of what we try to teach them is irrelevant and often useless.

Learning to read and write is a process of experiencing language. There is no end product. Fluency is not a state which is finally attained; one is continually arriving. We need to understand how we either limit or enhance development by the experiences we set for children. Activities which involve fragments of language, which discourage children from taking chances, which don't permit the exchanging of ideas can only make learning to read and write more difficult for children. Writing develops in many directions at once; it develops continually, sometimes inconspicuously, sometimes in dramatic spurts. Writing development needs encouragement and support, not a confining, prescriptive program.

Implications

We began by discussing some findings from a number of different areas of research. What should be apparent at this point is a common belief which connects them.

All of the research we've examined has demonstrated that the most fundamental concern of language users is making sense. From the earliest language exchanges between parent and child to the most sophisticated writing of a professional novelist the focus of language is on meaning. There are many kinds of meaning to be communicated: meaning about events and objects in the world, meaning about feelings, social distance, formality of relationships, and moral stance, for example. Some of these meanings are communicated through the words themselves, some by the ways in which the words are used. The complex orchestration of these different aspects of language is learned by participating in language. Young children learning to talk, a novelist working on a new novel are both learning about language by using it.

The vehicle for language development is language itself. Our experiences with all aspects of language are cumulative. Experiences with written language enhance our ability to interact with and create oral language; oral language provides resources for generating written language.

In addition, language development requires other language users to interact with; becoming a language user is a social activity. Because other people are involved and make judgments about one's effectiveness as a language user, learning language is a risky business. Yet, if no risks are taken, little can be learned. An integral part of becoming a proficient language user is the "messing around" with language that must go on. That means almost all language, in whatever form, is variable; there is no "perfect form" toward which we aim. Variability is an expected part of normal everyday language use. One doesn't learn language as a watcher from the sidelines; one has to be a participant in what's going on. Expecting children to produce exact, correct language, whether oral or written, places unnecessary pressure on them as language users. When the cost of making mistakes becomes too great, children cease to take risks. This effectively removes them from the language arena. As nonparticipants they have few opportunities for learning.

Classrooms have typically not been good language learning environments precisely because experimenting with language is discouraged. In a great many classrooms children are expected to read and write exactly. They are rarely allowed to explore ideas by talking with each other. Reading and writing are taught as separate subjects. That is not to say classrooms couldn't be good environments for language development. Making the shift, however, requires that we begin to try to understand how language functions and how children become language users in the first place.

To get a sense of how classrooms could be geared toward children's language development, we might well begin by looking at language learning in the home. Parents intuitively know how to create an environment in which children learn language. We need to re-

33

**Insights from Recent
Reading and Writing
Research and Their
Implications for
Developing Whole
Language Curriculum**

create that environment. Parents are concerned with making communication work. They understand communication necessitates a lot of filling in on their part—they know they must interpret the situation and then either offer confirmation or elaborate on the situation and by doing so provide their children with demonstrations of language in use. These demonstrations are the raw material from which children create their own language.

Figure 1–10 shows how setting a focus on making communication work can affect a child's writing. Colin's letter is somewhat cautious. He has written short sentences, used mostly "safe" words—words he's fairly sure he knows how to spell—and filled his page with a drawing. His letter has a simple structure: Say thanks; tell about things I've done; share events around here that might be of interest; now back to you.

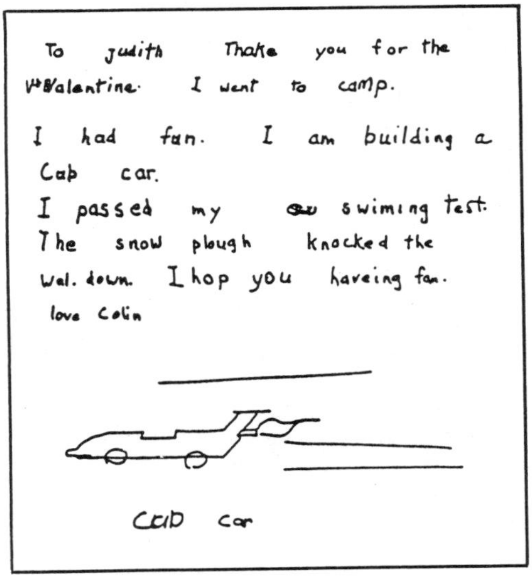

Figure 1 – 10
Translation:
To Judith, Thank you for the valentine. I went to camp. I had fun. I am building a cub car.
   I passed my swimming test. The snow plough knocked the wall down. I hope you [are] having fun.

love Colin

We can also see several strategies operating in his writing. He corrects mistakes which are evident to him— *valentine* and *swiming test*. He hedges his bets— *fun Cub*. When he isn't sure he checks with an adult—plough, knocked. Each of these strategies reflects some insecurity about writing on Colin's part.

Figure 1–11, written just three weeks later, is in answer to my reply to him. In my letter I shared what I was doing and asked him for more information about his camping trip and his cub car. My intention was to maintain communication with him. The first thing that's noticeable in this second letter is the increase in length. While Colin's organization hasn't changed much (he still includes thanks; answer questions; new information; and now back to you) there has been considerable expansion within each section. Instead of answering my questions with single sentences on a topic, Colin now has several things to say about each. He then introduces several items of his own: his ear tubes are out, he's now writing stories, his brother's not feeling well, he's earned some more cub badges. His "Now back to you" is also enlarged—he inquires about the weather and wants to know if

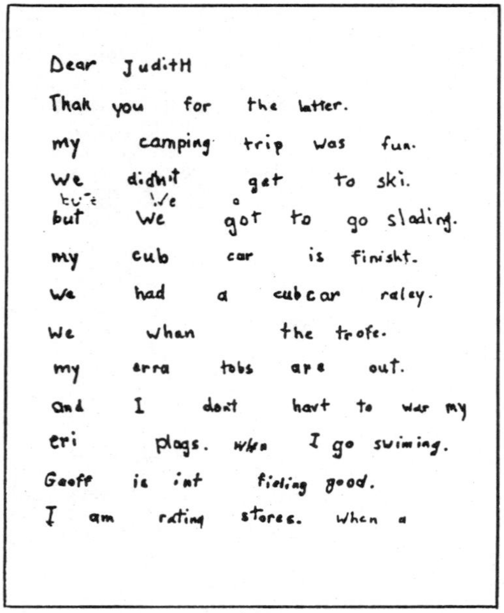

Dear Judith
Thak you for the letter.
my camping trip was fun.
We didn't get to ski.
but We got to go slading.
my cub car is finisht.
We had a cub car raley.
We When the trofe.
my erra tobs are out.
and I don't havt to war my
eri plogs. whn I go swiming.
Geoff is int fieling good.
I am rating stores. when a

(a)

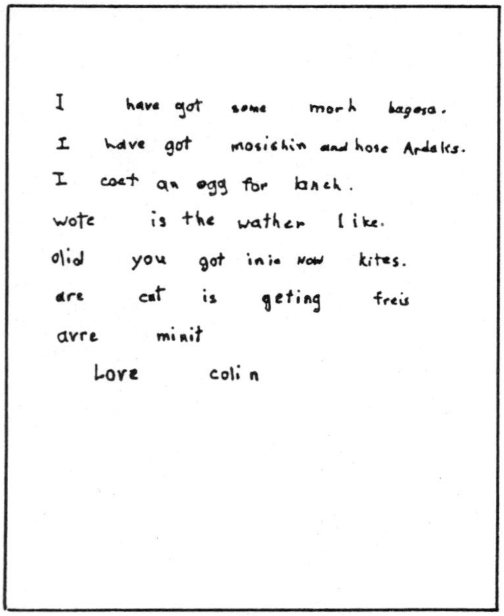

I have got some morh bagosa.
I have got mosishin and hose Ardeks.
I coet an egg for lunch.
wote is the wather like.
olid you got inia now kites.
are cat is geting freis
avre minit
Love colin

(b)

Figure 1 – 11
Translation:
Dear Judith
Thank you for the letter. My camping trip was fun. We didn't get to ski but we got to go sledding. My cub car is finished. We had a cubcar rally. We won the trophy. My ear tubes are out. and I don't have to wear my ear plugs. when I go swimming. Geoff isn't feeling good. I am writing stories.

When a [erased] I have got some more badges. I have got musician and house orderly. I cooked an egg for lunch. What is the weather like. Did you get any new kites. Our cat is getting fiercer every minute.

Love Colin

I've got any new kites. In addition to saying more, Colin is much less cautious in this second letter. Whereas in his first letter he corrected mistakes, hedged his bets, checked spelling with an adult, in this letter he's more concerned with function than with form. He uses functional spelling (instead of checking with an adult) in order to communicate what he wants to say (for example, *"latter"* for "letter," *"slading"* for "sledding," *"erra tubs"* for "ear tubes," *"trofe"* for "trophy," *"mosishin"* for "musician," and *"inie"* for "any"). This time he's more independent as a writer. Through Colin's letters we can see that shifting our emphasis from neatness and accuracy to sharing meaning can have quite dramatic effects on a child's writing.

But what about older students—fifth and sixth graders, students in junior and senior high school? The majority of examples I've used have come from younger children. That is, in part, because young children readily share with us their questions and insights about the world and about language. It is also because in young children's efforts we can see more clearly how the relationships among the many facets of language are being worked out. But every insight we've had into how young children learn about written language applies to these older students as well. Language development is the same process for them that it is for younger children. It is based on

35
**Insights from Recent
Reading and Writing
Research and Their
Implications for
Developing Whole
Language Curriculum**

the same strategies of text intent, negotiability, risk-taking and fine-tuning anguage with language. The main problem for older nonfluent readers and writers is that, in school at least, they've stopped negotiating, they've stopped trying to make sense, they've stopped taking risks. They've accepted that learning to read and write means coping largely with non-sense. The implications for classroom instruction we've drawn from the research we've examined apply equally to these older students. We need to encourage and support them in their efforts to make sense of reading and writing in just the same way we do with younger children. We do have one problem, however. We need to convince these older students that reading and writing are supposed to be meaningful activities before we can expect them to engage with literacy in any real way.

My experiences with a forty-four-year-old adult illiterate gentleman have some bearing on this point. When we began instruction he was unwilling to identify package labels or road signs with any confidence. He admitted he avoided written language. He found the business of daily living difficult, particularly since he operated his own business and had to face his inability to read many times every day. He had tried learning to read several times in the past, but had given up when he felt the instruction wasn't helping him.

I tried to establish a learning environment where he would feel comfortable exploring written language. We read together. I read slowly and carefully with him mumbling beside me. We read about four-wheel drive vehicles, winches, plumbing—subjects about which I know little. We would stop periodically and he would explain to me what we'd read. It wasn't long before he was bringing to the lessons materials he wanted to understand.

We wrote together as well. We carried on conversations in writing, two conversations at once, actually. We would ask each other questions and share experiences by writing to each other. We shared some fiction, too. That winter I read a lot of children's books trying to find some suitable material for this adult to read on his own. I had two criteria: the books had to be short and they had to relate to his life in some way. It is hard to recapture his pleasure at being able to read a whole book by himself.

We had been working together for about seven months when one day, having just completed a rather lengthy novel, he commented to me, "Do you know, I can read anything if it's long enough." This was an important observation for him to make. It showed he was beginning to understand what being a written-language user involves. He had learned that understanding was central to reading and writing. He had learned that even though he might not know particular words he could understand the sense of the text if he kept on reading. He was learning to become a risk-taker with written language.

Perhaps the most valuable insight from this experience for me was to realize that each learner must discover the strategies which allows him or her to be a functional written-language user. Frank Smith (1983) has described what he considers to be the one difficult way to make learning to read (and by implication learning to write) easy—that is, to attempt to understand what our students are trying to do and then help them do it. But in order to understand what our students are trying to do, we, too, must also discover (or rediscover) language for ourselves. It is only by observing language in use, by watching language users, that our own understanding of language can grow. And it is only from such understanding that we will be able to make curricular decisions which better match our student's intuitions about how language works.

What Teachers Are Demonstrating

Meredith Hutchings

A few years ago in September, I sat at the front of my Grade One class beside a blank piece of chart paper. "Yesterday," I said to the children, "we visited the post office. Now let's write a story about our trip. How shall we begin?" A number of suggestions were offered: "We saw the mailboxes." "I liked the way the machine stamped the letters." To each of these suggestions I responded, "That's a good idea; let's save it for later. How shall we begin our story?" One child offered, "Yesterday we visited the Post Office." "That's a good introduction," I replied. I printed this carefully, using the child's exact wording, at the top of the chart. "What did we do first?" I asked. Elements were added, following the sequence of the trip's activities. When I felt that the trip had been described, the chart story was finished. It was beautifully printed in bright marker colors. After the class read it together several times, the chart was displayed prominently so the children could read it. This activity is typical of the literacy learning activities found in many early elementary classrooms. Inherent in any instructional approach used for developing writing (or any other skills), there are always "demonstrations" being given the learners. Demonstrations are described by Frank Smith (1981) in the following way: "The first essential component of learning is the opportunity to see how something is done. I shall call such opportunities demonstrations which in effect show a potential learner 'This is how something is done.' The world continually provides demonstrations through people and through their products, by acts and by artifact" (p. 108).

As the post office story was being written, many demonstrations were being provided for the children about what writing and reading are all about. In this chapter I would like to consider several questions about the teacher's role with regard to the writing development of young children:

37

What are we actually demonstrating about the writing process to our learners?

Ideally, what do we want to demonstrate about the writing process to our learners?

How might we as teachers provide these new demonstrations in our classroom?

Recognizing the Existing Demonstrations

Using my post office language experience activity as an example, let's try to discover the demonstrations that I was providing about reading and writing.

If at the time I had been asked to describe a rationale for this activity, I might have produced the following list:

1. Every child's ideas are important.
2. Children build onto what they know. As teachers we must first find out what they know before we introduce anything new. Then new knowledge can be connected to what is already known.
3. Children need to verbalize ideas before they are asked to write. This makes writing easier, because the words have already been organized.
4. Writing is talk written down. To help children read and write fluently we must first help them to speak fluently.
5. Children begin to read and write more easily if their own experiences are the basis of these activities. Therefore they should write about things that they know. Sharing an activity as a class provides a base upon which reading and writing activities can be built.
6. Reading and writing are interconnected processes.

I could also have explained how I had applied this theory during the post office chart story activity.

1. No idea that was offered was refused or corrected. The order of ideas was organized but all of the ideas that were offered were used at some point in the story.
2. The content of the chart story came from the children's perceptions of the trip.
3. The group chart story activity preceded any individual writing activities about the trip.
4. The chart story was a copy of the children's spoken language, so that the vocabulary and syntax would be familiar and make the print easier to read.
5. The subject of the chart story focused on the trip that the class had just taken to the post office.
6. The chart was used as a reading activity when the writing was finished.

I intended to create a situation in which the children would feel relaxed about writing and would begin to write about their own experiences. As far as I could tell, my intentions were accurately reflected in the chart story activity and I expected that the children would make meaningful connections between this experience and their own attempts to write.

But did the children respond to writing in the way that I had anticipated? Were my intentions made clear as demonstrations to the learners? Frank Smith (198) suggests that the teacher's intended demonstrations are not always effective.

Learning is not an occasional event to be stimulated, provoked, or reinforced. Learning is what the brain does naturally, continually. . . . This is the time-bomb in every classroom—the fact that children's brains are learning all the time. They may not learn what we want them to learn. They may not learn what we think we are teaching them. . . . Learning is the brain continually updating its understanding of the world, we cannot stop the brain from doing this. The hazard of so much instruction is not that children do not learn, but what they learn. . . . In a sense most demonstrations are inadvertent but sometimes we can demonstrate one thing quite unintentionally when we actually think we are demonstrating another [pp. 108–109].

For the education system these are alarming, thought-provoking statements. What inadvertent demonstrations are ever-present in our classrooms? Do students learn, perhaps unconsciously, that their teachers value their own knowledge more than the knowledge that students might bring? Does this affect the students' acceptance of the teacher's information? Even those teachers who try to tailor the classroom environment to the students' interests and learning styles must unknowingly present many inadvertent and conflicting dem-onstrations. Teachers may try to conceal their own feelings and interests or lack of interest in topics but in doing so their true feelings may still be obvious to the learners. As Frank Smith (1981) points out, "Not only do we all continually demonstrate how things are done but we also demonstrate how we feel about them" (p. 109).

Perhaps becoming more aware of our own feelings about the programs we present in our classrooms may help us uncover some of the inadvertent demonstrations we may also be presenting. For example, at the time the post office story was written, writing was a difficult, avoided, and embarrassing activity for me. I did not want my feelings to be deliberately conveyed to the students. On the contrary, to compensate, I designed writing activities to seem as easy as possible. The invitation may have been delivered as "Try to write—it's easy" but may have been received by the children as "She's just trying to make it look easy. She doesn't really like it. Writing must be hard." Of course by being made to look easy, writing became a very different process. While trying to promote one aspect of the process— that is, to help the students develop a favorable attitude toward writing—I had altered the process of creating a written text.

From the students' perspective the demonstrations about the writing process transmitted by the post office story may have included the following:

• Writing is talk written down. First you say something, and then you just copy it down.

- You have one chance to write something down, so your printing has to be neat the first time.
- There's one way to organize a text, and that's to write things down just the way they really happened.
- In the classroom, things are written down so that children can learn to read.

The writing of the post office story can be considered a "first draft" approach to writing in which the first draft of any writing is the final finished product. In many classrooms first-draft writing activities are the only writing activities offered students. In first-draft writing, the student has time to attempt one piece of writing (perhaps a follow-up seatwork activity), and this piece of writing has only one function to fulfill—evaluation by the teacher. The post office story was not intentionally being used for evaluation but as one demonstration of how writing is done. However, prominently displayed, the chart story provided a definite example with which the children might compare and evaluate their own efforts.

During the year there were many charts, essentially crafted in the same manner. Each time my role was the same. There were very few other forms of writing that I demonstrated in the classroom. When the children were writing, I would assist, but I did not sit down and write with them. Each child frequently dictated stories that I would copy down, but the demonstrations of the writing process did not vary. Had I carefully observed these grade one writing efforts, the demonstrations they were actually receiving may have been evident. If I had become aware that their efforts were consistently first-draft reports or descriptions, as I recall they were, then I might have been able to change my demonstrations.

This interaction between the teacher, the student, and the demonstrations must be observed conscientiously and continuously. The students are the thermometers of the classroom climate. As Yetta Goodman describes this process:

Professional educators, whom I call kidwatchers, are always making judgments about how students are progressing and making decisions about what experiences and opportunities children may need to expand further on the child's progress or growth. It is this informal ongoing evaluation leading to continuous planning of instructional experiences for children that I have termed "kidwatching" [Goodman, 1982].

Ideal Demonstrations

The concept of demonstrations must not be confined to children's development. Everyone is surrounded by demonstrations constantly.

As teachers we must also contend with many different demonstrations about teaching and learning. From the teachers in the classrooms around us to workshop presentations and university courses, there are constant demonstrations which either reinforce or confront our own way of doing things. What produces real change in what we do is a shift in our underlying beliefs. Somewhere among the many demonstrations with which we have been in contact, we have been convinced to alter our fundamental beliefs. When and how this occurs is difficult to pinpoint because of the complexity of activities surrounding the event and because these changes are not always obvious. What we usually notice, in retrospect, are the differences between what we used to believe and what we now believe. Frank Smith describes this learning process as "engagement": "There has to be some kind of interaction so that 'This is how something is done' becomes 'This is something I can do.' ... Learning occurs when the learner engages with a demonstration, so that it, in effect, becomes the learner's demonstration ..." (p. 109).

In this way, over time, my beliefs about written language changed and a different theoretical framework was formed. It would be difficult and tedious to document all of the changes that occurred but the following are a few of the demonstrations about writing with which I "engaged."

- Written language is different from speech (see F. Smith, *Writing and the Writer*, chapter 6).
- We learn to write by writing, by reading, and by reading as writers (see F. Smith, *Writing and the Writer*).
- Writing is social. A writer is dependent upon an audience—upon readers (see F. Smith, *Writing and the Writer*).
- Writing is a "messy process" (see D. Graves, "Andrea Learns to Make Writing Hard," and L. McCormick Calkins, "The Craft of Writing").

These and many other ideas, forming a "whole language theory," were presented by theorists who practice what Harste (1982) terms "ethnography." This refers to research that is ongoing and strives to observe a process in action in its natural setting. More traditional research analyzes something away from the original setting, using variables and controlled experiments. However, as Harste points out, all teachers can be and should be ethnographers, carefully observing the process at work within their classes. Fundamentally, the teacher as kidwatcher and the teacher as ethnographer are performing the same role.

Putting Whole Language Theory into Action

For me several papers, authored or coauthored by teacher/ ethnographers, provided especially effective demonstrations of "whole language" writing theory in action.

Papers such as "The Craft of Writing" (Calkins, 1980) and "Questions for Teachers Who Wonder If Their Writers Change" (Giacobbe and Graves, 1982), depict the children as immersed in active, purposeful language environments. These environments, of course, are very difficult to describe because many forms of purposeful activities such as talking, reading, writing, listening, thinking, problem solving, and risk taking may be happening simultaneously. What is consistent within and between these environments were some shared fundamental beliefs held by the teachers. Smith (1982) may have summarized some of these beliefs when he wrote,

> . . . although children are capable of learning to write there is very little that they can be taught, at least in the sense of explicit rules and exercises that will transform non-writers into writers [p. 199].

> Instead it has been argued that writing is learned by writing, by reading and by perceiving oneself as a writer. . . . None of this can be taught [p. 199].

> The teacher must provide an environment in which a child will want to write and in which a child can learn about writing.

> The environment in which a child will want to write is an environment of demonstration, not just of "this is the way we do things" but also "these are things that can be done." . . . for demonstrations of what can be done children must see someone doing something. Before children will be motivated to write they must see writing being done [p. 204].

Some of the demonstrations these teachers intentionally provided were described in the articles. For example, in "The Craft of Writing," the teacher, Pat Howard, composed in front of her students. She had come to school with an idea for a story, a true experience, and she encouraged the children to interview her until she felt ready to write. Then she wrote her story in chalk, erasing and changing all aspects of the text, talking out loud about her reactions. The children offered suggestions that they thought might clarify or strengthen the story. Then they were encouraged to write their own texts by discussing their ideas with each other first. Once they had started, Howard suggested that they could make some changes to their texts, by trying several different beginnings or leads for the story, for example. Howard also initiated discussions of "leads" and texts where the children could discuss which leads they liked best. She instituted an editorial board of students, where the emerging texts could be read and the author receive some feedback in the form of questions and suggestions. She initiated discussions about good books to examine the strengths of effective writers.

Throughout, Howard asked questions and directed the students to new ways of doing things. A piece of writing might have the following reactions. "This is a good try. Try another beginning, OK?" "What's your main point?" "Let's read it and see where it picks up speed" or "What do you like best in this piece or writing?" By demonstrating, initiating, and questioning, Pat Howard was able to sense the students' needs. Here was kidwatching in action.

Similarly, Mary Ellen Giacobbe, a first grade teacher, provided an environment where childrens' writing strategies could develop naturally and purposefully. As a part of her kidwatching, she asked a set of prewriting and postwriting questions of her students during weekly individual conferences. Before they wrote she asked: "What are you going to be writing about?" (Children chose their own topics throughout the year.) "How are you going to put that down on paper?" "How did you go about choosing your subject?"

After they wrote she asked: "How did you go about writing this?"
"What are you going to do next with this piece of writing?" "What do
you think of this piece of writing?"

Giacobbe recognized that any real change in practice necessarily
reflects a change of beliefs both for children as well as adults.

It is important for us as teachers to recognize that children develop
their own theories about what the writing process involves. Because all
language learning is social, discussions can play an important role in
developing these theories. The more opportunity learners have to
discuss their ideas with others, the more meaningful the learning can
be. The research of Giacobbe, as well as Calkins and Graves, testifies
to the changes of their young writers in attitude and process as well
as product.

These teachers began with a set of beliefs about learning and
writing from which they developed sympathetic demonstrations in their
own activities and the activities of their students. Once in motion,
kidwatching helped to tell them if these were effective demonstrations
or if perhaps there were more powerful inadvertent demonstrations
occurring.

For me, what these teacher/ethnographers have provided is a set
of new demonstrations about the writing environment. They cannot
tell me exactly how to create such an environment; they have simply
recorded their own theory in action. They invite each teacher to ask,
"Does my theory, my set of beliefs, stand up in the real world of the
learner?" For teachers, kidwatching provides that critical feedback.
Because their kidwatching provides the proof, I recognize from
these teachers' accounts that their demonstrations effectively reflect
their beliefs.

The invitation for me now is to establish my own environment
to demonstrate my own beliefs about writing and then to kidwatch
carefully so that any inconsistencies (and there will always be
inconsistencies) might be recognized.

Only after I have identified my own beliefs about the writing
process can I begin to answer the questions: What am I actually
demonstrating about the writing process to my learners? Ideally,
what do I want to be demonstrating? How might I provide these new
demonstrations in my classroom? I've set the environment. There's
lots of paper at hand and the blackboard is uncovered, with plenty
of chalk on the ledge. But the real change will begin the first day of
school This year, writing may not be so easy. I expect that it will be
hard to create and recreate, to define and refine, but I feel ready to
learn about writing along with and from my students.

Andrew and Molly

Writers and
Context in
Concert

Wayne Serebrin

Ten minutes before dismissal on Friday, Andrew makes an urgent request: "Mr. Serebrin, may I please share my story with the class?" Molly, on the other side of the room, is intensely erasing a sentence which no longer sounds "right" to her, in the body of a letter she is writing to a classmate still on vacation. These two children, like the other five- and six-year-olds in my primary class, have been participants in a diverse range of writing events in their first year of school. An examination of Andrew's and Molly's written artifacts—taken from a single week in school and considered in conjunction with the environment in which they were produced—exposes the "alternate literacies" these very young children bring to a variety of different writing contexts. These children, like all language users, make complex, "orchestrated" decisions which must be seen in relation to the specific contexts in which they occur (Harste, Burke, and Woodward, 1981, p. 39).

Journal writing is a regular, ongoing activity in our classroom. Pencils pens, markers, erasers, lined and unlined scribblers are available in the writing center. The children are invited to write about whatever they find interesting—topics are not assigned; spelling is not given—they are encouraged to spell words the way they think they should be spelled; length and duration of writing is not circumscribed; and journals are never subjected to correction or grading. The children are free, if they wish, to share their writing with other children in the class, with volunteering parents, or with me. I write my own journal and select passages I am pleased with to read aloud to the class, demonstrating that for me journal writing is personally meaningful. The children see and hear me as my writing takes on a style and structure which is both uniquely my own while at the same time common to journal writing as a genre.

In just the same way that I experiment with what I will say and how I will say it in the genre scheme afforded by journal writing, Andrew conducts his own experiments. His first journal entry of the week introduces his topic—his March Break trip to Florida. In his second and third entries of the week Andrew begins to "shift gears": he narrows his focus and concentrates on a specific, personal recollection—the rocket ride and, more especially, the silver stick on the ride (Figure 3–1, a, b, and c).

(a)   (b)   (c)

Figure 3 – 1
Translation for Figure 3 – 1 (a), (b) and (c):
I had a very nice time in Disney World and
in Clearwater Beach. I went on a rocket
ride. It was fun. There was a stick to make it
go up and down. It was silver. Mum said,
"Go down." But it always made it go down.

Andrew chooses to write about a personally meaningful event—an experience about which he has something to say. He decides to adopt a journal format—his entries sound like a journal, look like a journal (brief, dated descriptions), and read like a journal. He organizes his descriptions in a logical order and shows clarity of thought as he moves from general to specific recollections. Andrew produces sentences which capture the flow of his thoughts; he has no difficulty expressing his intentions. He has conventional linearity, directionality, uniformity of print size; he is concerned about the spacing of his work—he starts the cramped ending of his second entry over again as a new entry on the next page—and his largely conventional spelling is "functional"—he solves each spelling problem as it occurs and keeps his marker moving.

Molly is also attending to the conventions of language use which apply to journal writing. Her first entry of the week, March 21, begins with a description of a possible future visit from her Aunt Elisabeth and cousin Meg (Figure 3–2, a and b). She describes the fun she will have playing with Meg and her older sisters, Jeany and Katy. Molly then brings this imagined experience to a close and discusses the more immediate future of playing this afternoon, first with her friend Kerry and then later with her two sisters.

Molly's second entries of the week seem to serve quite a different

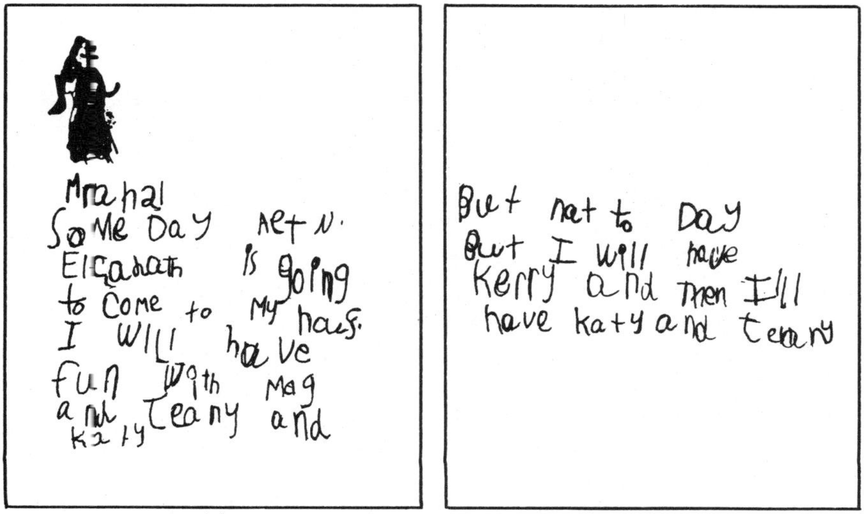

Mra hal
So Me Day Aet N.
Elcabath Is going
to Come to My haus.
I WILL ha Ve
fun with Mag
a nd Ky Ceany and
Kz ly

But not to Day
But I will have
Kerry and Then Ill
have katy and teany

(a)   (b)

Figure 3 – 2
Translation for Figure 3 – 2 (a) and (b):
Some day Aunt Elisabeth is going to come to my house. I will have
fun with Meg and Jeany and Katy. But not today. But I will have
Kerry, and then I'll have Katy and Jeany.

purpose (Figures 3–3, a and b). These entries—reflections on the
naughty behavior of her stuffed rabbit, Hoppy, and the lesser age and
jumping ability of Hoppy relative to her older stuffed toys, Yellowy and
Grayey—suggest to me that underneath the character of Hoppy may
be Molly herself (also the youngest of three siblings), engaging in a
little fanciful personal imagining. And while the symbolic intent of

March 22
I like Happy
But HOPPY Is
noty But I
do Mid

Hoppy Is Jongr
Than Yellowy and
Gray But They
Dont Caring it
Hoppy Cant jomp
as hi
Yollewy and Gray as

(a)   (b)

Figure 3–3
Translation for Figure 3–3 (a) and (b):
I like Hoppy, but Hoppy is naughty, but I don't mind. Hoppy is
younger than Yellowy and Grayey, but they don't mind it.
Hoppy can't jump as high as Yellowy and Grayey.

Molly's writing is purely speculative on my part, such a written exploration of personal emotions and knowledge would be suited to journal writing.

Molly does, after all, use her journal to explore ideas and feelings relevant to her; she knows that journal writing serves a pragmatic function. She at once makes decisions not only about what to say but how to say it—simultaneously she deals with meaning, syntax, and letter-sound relationships. Her conventional spellings—*"they," "come," "have," "like,"*—and her reversal of the letters *a* and *r* in *"March"* indicate that she not only uses her knowledge of letter-sound relationships, but also her knowledge of what these words look like. Molly also provides evidence of being a reader of her writing. In her first journal entry Molly originally wrote, *"Someday I will have my Aunt Elisabeth";* displeased with the sound of what she had written, she backed up and erased the *"I will have my"* that she had begun. And, when in her first journal entry, her pencil fell far behind her thoughts—she had started to write the *th* of the word *"with"* before the *w* and *i*—as a reader Molly caught this miscue immediately and self-corrected.

In their journal writing Andrew and Molly provide us with graphic displays in which meaning resides in a unique "textual shape" (Harste, Burke, and Woodward, 1981, p. 49). What they have to say cannot be separated from how they say it; their journal writing represents their current sense of how one manages such a complex cognitive, literary event. The decisions the children make provide them with inventive solutions which in turn keep their ideas flowing onto the page.

On the first day of the week from which these samples were collected, as a whole class we looked through a new wordless picture book, *The Bear and the Fly*. In a discussion of the book, the children offered suggestions about what was going on. Copies of this book were then left in the writing center and the children were invited to write their own text. The pictures and classroom discussion offered a potential semantic organization from which the writers could generate and compose their ideas. The context of this text-writing was, consequently, considerably different from that of the journal writing and, understandably, the children made significantly different literary decisions.

Text Translation for Andrew's *The Bear and the Fly*

The Three Bears were sitting down when suddenly a bee came buzzing along, so the Daddy Bear took the flyswatter and tried to hit him. First, he hit the Mama Bear trying to hit him. Then, he hit the wee-wee Baby Bear. He hit him [the Baby Bear] so hard that he fell down.
Written and Illustrated by Andrew

Andrew's writing for *The Bear and the Fly* illustrates what Harste, Burke, and Woodward (1981) call the "constraints" embedded in a specific writing context (p. 92). Andrew establishes a setting and characters, borrowing the names of the characters, I suspect, from *Goldilocks and the Three Bears*; note especially his use of the adjective "wee-wee" to describe the baby bear. His opening lead reads like a story, and his "written and illustrated" at the end of the story also signals that he believes he has written a story, yet the "episodes" in the middle of his story read like a series of loosely-connected frames: "The Daddy took the flyswatter . . . first he . . . then he . . . he. . . ." The constraints Andrew experiences are obvious; he knows that the situation (a stapled collection of photocopied pages) demands a story, but at the same time each picture also demands to be described. His "story," therefore, represents his attempt to juggle both of these demands at the same time.

For Molly this text-writing activity does not have the same con-straints as it did for Andrew. Rather, this activity provides Molly with an opportunity to try out quite a different use of language—experimentation with dialogue embedded in a full story grammar:

Text Translation for Molly's *The Bear and the Fly*

By Molly
One evening when some bears were having dinner a fly came in the window. The daddy bear almost got the fly. "He missed again," said the baby to the mummy. "It might sting," said the baby. "Ow!" said the baby, "that hurts!" The dog said, "Do not do that again." "OK," said the daddy. "I'll do it to you," said the daddy. Soon the three bears' dinner would be finished. Now it was.

Using storybook language, Molly establishes the setting: *"One evening when some bears were having dinner a fly came in the window."* She develops her episodes and characters through descriptions of the bears' actions and what they say: we know that the daddy bear is bent on swatting that fly regardless of where it lands—he says to the dog, who has cautioned him not to hit the child again, *"I'll do it to you."* The outspoken baby bear assumes the role of commentator: *"He missed again," "It might sting," "Ow," "that hurts."* The story is resolved by the ending of the bears' dinner: *"Soon the three bears' dinner would be finished. Now it was."* To my knowledge Molly had never written dialogue at school before. Her mother claimed no knowledge of Molly's having written any dialogue at home either. Molly's writing sample, hence, provides us with an instance of her experimenting with one of her latest language discoveries: making use of a particular kind of written language in a particular context. Her decision to write dialogue—her choice of words, the manner of delivery of those words, and the form those words take—is a decision which considers many elements of writing at the same time.

On Tuesday one of the children had brought the story *Jack and the Beanstalk* to school for me to read aloud. I read the story to the class and on Wednesday left another pile of textless *Jack and the Beanstalk* picture books in the writing center. Andrew readily accepted this invitation to write a fairy tale.

Text Translation for Andrew's *Jack and the Beanstalk*

This is the story of *Jack and the Beanstalk*. Once upon a time there was a little boy named Jack. He knew that there was a giant. If he climbed high into the sky he would find that giant. The end.

The text he created differs greatly in its "shape"—function and style of print, semantic and syntactic structure, and choice of words—from the text he completed just two days earlier. This picture book has a unique context, a particular "textual schema," which Andrew identifies with fairy tales (Harste, Burke, and Woodward, 1981, p. 49). For Andrew the task at hand is not to record what is in the pictures this time, but to write a particular kind of story with which he is very familiar. In fact, Andrew's grasp of the fairy-tale genre is so firm that he ignores the pictures altogether—there is no match between what he writes and what is pictured on each page. Semantically his text tracks like the setting component of a fairy tale: Andrew introduces Jack, the protagonist; he establishes the time frame, *"Once upon a time"*; and the physical setting, *"If he climbed high into the sky he would find that giant."* There are several possible reasons why Andrew stops short and attaches a predictable *"The end"* after dealing only with the setting component, but in answer to my question "Are you going to write any more of this story?" there came a very definite "no." We may speculate that he found this early component more memorable, that he ran out of physical space for writing, that he simply got tired or had nothing else to say. In any case, however, Andrew's prior experience allowed him to demonstrate both his understanding and stylistic control of the fairy-tale genre. These two wordless picture books call forth interestingly different responses from the same writer within the same week.

Text Translation for Molly's *Jack and the Beanstalk*

By Molly
Once upon a time there was a little boy; he was good. His mother said, "Go sell Bessy." "Yes, Mother," said Jack. Jack came up a beanstalk. He met a giant. It [the giant] came home. Jack hid. He took some money; it was Jack's. Then he came again the next day. He got something else. The giant found out. Jack chopped down the beanstalk. The end.

Molly's familiarity with the fairy-tale genre is also readily apparent. She has abstracted the underlying structural characteristics of fairy tales and uses this mental representation as a context for building her own story. In her semantic organization Molly includes a setting—she introduces Jack and his mother; the time frame—*"Once upon a time"*; the need to sell Bessy, their cow, for money; an initiating event—Jack climbs the beanstalk and meets the giant; a series of responses by the protagonist to the initiating event—Jack hides, steals his money back from the giant, and steals something else; consequences of the protagonist's actions—Jack is found out and a chase is implied; and final response—Jack chops down the beanstalk.

With such a clear text focus, Molly, like Andrew, is free to turn her attention to other aspects of her story writing. She continues to experiment with writing dialogue—choosing appropriate words and register within the constraints of this new context. In this activity, support for both Molly's and Andrew's writing came not from the pictures but from a rich exposure to the fairy-tale tradition. Drawing on the strength of language information acquired from listening to, reading, and acting out fairy tales, Molly and Andrew were able to test out their fairy-tale insights in their own writing.

On Thursday I read to the class from a magazine article about rabbits. I then asked them to tell me what they knew about rabbits and recorded whatever information they offered, in their own words, on a large piece of chart paper. I explained to them that I wanted to make a class book about rabbits (Easter was a couple of weeks away) and invited them to create a written contribution of their own. Once again, Andrew responded to my invitation (Figures 3–4, a, b, and c).

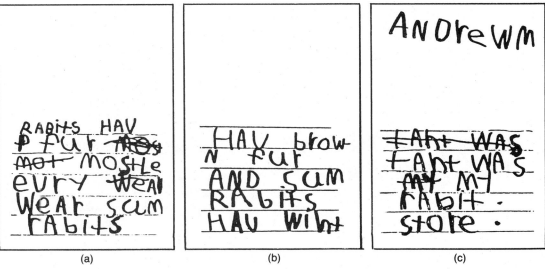

(a)   (b)   (c)

Figure 3 – 4
Translation for Figures 3 – 4 (a), (b), and (c):
Rabbits have fur mostly everywhere. Some rabbits have brown fur
and some rabbits have white. That was my rabbit story.
Andrew M.

His descriptive discourse intends to provide details about rabbit fur—where it is found and what colors it may be. Although Andrew writes *"that was my rabit store"* ("that was my rabbit story"), it is obvious from his lexical choice, short and to-the-point sentences, and semantic selection in the first place that this is not a story at all. I would speculate that he labels this a story because he is more familiar with story writing than with writing other types of discourse. I believe that he is relatively unfamiliar with descriptive, expository writing in terms of his own listening, reading, and writing experience and that this may account for the sparsity of detail he provides. It would seem that the abstracted store of stuctural information available to Andrew for expository writing is more limited than his "linguistic data pool" for fairy tales (Harste, Burke, and Woodward, 1981, p. 67). Frank Smith supports the plausibility of such an observation in his book *Writing and the Writer,* suggesting that "describing objects and situations in exposition is not something that children are often called upon to do in their world outside of school" (p. 194). Hence, Andrew may not only have found the "shape" of this rhetorical type elusive, but he may also have found the activity itself lacking a purpose.

On Friday I read the children a postcard which we had received in the mail from Craig, a child from the class still on vacation. I told them that I would be writing to Craig and that I would be happy to include a letter from any of them who wished to write. Molly decided that she would like to write (See Figure 3–5).

Figure 3 – 5
Translation:

Dear Craig,

Happy Passover. How are you doing? I hope you come back soon. I miss you.

From Molly.

There is no doubt that Molly understands the pragmatic function of a personal letter. Semantically her letter contains what one would expect a personal letter to contain. Structurally her letter is organized as a personal letter would conventionally be organized; it has a salutation, a message, a closing, and a signature. Syntactically her letter sounds like a letter and the graphic display looks like a letter. Yet, beyond these decisions Molly also demonstrates other contextually relevant concerns. First, as a reader, expecting written language to be meaningful, Molly found her "*Do you have nice sun* [?]" semantically unacceptable and attempted to erase it (it is much lighter on the original). Second, I did not give Molly any spellings, yet most of her words are conventionally spelled. Third, Molly puts a period at the end of all but one of her sentences (including one where convention would dictate the use of a question mark). And finally, her handwriting is much neater and more legible than in her other writing samples during the week. Taken together, these decisions suggest to me that Molly is demonstrating a sophisticated and sensitive response to print in this context—at the other end of this letter is a real audience who must make sense of what she has written, without her assistance.

Andrew and Molly, at age five, already demonstrate a sophisticated and complex understanding of writing in a variety of contexts. In the face of these differing contexts both children make a series of "orchestrated decisions" involving the use of pragmatics, semantics, syntax, format, word choice, punctuation, spelling, and even handwriting (Harste, Burke, and Woodward, 1981, p. 543). The products which result vary a great deal from activity to activity—emphasizing the importance of context to writing performance. When the children could draw on their knowledge of conventions, based on past writing, reading, and oral language experiences, they did so; when they could not, they invented their own personal conventions to fulfill their language needs. It is the latter which are the more interesting ones—the "generative" ones—they are the responses that show Andrew and Molly involved in "intention," "invention," "orchestration," and "experimentation" (Deford and Harste, 1982, p. 597). It is only when their responses are not conventional that we may see the particular constraints perceived by particular language-users in particular settings. The nonconventional responses tip us off to the constraints perceived by individual writers and allow us as teachers to support, augment, and extend the current strategies available to that writer.

The classroom implications are clear. Writers, big and small, need environments rich with all kinds of print. They need to be invited to choose from these materials, to read them, to listen to them, and to try their own hands at writing similar discourse in pragmatically and semantically functional situations. We must not confuse the products of their efforts with the processes operating within particular contexts. This means that their efforts must not be evaluated by the yardstick of correct form—conventional spelling, punctuation, and sentence structure—but rather in terms of decision-making events within specific contexts. To see only their products would be to miss the significant "language events"—language users bringing all they currently know to bear upon the task with which they are faced. To further enhance their learning, Andrew and Molly need teachers who are interested in understanding how language works and how language users learn and develop. They need teachers who will give them time to get where they are going and who will observe them with a view to the problems with which they are currently occupied. They need a classroom where they are supported and allowed to experiment in open-ended literacy activities.

Using Children's Books to Teach Reading
Judith M. Newman

"When you're reading and you come to something you don't know, what do you do about it?" This question was put to teachers attending a recent workshop on literacy to help them consider their own reading strategies. The list of responses was actually quite long. At this particular gathering, the teachers suggested that they often skip what they don't know, use surrounding context, substitute a word or phrase which seems to maintain the meaning, reread the passage, read ahead to see if what is coming clarifies the meaning, or try something else on the same topic.

In contrast, when the teachers were asked, "What would you do to help a student having difficulty reading?" they offered the following suggestions: tell them to look at the prefixes and suffixes, look for familiar small words within the word, or say the unknown word for them. The teachers' focus when their students are reading appears to be quite different from when they read themselves. In instructional situations teachers seem mainly concerned with students' identifying words correctly. When their students come to something they don't know, teachers seem to direct students' attention to the unknown itself as the source of needed information rather than shifting their attention away from the unfamiliar to the text as a whole to clarify meaning. In the instructional situation the belief seems to be that meaning is dependent on identifying particular words and that if these words aren't identified correctly there can be no understanding. Consequently, teachers correct students when they make mistakes rather than letting them correct themselves on the basis of what happens later in the material.

The comparison between what teachers do themselves and what they direct their students to do when encountering something unfamiliar is instructive. In their own reading, teachers are concerned with understanding. They use the flow of language to assist them; they focus on the whole rather than on individual parts; they rely on

55

what they already know to determine if what they're reading makes sense, and self-correct when it doesn't. However, teachers often encourage their students to view reading as a process of word analysis, to rely on external sources for correction, to depend on memorized rules for fragmenting words. Instead of helping students maintain a flow of meaning by using existing knowledge and information obtainable from what they are reading, teachers frequently have students stop and deal with the unknown, which interrupts the reading process.

This dichotomy between what teachers instruct their students to do and what they do when they read themselves is an illustration of the two views of the reading process which have emerged over the last several years. Traditional views of reading have seen the process as involving a passive relationship between the reader and the print. That is, the information necessary for reading is thought to reside exclusively on the page and to flow from the page to the reader. This view has argued that reading involves a sequence of steps beginning with the visual identification of letters and words followed by a pairing of the visual forms with their corresponding sounds to produce speech from which meaning is subsequently obtained. In contrast, the alternative view does not consider reading a primarily visual process. Instead, information from more than one source is seen to be necessary in order for us to make sense of what we are reading. Reading is seen to involve a transaction between the print cues and knowledge supplied by the reader (knowledge about how to read and where to look on the page, knowledge about the structure and flow of language, knowledge of the specific subject, and knowledge of the world in general). In other words, readers need to supply considerable information as they engage with written language.

A considerable number of research studies have supported this alternative view of the process. It has been shown that our knowledge about language and about the world affects the actual perception of print and plays an important role in the development of meaning. For example, the following marks on a typewritten page—IO—can be seen as either numerals or letters. What makes the difference is what we already know about the context in which these marks occur. If they appear within 3IO4 we see them as numerals, whereas if they occur in RIOT they are perceived as letters. This example illustrates that what we see depends as much on what is in our heads as on what our eyes receive from the page.

Since, according to this alternative view, reading involves the interplay of cues sampled from the text and cues supplied by the reader, it cannot be an accurate process but is one which results in many mismatches between what we anticipate and what the writer has written. When contradictions occur, when anticipations are not confirmed, we respond by reprocessing. When we come to something unfamiliar we have several strategies at our disposal. We can choose to read on and use subsequent information to help us build meaning; we can reread, or substitute something that seems to make sense for the moment.

It is significant, however, that reading instruction has been little influenced by recent reading research and the alternative view of reading that has developed from it. As we've seen from the teachers' responses about helping students having difficulty reading, in many classrooms, instruction still presents reading as accurate word identification. This accuracy view of reading underlies most basal reading programs used today.

For the last several decades considerable money and effort have gone into developing basal reading programs. They have been designed to constitute the entire reading program for a school. They include a range of materials from reading textbooks (the "reader") to student workbooks, worksheets, supplementary books, and teachers' manuals. These programs have been based on two assumptions: first, the complex process of reading needs to be broken down into simpler component skills; and second, if students are taught these "simple" skills in a particular sequence, they will emerge fluent readers.

Nowhere is this belief more evident than in beginning read-ing instruction. From the outset, the focus of most basal reading programs is the letter-sound relationship and accurate word identi-fication. This is based on the notion that once children are able to identify all the words correctly they will understand what they are reading. Consequently, the goal of reading instruction is to teach students to translate print symbols (letters and words) into their corresponding speech forms. The procedures used to achieve these decoding skills, as they are called, vary from teaching extensive sets of rules for pronunciation to the presentation of regular word patterns (fat, cat, sat, mat), to instruction in letter-by-letter sounding out. Although the preamble to some programs suggests the writers see reading as a meaning-seeking process, decoding receives heavy emphasis in both teachers' manuals and students' workbooks.

A problem, however, has arisen as basal reading program de-velopers have fragmented the reading process into more and more "simple" skills: more and more children have had trouble learning to read. But instead of examining the underlying assumptions of the instructional programs they've been using, teachers have taken the continuing failure of some of their students to be evidence of the severity of the children's learning deficiencies. The usual remedy has been to fragment the reading process still further, focusing even more intensively on words and parts of words with less and less attention given to meaning. However, the alternative view of the reading process which has been developing sees the cause of most reading failure to reside not in the children and their learning ability but in the way they are being taught. With their emphasis on accurate word identification, basal reading programs inadvertently make learning to read difficult. This is because the assumptions about the reading process on which these reading programs rest are at odds with what we understand about how language functions and how it develops.

Language is an important part of our knowledge and obviously plays a central role in reading. Much is now known about how language is comprehended. We know that the sentences a person produces do not convey meaning in any simple way. Meaning is not contained within the sounds of speech but must be provided by the listener. This fact was made apparent again to me recently when a friend, in lieu of showing me a picture, attempted to describe something of interest to us both as "a cross between a skull and a pod." Not until more information had been offered was I able to understand what he meant. The conversation was actually about small rowing craft: sculls, not skulls. My strategy for dealing with the ambiguity confronting me was the one we generally use. I encouraged my friend to continue talking while attempting to resolve the conflict between my understanding of "skulls" and "pods."

In both spoken and written language, then, we deal with uncertainty and ambiguity in the same way. Rarely do we interrupt the flow of meaning to identify a particular word. Instead, we construct an interpretation of the situation by establishing a tentative meaning and checking it against the new information being received. We build meaning on the basis of the whole. That is not to suggest we don't use acoustic information in the case of spoken language, or visual information in the case of written language, as we attempt to make sense of what is going on. Clearly we do use what we receive from outside, but that information represents only one source of the total amount of information available to us. We depend more heavily on the information we bring to the language situation to help us understand it.

The importance of our reliance on the meaning we supply for understanding what's being said has been emphasized by research on language development. Perhaps the most significant insight that has emerged from observing children learning to talk is that the search for meaning underlies all language development. Children begin with the intuition that the noises produced by people around them can be related either to what they already know or to what they can discover about the world. Children do not extract meaning from what they hear others saying; they try, instead, to relate what has been said to what is going on. Children seem to learn to talk by inventing their own words and rules: by experimenting with language. Children make statements in their own language for meanings which are perfectly obvious to adults and then wait for adults to put the statements into adult language so they can make a comparison. And parents respond entirely unwittingly by giving the children the information they need to develop language for themselves. They provide the adult form for the meaning expressed in the child's language. If the adult says nothing, or simply continues the conversation, the child assumes his or her utterance is correct. When adults "correct"—that is, expand in adult language what children have said—they are providing feedback. The adult and the child are actually speaking different languages, but because they understand the situation, the child can compare their different ways of saying the same thing. Comprehension is at the core of the interaction; both the adult and the child can make sense of what is going on. Adults, knowing what a child means, provide demonstrations of how adult language refers to the situation. The process is one of successive approximations toward adult forms of expression. The situation provides the meaning and the utterances provide the evidence for the child's language experiments.

Language development, then, seems to have the following characteristics. Language learning begins with immersion in an environment in which language is being used in purposeful ways. The environment is rich with examples of language in action. What aspect of the task will be experimented with, at what pace, and for how long is determined largely by the child. In fact, experimentation with language occurs whether or not an adult is attending. The environment is secure and supportive; the child's approximations result in expansions on the basis of shared meaning. Development is continuous, yet marked by considerable differences from child to child.

Yet, most basal reading programs operate on a number of assumptions which conflict with what we now understand about how language develops. There is, for example, the assumption that the vocabulary and syntax of beginning reading materials must be rigorously controlled and simplified in order for children to learn to read. This is accomplished by limiting the vocabulary used to a few words which occur with high frequency in the language (the, is, come, said, etc.) and repeating these words often in "simplified" syntactic structures ("Come, come," said Mother).

However, the research on language development raises serious doubt about using word frequency as a basis for preparing reading material for young readers. For example, in a young child's speech production the words most frequently used by adults are omitted. In fact, some less frequently used words may appear earlier in a child's speech than those with higher frequency of use because of their importance to the children for conveying meaning. It seems that intent to communicate meaning plays a more important role in learning oral language than the frequency with which words occur in the child's language environment.

The practice of simplifying the grammatical structure of basal reading materials is questionable as well. While what children say may be "simple," their language environment is complex. Children hear a full range of syntactic structures; and from this rich language environment they actively select and reconstruct those elements which they need to convey meaning. They begin by generating their own grammar, inventing rules which are later elaborated and refined on the basis of the demonstrations in their environment. Children respond to the flow of meaning, not to individual words and sentences It is meaning, as children understand it, in the context of daily life, that guides language development, not the sounds of language or grammatical rules in isolation. Language development consists first of grasping a whole which is subsequently differentiated. But in order for this differentiation to occur, the language available to children must be meaningful as well as structurally complex.

A second assumption underlying basal reading programs which needs examination is the importance of accuracy in identifying words. Implicit in most basal reading programs is the notion that unless children can say all the words correctly, they will be unable to understand. Again, a look at children learning to talk suggests such a belief is unwarranted. Language grows by approximation. Children's first language sounds little like their parents' language. Yet slowly over a period of months recognizable words emerge. The same is true with grammatical forms. The earliest structures are the children's inventions which are unlike anything they've ever heard (for example, "Mommy sock" to mean "Mommy, please put on my sock"). Yet, over a period of time, children develop mature grammatical forms. Vocabulary development involves an evolution as well. To start with, children use some words in general ways. Only later does the meaning become refined as a consequence of experience. A child's word "cup" may initially refer to any receptacle that can hold milk or juice, but later will become restricted to mean a small container with one handle. In other words, children don't start to talk with complete adult language. They begin by creating a baby talk, which slowly comes to resemble more and more closely the language they hear around them.

Parents intuitively encourage their children's language development. Their responses to what their children say is on the basis of meaning, not form. They enthusiastically support their children's language efforts. Yet many teachers often insist upon accurate word identification rather than helping children focus on the meaning of what they are reading. Such close attention to the surface features of words and parts of words is at odds with children's intuitions about how language works.

The most serious contradiction between what we know about how children learn spoken language and the way reading is so often taught resides in the third assumption inherent in basal reading programs; that is, teachers (and program developers) know all about what is to be learned and how to learn it and children know nothing. By and large, basal programs imply that learning to read is a difficult process requiring the careful intervention of a teacher using a carefully sequenced instructional program. The teacher controls the learning by asking the questions, giving instructions, assigning the skills exercises, and correcting errors. Yet the most important observation from watching children learning to talk has been the control they themselves exert over the process. Children learning to talk are most often responsible for initiating the interaction, for deciding the topic of conversation, asking the questions, conducting the experiments, soliciting feedback, correcting their own errors, even choosing when to stop the exchange. In learning to talk, children control their own learning and parents wisely follow their lead.

There is evidence which indicates literacy can develop in the same "natural" way as spoken language when the conditions for learning are comparable. There are several studies of children who have learned to read before going to school. These studies have demonstrated that children are able to learn to read without any deliberate assistance from adults. In many instances the children who were studied learned to read without either the children or their parents even being aware of it. What this research has confirmed is that children direct their own learning. They learn to read at the same time and in the same way as they learn to talk.

One of the necessary conditions for learning spoken language is an environment filled with spoken language. Similarly, one of the necessary conditions for learning to use written language is an environment filled with written language. The world bombards children with print (product labels, packages, posters, signs, magazines, wrappers, TV guides, storefronts, traffic signs, advertising, menus, mailboxes, bathroom doors), all of which has a meaningful function. Young children are aware of this environmental written language and recognize a great deal of it.

In addition, children who have learned to read before going to school, or those who rapidly become readers once they begin school, have been read to from earliest childhood. The most important outcome of these children's extensive experience with books and with other kinds of print is that they have come to understand how extended written language functions. They have developed the crucial insights about written language essential for learning to read and write. First, they recognize that print is meaningful. Second, they realize that written language, while related to it, is not exactly the same as spoken language. Third, they have discovered that both spoken and written language can serve the same functions. Children who have been read to know the enjoyment that can be obtained from stories and they can recapture some of their favorites. They have learned that information can be obtained from books and from the other written language around them. They have often started to produce written language themselves: writing their own names as well as some words which are important to them.

Children who have been read to have learned to follow plot and character development from their experiences with written language. Such knowledge is the foundation of comprehension. Children's knowledge of story structure underlies children's ability to predict what comes next when they are being read to and when they are reading themselves. Transcripts of very young children reading favorite stories show they continually strive to reproduce the story's meaning. They try to maintain the language of books, and they self-correct so that what they are saying makes sense and sounds like book language.

The experience of being read to, then, is extremely important for children. The being-read-to situation creates an atmosphere which fosters experimentation. The language and story of the book are being learned; attention is also being directed to figuring out the mysteries of print. The "rules" for relating meaning, symbol, and sound are gradually generated from the large samples of complex and complete language available.

Obviously, experience with all kinds of written language is essential for a child's literacy development. Equally obvious is that learning to read for many children begins well in advance of coming to school. The school reading program must build upon children's knowledge about written language and reading. The children should be involved in reading from the day they start school. They should be read new stories and encouraged to select their favorites for rereading. Their participation in the reading should be invited but not demanded. The focus of a reading program should be to help children figure out for themselves how written language works.

Whereas the instructional approach used in most school reading programs is formal and teacher-directed, the alternative is informal and child-controlled. Instead of beginning with fragments of language, such as letters and sounds, complete forms of written language such as stories, poems, signs, and cereal boxes are used. Instead of expecting children's responses to be error-free with little room for experimentation, children are invited to try, to do the best they can. Instead of the teacher correcting "errors," the children are encouraged to determine for themselves whether what they are reading makes sense and the language sounds acceptable.

There are several components to such a whole language literacy program. The approach offers children exposure to written language used in as many different ways as possible. They are offered involvement with *written language in and from the environment.* The functional nature of this kind of written language is emphasized by having the children participate in shopping activities, by making signs, posters, and notices, by preparing lists of what jobs or tasks are to be carried out, by writing letters. The inclusion of written language in meaningful contexts allows the children to begin to understand the relationship between meaning and the written language that represents it.

A whole language curriculum uses *predictable materials* such as songs, nursery rhymes, poems, as well as classical and contemporary children's stories. Predictable books are especially important. They have several characteristics. They use repetitive language patterns which allow children to anticipate what is going to come next. Predictable books have a good match between text and illustration. The children are able to use the pictures to help them figure out what the text might be likely to say. Predictable books are about things with which children are familiar. At the beginning of the year the teacher preselects the books and other materials, but as the year progresses the children are allowed to choose the books themselves. Each story may be read to the children many times until the language and the story are familiar. These favorite stories may be dramatized. They are available for later independent rereading. The children can also listen to, and read along with, taped readings of them.

A whole language curriculum also incorporates *language experience.* Language, whether oral or written, is learned through active "play" with language, through experimenting with different ways to express ideas, and exploring relationships between the children's language and their knowledge. Language experience stories evolve from the children's interests and activities. The writing becomes the communal record of what the children have learned or done. The language used for recording the activity or experience should come from the children themselves; there should be no attempts to limit or control the vocabulary used. Language experience stories are an excellent tool for helping children make sense of written language because they emphasize the importance of the connection between a reader's experiences and written language.

Shared reading is another important component of a whole language curriculum. One form of shared reading involves the use of enlarged books usually chosen from among the children's favorite books. The enlarged books allow the teacher to create an intimate atmosphere with a number of children at once. The large book sets a stage for involvement with both the story and the print since the children are all able to see what's on the page as they listen to and watch the teacher read and as they read along. It is through such shared reading that children begin to understand how print and meaning are related. The material used for shared reading should be predictable, have illustrations which are closely related to the narrative, have a clear plot, and/or be informative. The process of using a large book for shared reading involves repeated reading of the story until the children are able to read it on their own. The story may be dramatized. The children may listen to it on tape. They are encouraged to write about it, to discuss it, and to ask questions both about the story and about the print itself.

Story reading on a one-to-one basis with older students reading with younger students is another way of sharing reading. The older student reads to the younger, the younger to the older. Such sharing increases children's familiarity with books, increases their interest in print, and helps them recognize the difference between the function of picture and print. The activity helps build the children's fund of stories.

Shared story reading can involve parents as well. Both at home and at school parents are encouraged to read with their children new books as well as old familiar ones. Again the sharing is intended to extend the children's familiarity with stories and with the ways in which information is presented in books.

Sustained silent reading is another important reading activity in a whole language curriculum. Sustained silent reading is a brief time set aside each day when everyone (including the teacher) reads by him- or herself. Students select their own material. They are encouraged to spend silent reading time enjoying books on their own.

Of growing concern to many teachers is the literacy development of children from minority and disadvantaged families. A whole language curriculum offers a number of advantages for teaching children from families where a climate of literacy hasn't existed. The process of learning to read begins by reading to the children. The teacher reads to them; older students read to younger ones. New books, favorite stories, chart stories, posters, poems, even candy wrappers are read. Being read to helps make the children aware of the different structures and functions of written language. They begin anticipating how written language sounds. By being read to, children without previous exposure to books are given the experiences which lead to literacy which more fortunate children have had.

In addition, in a whole language curriculum children are given the opportunity to control their own learning. As with learning to talk, the environment offers the experiences but the children themselves initiate the interaction. They determine what books to read and when to read them. They may help turn their favorite stories into big books for a group to enjoy together. They can choose if and when to join in on the group reading, when to read on their own, when to read to someone else, when to ask someone to read to them. When reading is so pervasive, everyone gets into the act. Even children who haven't been exposed to books, who haven't been read to at home, participate as freely as those who have.

Because a whole language curriculum encourages experimentation, children lacking experience with written language are made to feel comfortable with print. In a relaxed, yet intensive, self-directed way they can read and reread their favorite stories to themselves or some noncritical audience (teacher, other children, adult visitors, pets). And as they read, based on their memory of what has been read to them, they move closer and closer to what the writer has written. To start with, the children's reading is based largely on what is remembered of the story, but it isn't long before they begin using the print.

Children's trade books are the cornerstone of a whole language curriculum. Such a program requires the availability in the classroom of a large number of different titles (both factual and fiction), many in multiple copies. The value of children's trade books as the vehicle for learning to read lies in the natural language children's writers use. There are neither controlled vocabularies, nor simplified syntactic structures. The illustrations are there to provide support for the text. In addition, children's trade books can be read in their entirety in a brief time and they have something relevant to say about children's lives. Consequently these materials allow children to assume control over their own learning.

Using funds currently locked into basal reading and other textbook programs for the development and purchase of large quantities of children's books covering a wide range of topics and for all school levels requires a major shift in curriculum policy, however. Furthermore, a move from a textbook-controlled curriculum to one which develops from a broad range of interesting books requires a major reeducation for teachers since greater responsibility would rest with them for deciding what and how their students should learn.

Some might argue that declining enrollments and financial cutbacks make it impossible to alter the status quo, to shift from our reliance on basal reading programs to a teacher-developed whole language curriculum. But perhaps now is the time to take a long, hard look at the alternatives. How we go about teaching children to read needs, certainly, to be examined. When I ask children, "When you're reading and you come to something you don't know, what do you do about it?" I get two kinds of answers. Children, no matter how old, who read confidently tell me they skip and read on, they reread, or put in something that makes sense. The children who are having difficulty seem to have a single reply: they "sound it out." My suspicion is that unfortunately these less fluent readers have learned, all too well, precisely what we've been teaching them.

From Sunny Days to Green Onions

On Journal Writing

Sumitra Unia

How does one progress from being an accuracy-oriented traditional teacher to a developing learner and teacher? My experiences with journal writing, previously at the grade two level and presently at the grade five level, help to illustrate my development. In retrospect, I can see a shift in my position from an impersonal, academic taskmistress to a more understanding person who recognizes the importance of collaboration between teacher and students. From using the journal as an ordinary writing assignment, I have learned to appreciate its usefulness throughout the curriculum.

I found journal writing enabled me to change my expectations of the students. My preoccupation with correct spelling, grammar, punctuation, usage, and neatness in written assignments had to undergo a close examination. I learned that these mechanical aspects of writing would have to be subordinated to the writer's message and purpose to enhance spontaneous written expression. My role shifted from being a mistake corrector to demonstrating the accepted conventions of written language through my own written responses to them.

It took a long time to overcome my compulsive marking habit. I now question the relevance of the traditional way of marking written work. The hours I spent in the past correcting children's work for spelling, punctuation, and grammar did not prevent the recurrence of the same errors by the same students. Besides, I had to keep double-checking to see if the students had corrected the errors I had detected. The task was laborious and devoid of joy. I realize now that my actions must have conveyed to the students the importance of correctness regardless of the nature of an assignment. To them, writing probably meant evaluation; they did not see it as a vehicle for communication. I have started to appreciate the importance of establishing communication as the fundamental purpose of written assignments. Writing is a much more meaningful activity when the constant threat of evaluation does not loom over it. The spontaneity encouraged in journal writing lends itself particularly well to fostering confidence and increasing written fluency.

My increased sensitivity to students' attitudes and expectations is a direct result of getting to know the children better through their personal writing. It has helped me to understand them better and to communicate with parents more effectively. Increasingly, I feel myself to be a partner with the students in the learning process rather than its sole director.

How Did I Begin Journal Writing?

Some years ago I taught second grade children. I wanted to see what difference writing regularly would make to young children who had had few opportunities to write meaningfully. We started with a class journal entry. After talking about the journal as a means of writing freely, I wrote on the board:

Dear Journal,

It is sunny today. We have school today. . . .

The children copied the opening sentences of our class journal entry. I explained that since the purpose of the journal was to record ideas, all spellings did not have to be correct; they could invent spellings for words they did not feel certain about. I would, however, help people if they were stuck, but they need not continue to work with me if they felt able to carry on without my assistance.

After the first two sentences, some children set out on their own; others took more convincing. They were so conditioned to thinking accurate spelling was essential that they kept lining up to have the words they needed spelled for them.

Probably because I kept my promise not to mark their journals for spellings, the children gradually asked for fewer words from me. Becoming more comfortable with the activity, the children were soon producing longer journal entries. The confidence they gained in journal writing facilitated other written assignments as well. Not only did they come to school looking forward to writing in their journals, but they also wrote and retold stories more easily. Hence there was no question of motivation. I do not recall any time when students were at a loss for ideas about what to write. A supportive environment and the opportunity to write were all that were required.

Students came to see journals as a vehicle of expression not requiring any correcting. Revising and editing were done in other contexts; book reports, stories, and projects were often taken beyond the first draft. It was at that time that we attended more closely to the conventions of writing, giving them their proper place. They did not make every task of writing formidable, either for me or for the students.

Reflections, Regrets, and . . .

As I examine the journals of those grade two students, I am both embarrassed and relieved. My views about the children's perceptions and my own reactions to their writing become evident in the samples below. They helped me see the changes I have undergone since I first started journal writing with that second grade class.

I find it appalling, for example, to realize how rarely I responded in the students' journals. I remember having had to struggle with the workload of reading the growing journal entries of a whole class on a daily basis. I would have liked to have written back regularly to each individual had I had the time to do so. As it happened, I managed to write to only a few students sporadically. My authoritarian and distrustful stance becomes apparent in that I did not consider discussing this problem with them. I now see that they might have suggested some very practical solutions to my difficulties. At that time, however, I did not appreciate the contribution students could make to my own development.

My occasional responses consisted of congratulatory or encouraging notes. It is a relief to see that very rarely in these responses did I worry about demonstrating correct spelling in what I wrote. To reassure the students that I had read their journals, I signed my initials in the margin. That I was interested, however, in the writer's message could scarcely be conveyed in this manner unless they took comfort in the absence of negative comments. My infrequent and brief responses probably had some effect on their writing. They wrote abundantly about their personal experiences but did not see the journal as a two-way communication between us.

Take Lisa's fourth entry (the first to which I responded):

Sept. 11

I saw my mom. I want four a walk with my clase. I like my teacher. I saw some machines and they were picing up rokse. My friend came to My hose and we played dolls and It was fun. I wore a dress today Im invited to melanie Birthday she is going to be 7.

I wrote back:

Dear Lisa,

You are doing your journal very nicely. I am very pleased.

Mrs. Unia

The child could have interpreted my response in a number of different ways since I had not explained what I liked about her journal. My compliment could have been for neat printing, for the quantity of writing, or for the variety of experiences she had reported. I would certainly write back to this child differently now, appreciating, as I do, the importance of communicating through writing. I might, for example, say:

Dear Lisa,

Your dress is very pretty. I hope you have fun at Melanie's birthday party. Do you like wearing dresses?

It is nice to be able to wear different kinds of clothes. I am glad I don't have to wear dresses to work all the time now. In cold or rainy weather, I prefer to wear pants. How about you?

Mrs. Unia

Lisa's entry of September 19 is an interesting example of the kind of writing produced spontaneously by my second grade children:

I saw some gerbils and they were cute. my brother hade some gerrbils frome the teachar and he took tham home and the cat kept on going on the cach.

My response:

Dear Lisa,

I am pleased to see you writing more in your journal. It is interesting to read your entries.

Mrs. Unia

While my reply showed an uncritical acceptance of what she wrote, I can now see that I lost a wonderful opportunity for inviting Lisa to extend an interesting story. I could have asked her what made the cat keep going to the cage, I could have wondered about how the gerbils must have felt to have the cat around, or I could have speculated about what might have happened if the gerbils got loose, which might have encouraged her to write more.

My effort to extend her next entry proved totally ineffective. She wrote:

Dear cjch I am going to the contest and It's going to be fun. I want to the vair and it was fun. I want to the Falie to pike some apples and pirs. and then we want to a plaes to eat awer lunch and It was fun.

I answered:

Dear Lisa,

You seem to have done a lot of exciting things at the weekend. What rides did you like at the fair? Where was the fair?

How many pears and apples did you pick in the valley? I would like you to tell me more about your weekend.

Love,
Mrs. Unia

My second paragraph demonstrates the contrived nature of my message in an effort to present conventional forms of some mis-spelled words. It also shows my dissatisfaction with the amount Lisa had written.

I now believe that my idea of writing back for the purpose of extending a story in a journal entry was somewhat misguided. I find that even my fifth graders rarely respond to my messages although they look for my written response and express disappointment when I have failed to write back to them. My writing seems to complete a link in the mutual writing cycle. It demonstrates my acceptance of their ideas and encourages them to go on. The dialoguing that does occur seems to take the form of postscripts. In October, Juliana, a fifth grader, wrote more than two pages about her weekend experiences and then realized she had something to say to me directly:

Dear Mrs. Unia,
   Thank you very much for the complement you gave me when I last wrote to you.

                                                                    Juliana V.

I had previously commented about how I enjoyed reading her journal.
   The same student had written barely six lines earlier in the month. Her entries for about three weeks remained quite brief before she returned to her normal volume. The lack of pressure from me may have restored her interest in writing. In the past, I might have required such a capable student to apply herself until she produced what I considered an acceptable quantity, taking over the control of the learning that the journal allows to occur spontaneously. I find that my trust in letting students determine their own learning is much greater now than before. If it is evident that a student is continuously unwilling to write much, I find sharing journal entries of volunteers helpful. One student reads his or her journal aloud to the class. The audience usually listens for the author's message ready with questions and/or suggestions. Exchanging journals with partners also accomplishes the same end.
   Occasionally a dialogue will develop between me and a student. Tina, for example, wrote about her younger brother catching chicken pox:

                                                    Monday, January 9th, 1984

Dear Journal
   On Saterday I washed tv all day and I hade to mind my brother that night I had to mind him to he got the chicken pocs. . . .

   My response was:

Dear Tina,
   I hope your brother is better now.
   Chicken pox must be spreading now as Ricky in Mrs. Stewart's class also has them.
   How old is your brother? I hope he's not feeling too miserable and that you don't catch them from him.

                                                                    Mrs. Unia

   She wrote back:

Dear Mrs. Unia,
   My brother is felling a lot better I don't Think I will ches them because I had the befor My brother is 7 hers old he is going on 8.
   P.S. Thanks for the little later.

                                                                    Tina Bennett

   Sometimes students will confide in me and relate personal problems. Other times they may ask for advice. Jeff wrote about a family quarrel:

   . . . I went over my mother's and we we're having a fight. I was yelling at her and arguing. She doesn't want me to go to her house any more unless

I apologize. I ain't going to go back there again because my father doesn't want me getting involved with her. He doesn't want me phoning her because she just causes arguments. . . .

Jeff had spent the Easter weekend with his mother and had brought back very nice gifts. I found it sad to read his entry and responded, partly to show empathy, and partly to offer my suggestions:

> Your rugby pants and Cooper bag are really smart, Jeff!
> When I'm angry, I don't see my fault, let alone apologize! But when I calm down, I find I need not have got so worked up and it doesn't require that much effort to say sorry. It makes the other person feel better and then I don't have a grudge against them! It takes a long time for me to make friends again sometimes.

Sabrina was an ambitious but talkative fifth grade student. She wanted to enter the junior high extended achievement program and expressed her concerns about that:

> Dear Mrs. Unia,
> I never thought of myself as intelligent and capable of learning a lot. I always thought I was just normal and my brother was the smart one. He's in advanced junior high program. Thats what I want to be in but it will take a lot of work. So I think I should sit by myself and you should be more strict with me and my work. I don't know if you would think the same about it if you were me. . . .
>
> Yours Truly
> Sabrina D.

I had taught Sabrina's brother in grade three and could appreciate her problem. I wrote back:

> Dear Sabrina,
> It's nice to see you are modest and ambitious.
> You should have no trouble going into Advanced Junior High stream if you work for that. You're welcome to sit at the spare desk. . . .
> I'm pleased Sean is doing well in junior high. . . .
>
> Mrs. Unia

Generally, I have found it difficult to give my fifth grade students the opportunity to write in their journals more than twice a week. To increase the frequency with which we write, we sometimes use the journals for science and social studies. For example, during our two-week study of maze learning by guinea pigs this year, students wrote in their journals daily. This was a convenient form for reporting their science activities. It also demonstrated the students' acceptance of journal writing as a worthwhile recording device.

The older children have a number of concerns about journal writing when they first start in the fall. Early in the year, it is not unusual to hear students protest, "But I never did anything interesting," before beginning their journals. They feel they must have interesting activities or experiences to relate. They also have a notion of how much they must write for their assignment to please the teacher. So I try to show that reporting daily experiences and activities is legitimate. Writing spontaneously about what is on one's mind, regardless of its degree of interest, is what must be attempted. They should write as much as they can in the time available. Some days they may write more than on others. The basic idea I want them to understand is that we get better at writing by writing. It takes a great deal of convincing before the students are willing to let their thoughts flow freely. However, as they gain experience as writers, they tend to write more coherently on subjects of greater sophistication. Chris wrote about an interesting experiment:

I have green onions.
My mom boght some at the store and I asked her if I could have some and she said "yes but you can only have the small ones" I said that I was going to make them biger for her. What I did first was I had to get a knife. Then I got some soil and a pot just a little one and then I took the knife and I cut the ends of the roots off. Then I planted them and tonight we are going to have them for supper.
There big enogh now. I am going to have to do it again it was fun wondering if it would work it did, and as I said it was really fun.

The
End

I only saw Chris's journal entry many days after he had written it. He had, however, obviously derived sufficient satisfaction from writing about his experience that he did not feel the need to share it with me immediately. I don't respond to the students' every journal entry, but I make the effort, at least once a week, to write to each one of them individually. This allows me to get to know students more personally and to share my ideas and experiences in a more informal context.

Students appreciate my problems and are more understanding in turn. One day I wrote about the restless night I had had because of my baby and how the lingering smell of oil paint around the school was particularly bothersome that day. Gregory wrote back saying how sorry he was that I felt so tired and hoped I would get some rest. He told me it was a good journal. I had to chuckle at his compliment; it was a reflection of the kinds of response I had used in the past. I have also learned to keep a journal as well. I try to write in it while students write in theirs. They react particularly well to my writing in my journal while they write in theirs. I exchange my journal with a student who finishes at the same time. I write back to this individual and encourage him or her to respond to my entry. This makes me a member of the writing group.

Sometimes there is a problem with privacy. There are journal entries which the students wish not to share. We have worked out a system whereby students put a red dot in the margin if ever they write something they do not wish me or someone else to read. A green dot indicates where one can begin reading again without intruding on the writer's privacy. The acceptance of this strategy shows the students' trust in their readers while allowing them to express freely what would otherwise not be written.

I also find the journal useful with parents on parent-teacher interview nights. They enjoy reading their children's journals; they too are able to see that the journal represents a meaningful use of written language. Like the teacher, they appreciate the insights journals offer. Parents, however, like many traditional teachers, are drawn to spelling inaccuracies. Occasionally, the journal is useful for showing concerned parents that their children spell a high percentage of their spontaneous written vocabulary correctly. Calculation of the percentage of misspelled words in sample journal entries helps to demonstrate that the problem is not as grave as it seems. The growth in the length of journal entries is also helpful for convincing parents that some learning is going on. Because the children do have the opportunity to become aware of and learn conventions of written language through revising and editing assignments meant for publication, parents are able to see that such skills are not being ignored. Consequently they become comfortable with the improvisation which is an integral part of journal writing.

It is interesting to hear what the children feel about their journals. Some like to save them so they can look back from year to year. Others have let me keep their filled journal scribblers, removing the pages of intimately personal entries. Some of the students I had had in grade two were in my fifth grade class this year. They really enjoy rereading their second grade journals. Often they're surprised they managed to write as much as they did. Children who were not with me earlier are amazed at the volume of writing produced by such young children.

Where Am I Now?

I see journal writing as an integral part of my curriculum. As the least threatening of all writing activities, it provides students with very special opportunities to become more confident and fluent writers. They take several risks: feeling free to express their own thoughts and ideas, considering them worth recording or sharing; trusting an adult to accept uncritically their ideas and expression without having to worry about accurate use of spelling and punctuation; putting the same trust in peers; believing that writing in this manner helps them become better writers.

My role is to be a facilitator. I no longer feel a need to demonstrate correct spellings and language conventions. The purpose of my writing back to students is not to extend their ideas; it is to create an awareness of my acceptance of their work and to encourage communication.

I see the journal as an important kid-watching tool. Continued experience has helped me to discover the many facets of journal writing I originally failed to perceive. It enables me to understand the student in academic as well as personal terms. I am able to evaluate the change in my own thoughts, attitudes, and actions in the teaching situation. It clearly illustrates the reciprocal relation of the teacher and the student, the partnership we share.

To Judith

A Look At A
Child's Writing
Development
Through His
Letters

Judith M. Newman

Jamie is a nine-year-old friend of mine. Recently, I was absent
from home for six months and Jamie was one of the people with
whom I corresponded. I was pleased to receive his first letter, which
accompanied letters from his mother and younger sister, and I
answered him promptly. Although he didn't reply immediately, I
continued exchanging letters with the rest of the family. That other
correspondence had an effect on Jamie, and about two months later I
received another letter from him.

I was astonished by the length and detail of this second letter
compared with the first one, and decided to see what I could learn
about Jamie as a writer from his letters. I realized I wanted to do
more than identify spelling mistakes or errors in punctuation and
capitalization, say something about his handwriting, or comment on
what he has yet to learn about letter writing form. By looking only at
his correct use of conventions, without regard for the context in which
the letters had been produced and the process by which they had
been created, I was aware I would completely lose sight of Jamie as a
writer. I would gain few insights into what he knew about producing
written language or what he knew about the social transactions
involved in letter writing. I needed, instead, to develop a sense of the
complexity of the process in which Jamie was engaging as he wrote. I
needed to try to understand the decisions Jamie was making as he
worked out what he wanted to say and how he wanted to say it.

Figure 6–1, written toward the end of January, is a thank-you note
for my Christmas gift—a kite which I had given the family. While
Jamie has known me for some time, this was the first occasion he
had had to write me. His caution is evident. The length of the letter
tells us he didn't have much to say. The tone ("To Judith" instead of
"Dear Judith") suggests there may even have been some coercion
involved in his taking on the task in the first place.

However, having accepted the responsibility for writing a thank-you

Figure 6 – 1

note, Jamie was faced with some decisions about how he would go about it. He knew he couldn't just say:

Thank you for the kite.
From Jamie

He had to enlarge on that somewhat. His problem arose when he found that what he had to write didn't use very much of the available space. Realizing he had to say more, he now had to consider what would constitute appropriate news to write about. It's not difficult imagining the conversation which probably took place between Jamie and his mother as he was writing:

Jamie: I've said thank you, now what do I write?
Mother: Well, you could tell her about what you've been doing at school, or you could say something about your swimming and gymnastics.
Jamie: OK. I guess I'll tell her about the diving.

Telling me about his participation in a couple of upcoming diving competitions produced what looked like enough writing. Satisfied with that amount, Jamie used a time-tested ploy: he filled the remaining space with a picture. Like the rest of us, Jamie is clearly operating on the principle that letters should fill the page. He has a sense of how much writing looks like enough and a convention which allows him to complete his letter with a drawing.

Next I asked myself what were some of the specific strategies Jamie used as a writer. It is clear the most important decision Jamie makes from the outset is to write what he wants to mean. Unlike many more cautious writers, Jamie decides to say what he wants to say whether he knows how to spell the words he wants to use or not. This decision is most fortunate since it allows us direct access to Jamie's decision making as a writer/reader.

There are several instances, for example, where we can see Jamie saying to himself, "This doesn't look right!" We can see where he changed several words: *"key"* was changed to *"kit"* (for kite); *"nat"* to *"not;"* *"dut"* to *"but;"* *"sume"* to *"some."*

These changes are direct evidence of the interplay between what Jamie knows about written language from being a reader and what he knows about spelling. They let us see the considerable extent to which Jamie's visual memory influences his spelling decisions. His spelling of *"flon"* ("flown") and *"Halafax"* ("Halifax") shows his awareness of sound/symbol relationships. The changes he makes in *"not"* and *"some"* shows he knows what those words look like. His initial spelling for "but" (*"dut"*) is a holdover from earlier years when he was unsure about how b's and d's were written. His change indicates he is now able to self-correct. (Note that he made the appropriate initial decisions for *"Diving, and,"* and *"Judith."*)

Jamie's changing the spelling of *"conpeyt"* ("compete") to *"conpet"* later in the letter is particularly interesting. Dissatisfied with his first attempt (which was based on a spelling generalization: spell /e/—ey as in *money* or *honey*) Jamie tries spelling the word another way, which is closer to how he remembers that word looking. His trying an alternate spelling at some later point in the letter demonstrates how the constant revision or updating of knowledge comes about through the use of written language itself. Jamie is in effect saying, "I'm not sure about that word. I'll try it a different way this time." What's important is that he doesn't let his uncertainty about how to spell something stop the flow of meaning.

Jamie makes other changes as well. The capital H written over the lowercase h in *Halifax* shows Jamie's awareness of some rules for capitalization. (Again, note his use of capital letters for the names of persons: *"Judith," "Jamie."*) He also uses periods in a somewhat unconventional way; he uses them to mark a topic shift rather than to signal a sentence ending.

We see two other interesting changes in this letter.

7 I will conpeyt

The c underlying the I is an example of the writer's head getting ahead of his hand. Jamie had figured out what he was going to say before his hand had caught up with his thoughts. Because he was writing with a pen, he chose to write over this anticipation.

the 14 We

The mark between the "the" and "14" informs us that Jamie paused to make a decision. Jamie's pen was on the paper waiting to write while he was trying either to recall the date of the diving meet or to decide whether he wanted to write "fourteenth" or "14." His *"7"* and *"14"* for "seventh" and "fourteenth," by the way, are examples of his choosing to use an alternate communication system.

Even in such a short writing sample we begin to sense the complex orchestration required to produce any written document. Jamie's determination to place meaning ahead of convention is important for him as a developing writer. His commitment to meaning allows him to explore written language freely, to make whatever decisions he deems appropriate for maintaining communication. His commitment to meaning is equally important for us as kid watchers. His slips of the pen, his overwriting, his use of functional spelling all provide opportunities for us to observe some of the strategies Jamie has developed for generating written discourse.

We learn a great deal about Jamie as a written-language user from this letter. We see he has learned that letters have several components: salutation, body, closing. We find Jamie being a risk-taker with language, not unnecessarily concerned about neatness and accuracy, willing to invent spellings and other conventions in order to say what he wants to say. We are also able to see how knowledge about written language, developed by reading, is used as Jamie writes—evidence of the important and intimate relationship between reading and writing.

Let's turn, now, to Jamie's second letter (Figure 6–2, a, b, and c), keeping in mind what we've observed so far.

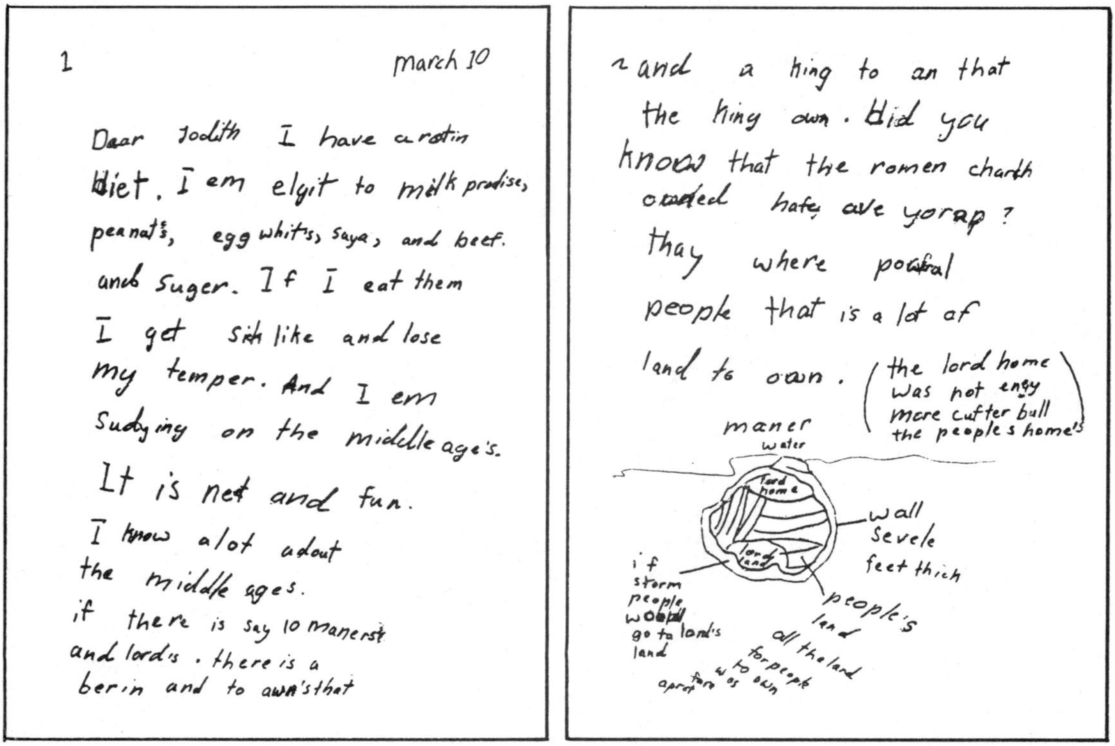
1 March 10

Daar Jodith I have a rotin diet. I em elgit to milk pradise, peanat's, egg whits, saya, and beef. and suger. If I eat them I get sik like and lose my temper. And I em sudying on the middle age's. It is net and fun. I know alot adout the middle ages. if there is say 10 manerst and lord's. there is a berin and to awn'sthat

2 and a king to an that the king own. did you know that the romen charth oned hafe ave yorap? thay where powful people that is a lot of land to own. (the lord home was not engy more cufter bull the people's home's)

(a) (b)

Figure 6 – 2

Several differences are immediately apparent in this second letter. The most striking difference, of course, is the increased length; Jamie has a lot to say this time. He gets very involved explaining two things which currently interest him: his *"rotin"* ("rotten") diet and what he's been learning in school about the Middle Ages. Notice, in fact, that his discussion of the Middle Ages takes on the character of a school report with an underlined heading (*"To be a Knit"*) as well as a final *"Thend."*

Jamie has little difficulty describing his diet and its effects on his behavior. He does, however, run into trouble when he begins writing about the Middle Ages. He has so much to say and he can't get it down quickly enough. I had some difficulty reading his description of land ownership:

WHAT HE WROTE	TRANSLATION
If there is say 10 maners and lord's.	Suppose there are ten manors.
There is a berin and to own's that	Each manor is owned by a lord.
and a king to and that the king own.	There are barons and a king, too, who own land.

Having begun with a rush, Jamie then settles into his topic, informing us *"the romen church owned hafe ave yorap"* ("the Roman Church owned half of Europe").

Next Jamie decides to diagram a typical manor. He titled his drawing and provided explanatory notes. His decision to shift from

people how do all the work have to pay taxis to the lord and thay bow when the lord Come's, tha

To be a Knit

A lord would send his sun to a place where he code lorn to be a Knit. at it thay would get thing for the lord and Hesse him and get food for him and then play a game of chess. at 21 he get's the Knit sat and gos to be a lord in a nother maner. thend

love
Jamie

(c)

writing to drawing allowed him to describe more easily, and in greater detail, what he understands about land use. His comparison between the living conditions of the lord and his peasants (*"the lord home was not eney more cufter bull the peoples home's"*) ("the lord's home wasn't any more comfortable than the people's homes") is clearly an afterthought; he has placed this information between the writing and drawing and enclosed it in parentheses. At this point, Jamie has become so involved in sharing what he knows that he chooses to write a third page.

Why, we might ask, has Jamie decided to write such a lengthy exposition? It is obvious his diet is important and he is interested in what he's currently learning at school, but there are other subtle influences operating as well. For example, Jamie's mother and I had been corresponding about his diet. In my last letter to her I had expressed interest in Jamie's reactions to having his choice of foods so severely limited. She had shared that part of her letter with him. Jamie actually begins his letter by answering a question I had asked his mother.

Furthermore, in the time between Jamie's first and second letters, I had exchanged two letters with Jamie's younger sister, Jillian. Her first letter, a single page, had included a story. In my reply, I had complimented her on it. Needless to say, in her next letter, three pages in length, she had included another story. Again I responded enthusiastically. I also enclosed a small gift. Jamie's letter is influenced to some extent by my correspondence with Jillian. She was getting letters because she was writing to me; he wasn't. She also received a small present; he hadn't.

As Jillian and her mother were writing once more, Jamie decided to get into the act himself. I learned later that he had come into the dining room, where the other two were working, watched for a few moments, asked for some paper, then disappeared for about a half an hour. When he returned he handed his letter to his mother to send with hers.

We can imagine Jamie saying to himself as he started writing: "Hmmm, Judith wants to know about my diet. OK, I'll tell her about that. Hmmm, Jillian got some stickers when she told Judith about losing hers. Judith also likes long letters (she writes three pages to Jillian). What can I write about? I'll bet she'd be interested in what I know about the Middle Ages." Hence: *"Dear Judith . . . love Jamie"* and his report-like tone.

I did in fact respond to his letter as Jamie had predicted I might. I had seen in a bookstore a kit for making a model of a medieval village. I didn't send it to Jamie, though; I sent it to his mother for the family to work on. Nevertheless, when the present arrived, Jamie commented, "I'll bet she meant that for me but she didn't have anything for Jillian!" So much for adult subtlety. Jamie had watched my correspondence with the others, figured out how I would probably respond to a serious effort if he chose to make it. He decided to test his theory with this lengthy letter—to my knowledge the longest document he'd ever written.

Now let's look briefly at Jamie's decision making in the process of writing. Again, his functional spelling, overwriting, crossing out, slips of the per, etc., help us understand how he handles the writing process. Once more, we notice Jamie placing meaning ahead of convention both in terms of punctuation and spelling, yet his knowledge of both is considerable. Whereas we might have concluded from his first letter that Jamie needed to be taught about beginning sentences with capital letters, in this letter he uses that convention. He even corrects himself twice:

my temper. And I em
A lord would send his Sun

(When he gets involved in his topic he drops the capital letters although he retains the periods.)

Jamie is also experimenting with apostrophes: *"peanut's," "middle age's," "come's," "get's," "lord's," "people's."* It would seem that he has only recently become aware of this particular punctuation mark and is still unsure of its application. He uses apostrophes with plurals and third person singular verbs as well as to show possession; wherever he has a final *s*.

Again, we see Jamie deciding, "This spelling doesn't look right": *"Da"* becomes *"Dear," "rs"* becomes *"rotin," "biet"* becomes *"diet," "ave"* becomes *"of."* We notice him overwriting some letters (the *w*'s in "know" and "own," for example), forming them more legibly. He combines words in his haste to get his ideas down: *"ang"* is corrected to *"and get"; "thend"* wasn't noticed.

Jamie's spelling strategies continue to reveal the intimate relationship between reading and writing. There is evidence of his knowledge of sound-symbol relationships as well as his knowledge of how words look. We can see him solving the problem some words present by deciding to spell them the way he spells other words: *"cufterbull"* ("comfortable"); *"taxis"* ("taxes"); *"where"* ("were"); *"sun"* ("son"). We have evidence of his knowledge of spelling generalizations: *"suger"* ("sugar"); *"maners"* ("manors"); *"neet"* ("neat"); *"eney"* ("any"). We see him deciding to place-hold meaning with some vague approximation for a word he knows he's never thought about before: *"elgit"* ("allergic"); *"prodise"* ("products"); *"swt"* ("sword"). While a quick reading of his letter may leave the impression that Jamie's spelling is highly unconventional, of the 221 running words he has written here, 78 percent have been spelled conventionally.

What do we learn about the writing process from Jamie's second letter? First, we observe the importance of the writer's willingness to take risks. While Jamie had been a risk taker in his first letter, committed to saying what he wanted to say, he'd written very little. Not until he'd received a reply and observed my correspondence with Jillian and his mother did Jamie really decide to be a writer himself. Jamie had learned that letters to friends are first-draft affairs; neatness and accuracy aren't obligatory. Consequently, he shows little hesitation on this occasion in selecting a topic, organizing what he wants to say, and writing about it.

Jamie's second letter confirms the necessary interplay of reading and writing. Jamie makes many more decisions where we see what he knows as a reader influencing what he decides as a writer. His spelling decisions, organizational and formatting decisions, and self-corrections are all affected by his previous reading experiences. We become aware of the continuous interaction of the decisions he makes as a writer and the decisions made as a reader, both in the process of putting the marks on the page and as he reflects on what he's written.

Jamie also provides us with an opportunity to see that learning isn't linear. His letters demonstrate, in fact, that learning occurs on several fronts at the same time. The coordinating of ideas, use of formatting conventions, and attention to audience must all be considered on every writing occasion. It is not possible to master one aspect of the process before tackling a second; learning to write involves evolution on many fronts at once. The writer is constantly involved in experimenting. Jamie's use of apostrophes is an example of just such experimentation. Whether his awareness of this punctuation mark has come from reading, from something the teacher has said, or from watching the other kids write, Jamie has chosen to experiment with it here. He has some of the features of its use worked out: an " ' " is often followed by an *s*. In the process of experimenting he naturally uses *s* correctly; but his experimentation leads to errors as well. Those errors are important; they allow us to observe how a learner's knowledge is continuously refined by experience.

Jamie provides other evidence that learning isn't linear. We see that writers don't always use everything they know when they write. Jamie demonstrates his knowledge of how to use capital letters and periods to begin and end sentences, but as he becomes more involved in drafting the letter he frequently omits the capitals. Jamie also knows a great deal about conventional spelling (he corrects *"melk"* to *"milk"*; *"ond"* to *"owned"*; *"wood"* to *"would"*; *"wen"* to *"when"*; *"ave"* to *"of"*), but in his concern for getting his meaning on paper he often chooses to spell functionally. Although writers may know about certain conventions there is no guarantee they will use them all the time. The reasons for writing, knowledge of audience, confidence of the writer, and the flow of ideas all affect whether a particular convention will be used or not.

The most important thing we learn from Jamie's second letter is the complexity of the context which affects a writer's decisions. Our notion that the writing context can be determined from what is written in a teacher's lesson plan is clearly erroneous. The influences which operate either to expand or constrain a writer's opinions extend far beyond the narrow situation of a writing lesson in school. A child's decisions as a writer are affected by a multitude of factors many of which only become apparent after the child has written. In the case of Jamie's second letter, that context included what was going on at school which interested him, his diet and the effect it was having on his life, what he'd been reading, what he was able to observe about the social transactions involved in letter writing from other correspondence, and what he was learning directly from what I had chosen to write him in my reply to his first letter. All of these factors affected what Jamie said and how he said it.

As teachers, then, we need to look beyond neatness and accuracy when examining children's writing. We need to become sensitive to the experimenting that's going on each time a child writes. We need to understand what children's "mistakes" reveal about their knowledge of the writing process. Kenneth Goodman has referred to those "mistakes" as "windows into the process"; they provide opportunities for insights into the kinds of sophisticated decisions children are capable of making.

We also need to understand that knowledge about writing comes from many sources: from reading, from watching others write, and from writing itself. The curricular implications are straightforward. The only way we can help children become fluent writers is by letting them write—for many different purposes, on topics of their own choosing, and for audiences of their own.

As we've seen with Jamie, letter writing is a particularly useful vehicle for facilitating children's writing development. Letters to friends, teachers, older students, and family are informal, legitimate first-draft writing where the focus is on meaning, not on convention and form. Letters provide opportunities to experiment with writing where the cost of being wrong is low. Letters provide their own feedback; they invite replies from those who have received them. Letter writing is highly contagious. A message board, to which notes can be pinned, is quickly covered with letters the children write to one another. A section of the blackboard reserved for reminders is soon filled with notices. There is no need for a child to ask, "What should I write about?" when writing to an older or younger student in the school who's become a pen pal; there's lots to share. A personal reminder from the teacher to a child, tucked into a lunchbox or pocket, is sure to prompt a reply. A young friend of mine, for example, has to take pills with each meal. Not long ago the teacher was sending the pill container home to be refilled. She'd enclosed a note saying her supply was low. The box was returned to school with a reply from the child himself on top of the pills.

The most useful thing about letters as a vehicle for helping children develop as writers is that they circumvent our compulsion as teachers to correct everything in sight. Whoever heard of returning a letter to its sender with the mistakes circled in red? Letters are to be answered; they highlight the importance of meaning. Maintaining that focus on meaning, more than anything else, is crucial for becoming a writer.

I received a third letter from Jamie shortly before I returned home (see Figure 6–3, p. 82). Once more the complex decision-making required of a writer is evident. We are able to see how the continuous evolution of a writer's control over the process is facilitated by the process of writing itself.

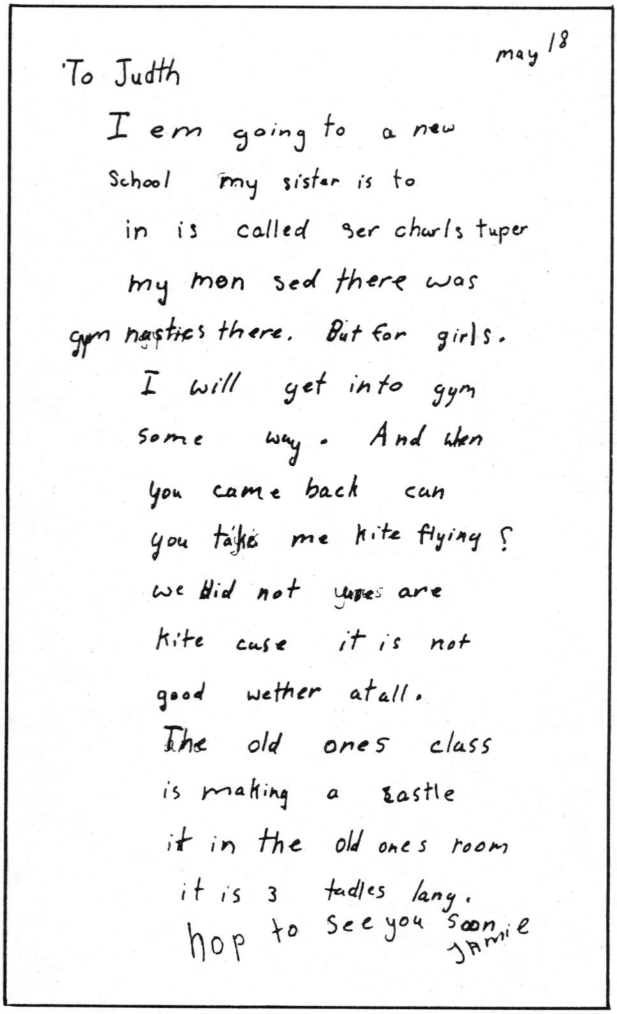

To Judth

    I em going to a new
School   my sister is to
    in is called ser churls tuper
    my mon sed there was
gym nasties there. But for girls.
    I will get into gym
    some way. And when
    you came back cun
    you take me kite flying ?
    we did not ywses are
    kite cuse it is not
    good wether atall.
    The old ones class
    is making a castle
    it in the old ones room
    it is 3 tadles lang.
        hop to see you soon
                         Jamie

may 18

Figure 6 – 3

Learning to Spell
Olga Scibior

The writing sample in Figure 7–1 was produced at the beginning of the school year by Michael, a boy in my third grade classroom, who was one of the weakest spellers in the class. In looking at his spelling attempts, I had to decide, as his teacher, how best to help this child develop as a writer.

According to current provincial spelling curriculum guidelines, I should have marked Michael's misspelled words and had him add them to his personal study list. The guidelines then suggest:

One 15-minute period each week can be devoted to their [the students'] weekly study list. A recommended study procedure is: See the word in isolation. Say the word. Look carefully at the word, noting the relationships among sounds, structure and unusual letter combinations. Write it. Check the spelling. Repeat the process if the word is misspelled. . . . The self-corrected test is the single most important factor contributing to the successful study of the spelling words [*Spelling 2-8,* N.S. Department of Education, 1979, p. 16].

Figure 7–1
Translation:
The Space Battle Poem
space battle, space battle, face battle,
face battle, we're losing, we're winning,
we're falling, we're spinning
the enemy's here, the enemy's here
get to your gear!
the end

> The Spase Bael pom
> spase Batel spase Batel fase Batel
> fase Patel wer loosing wer wining
> wer falling wer spening
> the enemes Her the enemes Her
> Getowt your Ger!
> The end

I wondered, however, whether this was really how children learn to spell. A great deal of recent research evidence suggests it isn't. This recent research, based on observations of children's writing, suggests, in fact, two things. First, learning to spell is a natural developmental process for children; they naturally evolve systematic strategies for spelling. Second, the process of learning to spell involves rule generation and hypothesis testing.

Read (1971, 1975), for example, demonstrated that preschool children quite naturally begin making sense of English orthography and actively construct written language by using their intuitive understanding of English speech sounds in their spelling attempts. In their earliest writing, he found children frequently represent sound by using letters whose names approximate the sound they want (e.g., "HARE"—"cherry"; "GRIV"—"drive"; "BOT"—"boat").

Beers and Henderson (1977) were able to show a progressive development in the use of vowels and morphological endings *(-ed, -ing)*. They proposed four spelling stages through which school-age children from kindergarten to grade two seem to progress:

1. Prephonetic—some essential sound features of words not represented (e.g. omit vowels) but usually correct beginning and/or ending consonants (e.g. MTR—monster; SM—swimming).
2. Phonetic—letters used on basis of sound and all sound elements represented in a letter-name strategy (ATE—eighty; BAD—bed).
3. Transitional—awareness of some of the conventions of English orthography (e.g. vowel markers, vowels in every syllable, acceptable letter sequences) and rule generalization and overgeneralization.
4. Correct Forms—words spelled conventionally.

Beers *et al.* (1976) also demonstrated that children's spellings reflect their exposure to words such that words with common vowel spellings which occur with high frequency in the language were found to be spelled conventionally more often than those which occurred with low frequency.

It seemed necessary to me to look at Michael's writing, particularly his spelling, in terms of these research findings. I was interested in what I could learn from his spelling attempts. What did he know already about the spelling system? What rule-generating strategies was he using?

These questions about Michael led me to investigate the development of children's spelling strategies (as used by third grade children) and to follow the evolution of these strategies in a language environment which allowed children to use language in meaningful contexts; an environment which allowed them to construct meaningful written language and which permitted them the freedom to experiment with spelling.

I tried to create such a learning environment by (1) encouraging the children to generate their own spelling in their writing; (2) having the children write daily in journals, making books, doing projects and other open-ended language activities; (3) pointing out informally certain spelling generalizations if the children asked about them or if it became apparent to me that such information might be helpful. (No formal spelling program was used at any point during the year.)

I observed the spelling strategies of Michael and four other children (two of whom were able to spell well, two of whom were average spellers) over the entire school year. The writing samples I collected were drawn primarily from the children's daily journal entries. The children's writing reflected their judgments about spelling and revealed a range of strategies.

The percentage of conventional spelling was compiled for all children on a monthly basis. This tabulation showed a general, steady progression in the development of conventional spelling over the school year:

CONVENTIONAL SPELLING (PERCENTAGES)

Month	Student				
	Traci	Kelly	Kelcey	George	Michael
September	85.9	87.1	76.7	76.4	[b]
October	90.0	91.1	80.5	69.0	51.2
November	91.6	91.5	78.9	73.1	66.2
December	93.8	93.6	84.7	78.3	64.9
January	92.5[a]	91.8[a]	81.8[a]	80.6	66.4
February	93.0	87.9	89.2	80.9	63.2
March	93.3	92.1	81.3	75.7[a]	67.7
April	93.5	90.8	81.3	73.7	69.9[a]
May/June	93.4	90.0	83.2	87.3	71.4

[a] Consistent changeover to cursive writing in samples.
[b] Michael's initial reluctance to risk writing on his own resulted in his copying for the first month.

There were some fluctuations in the percentage of conventional spelling. One particularly noticeable fluctuation occurred during the period when the children were shifting from printing to cursive writing. I found that words which had been spelled conventionally by some of the children earlier in the year were being written incorrectly when the children were trying cursive writing; letters were unintentionally left out, some letters were positioned in the word incorrectly. At this time the children seemed to be contending with the uncertainties of controlling their pencils, which interfered to some extent with their knowledge of spelling. The children's spelling also seemed to deteriorate somewhat when they shifted to using more multisyllabic and low-frequency words. This became increasingly the case toward the end of the school year as the children were trying to write longer and more elaborate pieces.

I also followed certain elements of the spelling system in the children's writing such as the use of short vowels (a, e, i, o, u as in pAt, pEt, pIt, pOt, pUtt, pUt), the use of long vowels (as in cAke, PEte, dIme, stOve, tUne) and the use of e-markers on long vowel words (e.g., cAkE). Percentages of conventional spellings used for these categories were compiled for the beginning, middle, and end of the school year to find out how the children's use of these spelling generalizations developed.

In addition, I observed the development of the children's use of vowel digraphs such as:

LONG VOWEL

ai (rain)	ee (see)	igh (night)
ay (hay)	ea (mean)	ie (pie)
eigh (sleigh)	ie (field)	y (sky)
	ie (receive)	

ow (snow)	ue (blue)
oe (toe)	ew (knew)
ough (though)	oo (moon)

SHORT VOWEL

oi (point)	ow (cow)	oo (took)
oy (boy)	ou (cloud)	ou (could)
au (because)	aw (draw)	ea (head)
	augh (daughter)	

I also included observations on the use of vocalic r as in ar, or, ur, er, and ir, as well as the children's use of simple morphological endings: -ed and -ing.

An increase in the use of conventional spelling seemed to develop in some categories more quickly than others, and this development seemed to be related to the frequency with which these words needed to be used by the children (reflecting, to some extent, their frequency of occurrence in the language). For example, short and long vowels occurred considerably more frequently in the children's writing than vowel digraphs:

Number of Occurrences	
Short vowels	3468
Long vowels	1347
Vocalic r	870
Long vowel digraphs	797
Short vowel digraphs	453

An examination of the writing samples showed the children were spelling short and long vowels conventionally more frequently; they were needing to write such words often and consequently developed a sense of the conventional spellings for words with these features. By February, the spelling of short and long vowels, e markers for long vowels, and morphological endings -ed and -ing were conventional most of the time. Vowel digraphs were more difficult for the children initially, and continued to present difficulty for some throughout the year.

CONVENTIONAL SPELLING: SHORT VOWELS (PERCENTAGES)

	Traci	Kelly	Kelcey	George	Michael
September	96.5	98.0	95.7	91.2	89.4[a]
February	100.0	97.8	97.0	91.3	92.4
May/June	98.9	98.5	98.6	97.9	99.0

CONVENTIONAL SPELLING: LONG VOWELS (PERCENTAGES)

	Traci	Kelly	Kelcey	George	Michael
September	96.7	99.2	97.4	97.6	90.1[a]
February	98.9	100.0	100.0	96.6	93.2
May/June	99.2	96.0	100.0	98.9	96.0

CONVENTIONAL SPELLING: E-MARKERS (PERCENTAGES)

	Traci	Kelly	Kelcey	George	Michael
September	92.3	97.6	85.2	71.4	65.5[a]
February	93.3	62.5[b]	100.0	100.0	92.6
May/June	100.0	—	100.0	100.0	100.0

CONVENTIONAL SPELLING: VOWEL DIGRAPHS (LONG) (PERCENTAGES)

	Traci	Kelly	Kelcey	George	Michael
September	83.3	88.4	82.2	28.6	34.7[a]
February	93.7	80.4	89.7	74.4	47.5
May/June	99.2	96.8	82.6	91.7	50.0

CONVENTIONAL SPELLING: VOWEL DIGRAPHS (SHORT) (PERCENTAGES)

	Traci	Kelly	Kelcey	George	Michael
September	78.6	89.7	68.8	22.2	40.0[a]
February	97.9	95.8	72.8	71.4	22.2[b]
May/June	100.0	100.0	70.0	90.0	60.6

CONVENTIONAL SPELLING: VOCALIC R (PERCENTAGES)

	Traci	Kelly	Kelcey	George	Michael
September	95.6	96.0	83.8[b]	79.2	61.9[a]
February	97.3	92.1	95.0[b]	88.8	93.9
May/June	98.3	89.5	88.5	90.9	68.2[b]

CONVENTIONAL SPELLING: -ING (PERCENTAGES)

	Traci	Kelly	Kelcey	George	Michael
September	100.0	81.8	80.0	100.0	100.0[a]
February	100.0	100.0	100.0	100.0	100.0
May/June	100.0	100.0	85.7[b]	100.0	71.4

CONVENTIONAL SPELLING: -ED (PERCENTAGES)

	Traci	Kelly	Kelcey	George	Michael
September	97.4	87.9	100.0	—	100.0[a]
February	100.0	75.0	100.0	66.7	100.0
May/June	100.0	100.0	100.0	100.0	100.0

[a] For Michael's first writing in October.
[b] Reflects some repeated misspellings.

The frequency of use seems to be a factor in the development of conventional spelling. For example, I found that the long vowel digraphs *ay, ee, ow,* and *oo* were spelled conventionally earlier in the year than the less common ones *eigh, ei, ie, oa, oe, ui,* and *ough.* Also, the short vowel digraphs *ow, oo,* and *ou* were spelled conventionally earlier in the year than *ea, oi, ough,* and *augh,* all of which continued to cause the children difficulty at the end of the year.

What of Michael in all of this? What did I learn about his spelling development? In looking back at his spelling attempts at the beginning of the year, I could see that he was spelling short and long vowels conventionally most of the time. He was also using *-ing* and *-ed* appropriately. He was, however, having difficulty with vowel digraphs. In some samples, Michael used a letter-name strategy for vocalic *r* (*"spidr"* for "spider," *"supr"* for "super"), but he was using e-markers for long vowels and could use the long digraphs *ee* and *ay* and the short digraphs *ow* and *oy* conventionally much of the time.

What did I learn about Michael's spelling development? As the year progressed, I could see Michael was using letter-naming strategies less and less. By February, he was using conventional spelling for vocalic *r* and he was beginning to use more vowel combinations appropriately. Although he was still having some difficulty with vowel digraphs at the end of the year, he had sorted out a great deal of spelling information, as Figure 7–2 attests.

By watching the children as they tested their spelling hypotheses, tried out their own rules, and solved their own spelling problems, I certainly came to question the utility of assigning lists of unrelated words to be memorized for a weekly test for helping children learn to spell. From this study I learned, instead, that children's spelling development does proceed naturally if they are allowed to write a great deal and are permitted to spell functionally. I came to see that learning to spell is a function of experience; the more writing the children did, the more opportunities they had to spell, the more likely

Figure 7 – 2
Translation:
On june the 30th I'm going to white point beach. and on july the 7th I'm going home. this is what my new Dinky [looks like].

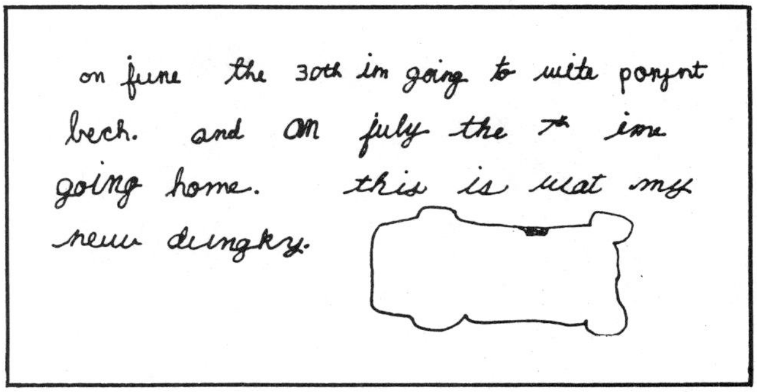

they were to spell the words they were using conventionally. I came to understand that the way to help children's spelling development is by encouraging the children to use their own judgments about how to spell, and by letting them read and write.

The Message Board

Language Comes
Alive

Reta Boyd

With gaping mouths and horror in their eyes, the three boys stared in disbelief as the insensitive teacher ordered the removal of Jason B., buddy, coworker, the third side of the triangle, from Table Five. Never, not even during their loudest arguments, had they thought of such an occurrence. This could not be happening. No more on-the-side sharing their stories, no more assisting one another with the math, no more discussing the pros and cons of why Jimmy hit Tony, should there be commercials in the videoing of the CHS News, etc. This couldn't be happening. They could not function separately. This was the end of the Three Musketeers or WAS IT?

What followed this event was the first of many exchanges between these three boys and myself during the months of November, December, and January. One hour after the change of seating the following note to me appeared on the class message board (see Figure 8–1):

> *please would you let Stephen*
> *set back her were he*
> *wore befor. We are begining*
> *to miss each other all ready.*
> *If you moue us back we*
> *will promis not to talk*
> *nearly as much,*
>
> *Jason Bradley*

Figure 8–1
Translation:
Please would you let Stephen sit back here where he was before. We are beginning to miss each other already. If you move us back we will promise not to talk nearly as much.
Jason Bradley

I wrote in my reply that I had a responsibility to the other members of the class. They too had rights. The talking trio was to show us that they could be considerate of others.

Before the class was dismissed for the day, a message from Stephen, one of the boys involved, emphasized Jason's request (See Figure 8–2).

Figure 8 – 2

And I replied (Figure 8–3):

Figure 8 – 3

Several weeks went by; December brought a Christmas card with another request (Figure 8–4).

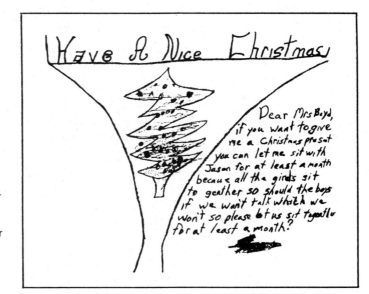

Figure 8–4
Translation:
Dear Mrs. Boyd,
If you want to give me a Christmas present you can let me sit with Jason for at least a month because all the girls sit together so should the boys if we won't talk which we won't so please let us sit together for at least a month.

My message to the boys was a noncommittal "Let me think about it."

On the first day back after the Christmas holidays, our correspondence continued. Obviously the boys had discussed their problem and their plan of attack; on the message board first thing in the morning appeared the following (Figures 8–5 and 8–6):

Figure 8 – 5

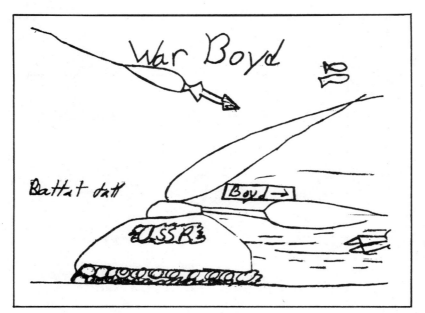

Figure 8 – 6

Noticing these two messages on the board, I responded, "Says who?" and initialed it, to which Stephen replied, "Me."

We had no sooner engaged in this exchange when all other communication was cleared from the message board and centrally displayed was the following brightly colored scroll (Figure 8–7):

Figure 8 – 7

The two boys were out for blood. The next morning before I had a chance to respond to their scroll, these notes appeared on the message board (Figures 8–8, a and b; and Figure 8–9):

(a)

(b)

Figure 8 – 8

Figure 8 – 9

Ignoring this threat, I instead replied to the proclamation (Figure 8–7):

> Fair! Who says I have to be fair?
> Give me some reasons why Jason should sit with you.
>
> R.E.B.

Moments later the "King's Note" (Figure 8–10) was posted accompanied by a paper crown.

Kings Note
1. Because he is our friend.
2 We think it's not fair that the girls get to sit togeather.
3. Because we work better togeather.

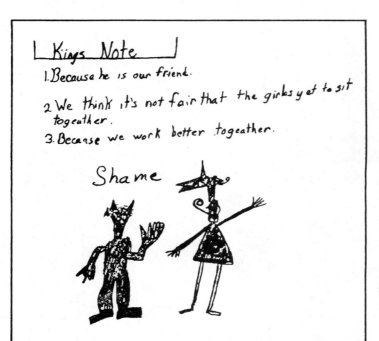

Figure 8 – 10

Apparently much had gone on behind the scenes; the boys had decided to enhance my prestige, hoping to make me feel better and help sway me in their favor. The presentation of the crown prompted me to respond (Figure 8–11):

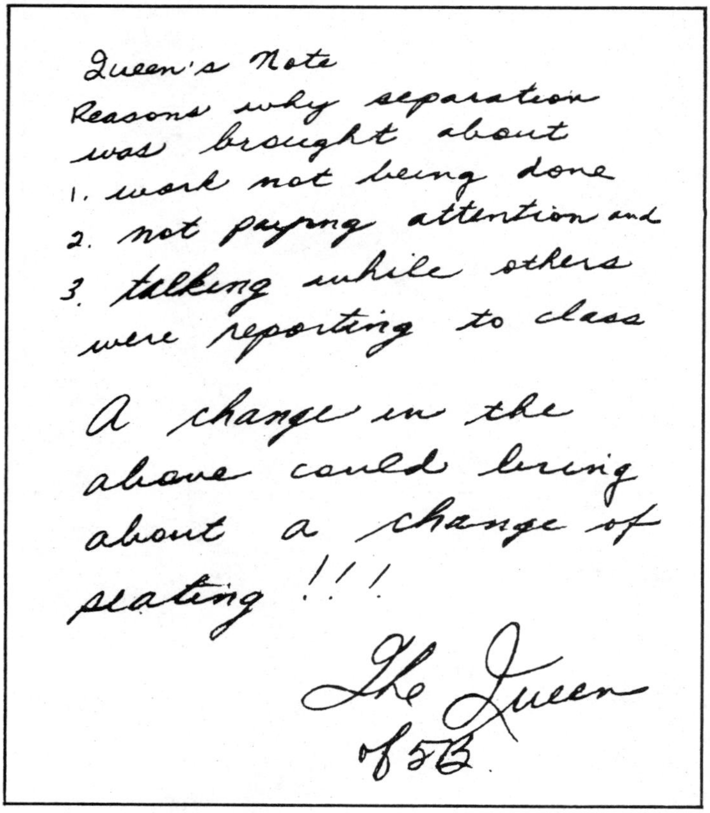

Queen's Note
Reasons why separation was brought about
1. work not being done
2. not paying attention and
3. talking while others were reporting to class

A change in the above could bring about a change of seating!!!

The Queen of 5B

Figure 8 – 11

These students had zeroed in on their teacher's weakness: a decision made under pressure is not always the best one. The message in the next note was clear.

Figure 8 – 12

My response was a smile with silence. However, the trio was undaunted. The following day, another brightly decorated King's Note greeted me (Figure 8–13). This time it was from a humbled king.

(a)

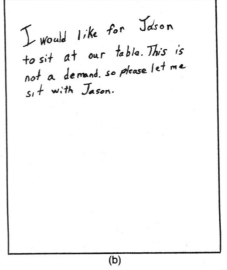

(b)

Figure 8 – 13

In setting up the message board, I chose a bulletin board about one and a half meters square inside the classroom near the entrance. I covered it with white paper, applied an attractive border, attached holders for tacks, paper of various sizes, and a pencil, and titled the bulletin board *MESSAGES*. The first day of school, I wrote an open message to everyone welcoming them to grade five and expressing the hcpe that we would all have an exciting year.

I also posted the directions for using the Message Board.

Who can use it?
Everyone.

When may one use it?
Before opening exercises, immediately after recess and/or whenever you have a few free minutes.

Why might one use it?
For sending personal messages.

How might one use it?
Use the materials on the Message Board and include the receiver's and sender's names.

The message board, originated by Carolyn Burke at Indiana University, demonstrates the functional nature of written language and requires the involvement of more than one individual. The social interaction may be between two people, several people, or the whole class. In this activity the emphasis is on meaning, and many of the messages demonstrate that language exchanges are ongoing processes which lead to writing, reading, more writing, more reading, and decision making.

The message board activity has two parallel purposes. It serves as a vehicle for communication: for reminders that help is wanted, that jobs need doing, that an assignment is due, or that greens are needed for the guinea pigs. Here, I, or any member of the class, can communicate with the whole group, a small group, or an individual. On a more personal level, it provides an opportunity for me to acknowledge students helping other students solve a problem, the spontaneous written poem on Tall Ships, an oral presentation, or the finishing of a difficult task. These notes take little time and help develop greater rapport with the students.

The second purpose of the message board is the development of language fluency. It supports learning in several ways. The students may write to inform, to respond, to persuade, to give an opinion, to inquire, and to describe their feelings. It encourages writing, reading, questioning, the sharing of ideas, and also allows the teacher an opportunity for demonstrating the functional nature of language. This informal, expressive writing provides even the reluctant writer the chance to explore written language. This year, the notes from many of the students, nonfluent writers and readers included, not only gave me insights into group and individual problems, but continued to demonstrate the usefulness of the message board.

How did this problem that I have shared with you end? After reading Stephen's final note, and sensing the change of attitude, I agreed to let Jason sit with his buddies. Yes, the boys did get back together for a while. By releasing the reins and demonstrating that the message board was there for the class's use, we worked through a social problem. All four of us enjoyed every exchange, and a closer relationship resulted.

What about Reading?

Judith M. Newman

For quite some time teachers have been concerned about their students' reading fluency. It's clear there's a need for continually planned instruction in reading throughout a student's school career since many students seem unable to handle the range of materials we'd like them to read. However, improving students' reading fluency doesn't rest only with the teaching of English or Language Arts. Instead, it's important that reading instruction be provided throughout the curriculum. We need to consider how we can adapt instruction across the curriculum to foster reading development. We need to examine ways of integrating instruction in reading with subject instruction as well as explore ways of helping students develop adequate background knowledge so they can read what we want them to read.

Let's start by looking at the reading process. Many people believe reading begins with the print. But consider the example in Figure 9–1. At first glance it's unintelligible. Why is that? Our eyes are receiving information from the page; but something is clearly missing. What's missing is the interpretive information we must supply. If I tell you the

Figure 9–1

example is a word, some of you will be able to see it. If I add that the word has been written in white against a black background more of you will find it. I might even need to tell you the word in the example is "ART" before you will be able to see it.

This example illustrates a fundamental point about seeing: that is, seeing is not primarily a visual process (Kolers, 1969). Neither is reading. We gain some information directly from the print through our eyes. Frank Smith (1971) called this "visual information." But this isn't the only source of information we use. We also have considerable information stored in our heads, in memory, which we need to use when we're reading. Since this information is available, as Smith (1971) says, from behind the eyes, it can be called "nonvisual information." We don't need to identify every print element in order to understand what we're reading. Our nonvisual information (that is, our knowledge of the world together with what we know about language and how it works) affects the actual perception of print and contributes substantially to our understanding.

Let me illustrate this, with the following print symbol:

$$\mathit{13}$$

How it's perceived depends on the context in which it occurs. When it appears in

$$\mathit{13LACK}$$

we see it as a letter. When it occurs in

$$\mathit{413-7609}$$

we identify it as two numerals. The visual information is the same. What makes the difference is the nonvisual information we've supplied.

The skill that's developed in becoming a fluent reader is learning how to use relevant prior knowledge to select the fewest, but most productive, print cues. The amount of attention we need to give the print will vary from moment to moment. If we have a great deal of nonvisual information we need to pay relatively little attention to the print. If, on the other hand, we have little prior knowledge to supply, we have to attend more carefully to what's on the page. The more we know in advance, the easier it is to read; the less we know beforehand, the more difficult it is to understand.

The conceptual information we supply is crucial for understanding written language. Many students, both younger and older, have difficulty reading school materials, not because they don't know how to read, but because they lack sufficient nonvisual information. Having insufficient nonvisual information is a common experience for everyone. Consider the following passage:

In this example the modulation to E is a passing modulation. The suspension in the inside voice is helpful in avoiding the cadential effect at each final chord of the pattern. The first transposition moves down a major third and the second down a minor third, it being impossible to divide the interval of a perfect fifth (from the intitial key, G-sharp, to the desired destination, C-sharp) into two equal parts [Piston, 1962].

Just as with the "ART" logo and the print symbol that could be either the number 13 or the letter B, the information we need to understand this passage is not on the page. In order to make sense of the paragraph we need to have some fairly sophisticated knowledge about harmony before we read. Although we have some clues that we're reading about music, if we lack any knowledge of the terms used in the study of harmony, we find the meaning of the text is still largely a mystery.

The point being made is this: whether we are fluent readers or not depends largely on the background knowledge we have available to bring to the print. Fluent readers can have difficulty reading when they have little or no prior knowledge to supply. The opposite is also true; less fluent readers can read more easily if the material they are reading is about something with which they are already familiar.

What does this distinction between visual and nonvisual information mean for instruction?

Because we know reading is easier when we can bring some prior knowledge to the text, we can simplify reading by making sure our students have adequate background knowledge before asking them to read. Since understanding depends on our being able to relate new information to what we already know, we must help students develop the conceptual background necessary for reading.

How can we help students develop background knowledge? There are a variety of ways we can do that. The instructional choices we have available depend on what the students know already. In some situations students' general knowledge is adequate for understanding. What is required is that their attention be drawn to what they already know. One useful way of doing that is having students brainstorm the topic before they read, to make them aware of what information they possess. This enables them to read actively; their reading is guided by the information they have considered in the brainstorming discussion. The questions raised during brainstorming lead them to read for answers.

Most teaching, however, is concerned with helping students develop new knowledge. There are many situations in which it's helpful to provide practical experiences. Students will find a text on animal classification easier to read if they have had an opportunity to observe and sort specimens first. Math books make more sense when students have explored concretely the concepts about which they are reading. History is also easier to understand if a novel or a film about a particular period has preceded a difficult chapter from a textbook or if appropriate artifacts are examined and discussed.

Another way of building background knowledge is through reading itself. The information from one selection on a topic can serve to support reading of another selection; what we learn from the first becomes the foundation for subsequent transactions with text. Sometimes reading a brief selection, simply written, can serve to support students' reading of a more complex passage. Where the ideas are complex, and perhaps difficult to grasp, information from several sources can be used to help students build a general understanding of the topic under discussion. The supporting selections can come from books other than the ones we want the students to be able to read and understand, or they can, if necessary, be written by the teacher.

Developing students' reading fluency requires more than attention to word identification or word analysis. We can affect our students' reading more directly by helping them develop the knowledge they need for understanding and interpreting a text before we ask them to read it. We need to keep in mind it's the amount of nonvisual information readers have that makes reading difficult or easy. If we expect our students to read, without first ensuring that they have some background knowledge, then we're making reading difficult; if, on the other hand, we draw their attention to what they already know, if we discuss previously learned concepts and anticipate where they might lead, if we take the time to provide concrete experiences, as well as a range of reading selections on the same topic, we'll be making reading easier.

We've been discussing nonvisual information, prior knowledge, in general terms. We need, however, to consider its precise nature. Specifically, we need to examine the language cue systems which contribute to understanding. Let's begin with a sentence:

Jimmy lived in a small

Suppose we'd encountered this part of the sentence at the bottom of a page. Even before turning the page we've some information about the next word. We know, for example, that it is likely to be a noun or an adjective because other types of words such as verbs, adverbs, prepositions, conjunctions, or articles don't usually follow an adjective. We wouldn't expect to find:

Jimmy lived in a small eat

or

Jimmy lived in a small of

We'd expect, instead, the name of a place or a type of dwelling to occur next, although another descriptive word would be possible:

Jimmy lived in a small white

Knowing the next word is a noun or an adjective is part of our knowledge about language. Our ability to anticipate a particular part of speech is based on our syntactic knowledge—what we know intuitively about the grammatical rules which govern how language is used.

We also know the next word won't be *elephant* or *telephone,* and it probably won't be *submarine* because although these words are nouns their meaning is inappropriate; they don't refer to small places in which people usually live. Our semantic knowledge, what we know about meaning, restricts our choice of words.

If I added a bit more to the example:

Jimmy lived in a small c . . .

we could make some guesses about what the word might actually be. We know the next letter won't be *b, f,* or *g,* because these letters don't follow *c* in common English words; after *c* we expect to find either a vowel or an *h, l,* or *r.* Our intuitive knowledge of the spelling patterns used in English, orthographic knowledge, is acquired through experience with reading and writing and helps us anticipate what specific words would occur next.

	cabin
Jimmy lived in a small	church
	clearing
	craft

In other words, we bring to reading our knowledge of language structure—syntactic knowledge, knowledge of the meaning of words and of how certain meanings fit together—semantic knowledge, and knowledge of spelling patterns commonly found in the language—orthographic knowledge. Syntactic information, by indicating the relationships among words, limits the grammatical choices possible; the semantic cues help us predict appropriate meanings within the syntactic constraints. The orthographic cues help us predict specific word choices.

These sources of information—the language cue systems—are used interactively with visual information. The more syntactic, semantic, and orthographic knowledge we can supply, the less we have to rely on the print because we already have some sense of what we expect to see. As we read we use the language cue systems to anticipate what is coming next, to confirm our expectations, and to integrate new information into what we already know:

It was still dark but there was a faint suggestion of a grey luminosity in the east as we felt our way through the bordering poplar bluffs to the slough.
Through the blurred screen of leafless trees, I beheld the living silver of the slough, miraculously conjured out of the dark mists. The shimmering surface was rippled by the slow, waking movements of the green-winged teal.
As the dawn approached, the red glare of the morning sun fell on the immaculate mirror of the slough; and then the ducks came to the pond with a great whoosh. They came in such numbers that it seemed the slough would be too small to hold them all.

There is a word in this passage—*slough*—which many of us haven't seen before. Using our syntactic knowledge we can tell it's a noun because it's preceded each time by *the,* used to identify a noun. We also can say something about what the word means. We're able to tell it's a place surrounded by trees which for the moment are leafless perhaps because it's winter or early spring. Its surface is being rippled by the movement of the ducks. From the semantic cues we understand the place must be some kind of a pond or small lake.
Many of us won't have ever heard the word used, but we do have

some idea how it might be said. It could be like *cough,* or *though,* or *rough,* or *plough,* or *through.* However, being unsure of its pronunciation doesn't prevent our knowing what the word means. Pronunciation isn't necessary for understanding the meaning, which we've been able to construct by using syntactic and semantic cues.

What the example illustrates, I think, is that an emphasis on pronouncing words detracts from the more important business of understanding them. While it was possible to establish a tentative pronunciation for the word, our semantic and syntactic input contributed substantially more to our understanding.

Yet, instruction is often based on the premise that if we can say a word we'll understand it. That may be true if the word is one we've heard before and we recognize it. However, we meet many words we've never heard used, and being able to say them won't help with understanding. What will is using the syntactic and semantic cues to formulate a tentative meaning, which we'll revise as we gather further information from reading.

How can we make use of this information about the language cue systems for reading instruction?

I want to emphasize that I'm not advocating we teach our students about the language cue systems in any formal way, because I'm not sure that making this knowledge explicit would be of much use to them. Being able to talk about the language cue systems is not necessary for fluent reading any more than being able to analyze and describe what we do when we talk makes us better talkers. It is important, however, for teachers to understand what's involved in reading so we can create instructional situations in which students are enouraged to risk using the range of knowledge they have available to them.

In fact, without our realizing it, many of our students have become rather adept at using the syntactic cue system. We've often assumed they've understood the concepts we've wanted them to learn when they've been able to answer our questions. By using word order, function words, inflectional endings, and punctuation, they can often supply "answers" and still lack understanding.

For example:

In Scrangle, wizzets were crailing because most furples were glinking a targ of pranialism. This targ of pranialism was the result of many pranial fwumps wanting their own persats.

Why were wizzets in Scrangle crailing?
Because most furples were glinking a targ of pranialism.

Why was there a targ of pranialism?
Because many pranial fwumps wanted their own persats.

Is the following situation, in which students are asked to read and answer questions about the text, very different?

In Europe, tensions were rising because most countries were experiencing a surge of nationalism. This surge of nationalism was the result of many national groups wanting their own governments (Tait and Mould, 1973, p. 307).

Why were tensions in Europe rising?
Because most countries were experiencing a surge of nationalism.

Why was there a surge of nationalism?
Because many national groups wanted their own governments.

These "answers" may be demonstrating an ability to manipulate syntactic structure and not an understanding of the concepts.

If we shouldn't formally teach students about the language cue systems, how, then, can we help them become more adept readers? We can begin by emphasizing that the goal in all reading situations is understanding. We can help them realize that they don't need to identify every word in order to develop a sense of the passage. We need to help students become aware of how they make use of the language cue systems, how they make decisions for handling what doesn't make sense.

Knowledge about the kinds of decisions readers can make, another aspect of nonvisual information, is largely intuitive. That is, we don't actually say to ourselves, "What do I do now?" when we encounter something unfamiliar. But as we read, we're engaged in deciding when to go back and try again and when and how to keep on going. Such decisions are called reading strategies (Goodman and Burke, 1980).

There are three basic types of reading strategies. We predict what is coming next. We confirm our predictions and correct when our expectations are not verified. We integrate new information into existing knowledge.

Predicting strategies consist of generating expectations on the basis of information from any or all of the available cue systems. Confirming strategies are the result of asking ourselves if what we're reading makes sense. Integrating strategies are involved in the complex process of incorporating the meaning we're constructing into the knowledge we bring to the reading situation. We integrate meanings for unfamiliar words; we integrate complex ideas and relationships as well. We predict, confirm, and integrate on the basis of information from all the cue systems. Try the following passage:

People usually shudder when we mention ———.

(snakes, spiders, slugs, murder, war, inflation)

This is unfortunate because most ——— are harmless and interesting little creatures.

(Cross out murder, war, inflation— they're not creatures.)

The mother ——— cares for her baby just as carefully as a human mother

(Maybe snakes do; slugs and spiders lay eggs and leave.)

The ——— carries her baby with her for the first two weeks of life.

(I don't think snakes carry their young around.)

Like all mammals, she provides it with milk by nursing it.

(Snakes aren't mammals, anyway.)

By the time it is two weeks old, its wings are ready for flight.
A ———'s wing is unusual. It really is a thin skin that stretches from the arm-like front limb, along the body, to the hind leg. The flying habits of ——— are amazing. Although they fly only at night when it is dark, they never strike an object. ——— cannot see in the dark, but they have a special sense that warns them before they fly into an object.

(mammals, wings: bats?)

(BATS!)

(I didn't know that.)

The passage demonstrates how we use predicting, confirming, and integrating strategies. Reading such a passage helps us realize that meaning is constructed from the text as a whole. Through a sampling of the print, readers confirm predictions and predict subsequent meaning; tentative meanings are confirmed or disconfirmed depending on information met later in the passage. Having tried a number of different possibilities—snakes, slugs, war, inflation—most of us have realized we are reading about bats with the reference to wings. Knowing bats are the only mammal which can fly allows us to establish a meaning for the missing word. The remainder of the passage provides confirmation, at the same time offering what may also be some new information. These aspects of reading—predicting, sampling, confirming, and integrating—operate both continuously and in concert.

How can we help students develop more fluent reading strategies?

One major objective should be to help them overcome the obstacle of unknown words. Because many nonfluent readers think reading is an exact process, involving the accurate identification of every word, they usually stop when they come to something they don't know. Many of them try at that point to "sound it out," usually with little success. In the meantime, they've forgotten what they've been reading about. We need to help students understand that the meaning of the whole doesn't depend on being able to identify every word. We can help them realize there are a variety of decisions they can make when encountering something unfamiliar. They can do what fluent readers do:

- They can try reading on to see if what comes later in the passage offers more information.
- They can try substituting a "placeholder"—something which makes sense—until some new information makes it necessary to try something else.
- They can choose to reread, to see if they've missed something which would help specify the meaning.
- They could decide to make no decision for the moment, to read on and later return to what's unfamiliar if it seems crucial.

In other words, we want to encourage students to predict, confirm, and integrate.

An activity which is particularly useful for helping students make meaningful substitutions when they encounter something unfamiliar is *Synonym Substitution* (Goodman and Burke, 1980). In this activity, readers are encouraged to substitute something which makes sense for anything in the text they don't know. The emphasis is upon creating meaning from a context. The students are forced to integrate actively both semantic and syntactic information in order to supply a reasonable "placeholder." The activity demonstrates to students that they possess nonvisual information which can be used for interpreting text. It also encourages the processing of large chunks of language. Students are helped to focus on meaning rather than to rely on the print.

The lesson is used most effectively with small groups. First, each student is asked to read the passage silently. Then each group reads the text together, trying to supply a minimum of two substitutions for each underlined word. The substitutions are written down and discussed later. The most important aspect of the activity is the discussion about meaning which takes place as students try to create an interpretation of the text. This discussion allows them to recognize that there may be a variety of ways of conveying meaning.

For students having considerable difficulty reading, it is useful to begin with an excerpt from a familiar story or fairy tale. With more proficient readers an excerpt from a textbook is appropriate. Let's try a passage ourselves:

The sea is our ecosystem of last resort. Destroy or seriously *impair* the oceans and we *obliterate* not only the diverse and bountiful life *harbored* there, but, *ultimately,* ourselves as well. A dead ocean *portends* a dead earth. Most marine experts are *profoundly* disturbed about this possibility.

For millennia, man believed that the sea was a bottomless pit into which his *offal* could be dumped endlessly because the oceans recycled the products of life on earth with ease. However, every time we put something in or take something out, it has *an impact.* Despite its vast self-healing ability, scientists are learning how *vulnerable* the sea really is [adapted from Fisher, 1977].

Now let's try substituting for the italicized words.

The sea is our ecosystem of last resort. Destroy or seriously *impair* (spoil, damage, injure) the oceans and we *obliterate* (wipe out, exterminate, destroy) not only the diverse and bountiful life *harbored* (which lives, which is sheltered or protected) there but, *ultimately* (finally, in the end, eventually), ourselves as well. A dead ocean *portends* (means, threatens, foreshadows) a dead earth. Most marine experts are profoundly disturbed about this possibility.

For millennia, man believed that the sea was a bottomless pit into which his *offal* (garbage, waste, rubbish) could be dumped endlessly because the oceans recycled the products of life on earth with ease. However, every time we put something in or take something out, it has *an impact* (an effect, serious consequences or repercussions). Despite its vast self-healing ability, scientists are learning how *vulnerable* (fragile, defenseless, open to damage) the sea really is.

Notice that the substitutions need not be single words; sometimes we need to substitute whole phrases and rearrange sentences as we try to understand what we're reading. The activity legitimizes the substituting of something meaningful for something unfamiliar in the text. It helps students overcome their fear of unknown words.

Another activity which has the same kind of objective—that is, helping students deal effectively with something (words, sentences, paragraphs, even whole texts) unfamiliar—is *Reader Selected Miscues* developed by Dorothy Watson at the University of Missouri. This activity helps students become aware of the range of options available to them as readers when they encounter something unfamiliar. The students receive a copy of a selection and read it silently, marking either with pencils or highlighting pens anything they don't understand or about which they have questions. When they have finished reading and marking the reading material, they take turns discussing what they have marked. They are encouraged to consider which of the items they marked were significant and which were not; which affected their understanding and which didn't. During the discussion the students are encouraged to return to the material for clarification. Either factual or fictional material can be used for the activity.

Again what the activity demonstrates is that reading involves making sense. Through social interaction students are helped to see that not everyone creates the same interpretation from reading; that one's interpretation is determined by what one knows. What the discussion allows is the development of a consensus and a collective working out of what wasn't understood. The activity demonstrates that it isn't necessary to identify every word on a page in order to understand. It also shows students that the meaning of something unfamiliar can be created from understanding the whole. *Reader Selected Miscues* makes *"not* understanding" legitimate. It helps develop a willingness to use what is understood for clarifying what is unfamiliar.

Not only are we concerned with helping students overcome the obstacle of unfamiliar words, we also want to help them integrate the complex ideas and relationships they are reading about. *Say Something,* developed by Jerome Harste of Indiana University, helps students explore the relationships between what they know and what is offered in a particular reading selection. In this activity, students choose partners. Each student takes a copy of the reading selection. Before reading, students decide how they will read (orally—in turns or in unison—or silently) and how much they will read before stopping and reacting. Students then read and stop at the predetermined points to "say something." The "something" can be questions they might have which they can discuss; it can be a reaction to what they've read; it might be information they have from other sources which confirms or contradicts what is said in the current selection. After the students have completed reading and discussing the selection they can share their insights and interpretations with other pairs of students.

Say Something allows students to react to the information in a selection and relate it to what they know. The opportunity to discuss what they are understanding as they read permits students to see how others make sense of written language. The sharing of knowledge facilitates the development of understanding.

Another activity which serves the same purposes was developed by Carol Cillis, a teacher in Columbia, Missouri: *Estimate/Read/Respond/ Question.* In this activity, students begin by glancing through the selection and estimating how far they think they will be able to read with some understanding. The reason for this is to let students see they are often able to understand more than they thought they could. Next they read the selection. They can choose to read independently, in pairs, orally, or silently, stopping for discussion or reading straight through. Now they respond/retell by discussing what they think they've learned from reading and their reactions to what they've read. At this point, the students write a general question concerning some aspect of the selection that interested them or where they found the meaning unclear. They exchange questions with a partner and answer the questions either orally or in writing. Once again, the activity helps students see the relationship between what they already know and what they are learning from a particular reading.

What all of these activities I've described have in common is a focus on understanding. It is important, at this point, to raise a question which concerns many teachers. Shouldn't students be able to read accurately? By that, most teachers mean shouldn't students be able to replicate what's on the page. The answer is, however, that an interpretation which approaches what an author has intended comes not from closer attention to the print but from being able to supply appropriate nonvisual information to the transaction with written language. What each of the foregoing activities emphasizes is that reading is an interpretative process. As students become fluent readers they learn to take risks, to ask an essential question: "Is this making sense to me?" They become less and less concerned with getting the words right and more and more concerned with creating meaning. They learn not to depend on the print as their only source of information. Rather, they sample the text on the basis of what they know about language and about the world. They construct meaning which is confirmed or disconfirmed depending on subsequent information. They do a great deal of interpreting and filling in. The social interaction, an integral aspect of each activity, provides the means by which interpretations can be compared and related back to the text itself. The need to understand the author's intent develops from exchanging and comparing interpretations.

As teachers, we must keep in mind that it is the students themselves who must construct meaning. No two individuals reading the same passage will arrive at exactly the same interpretation. Our interpretations are influenced by our prior knowledge, which is different for everyone. Our role is not to impose our interpretations on our students, but to help them construct understandings of their own. If we want to help students become more fluent readers, we need to encourage them to deal with unfamiliar words and concepts in a variety of ways. We need to help them become more aware of how contextual cues (both syntactic and semantic) can be used to construct a tentative meaning. We need to direct students to construct a general understanding of what they are reading before we ask them to consider the details. If we emphasize only the detail, we are likely to force them to become overly concerned with identifying words. We have to create activities in which students are willing to risk being wrong.

The following language story illustrates, I think, the sort of understanding about reading we must help students develop. I was reading with a fifth grader who was having some difficulty in school. I handed him a passage to read from which several words had been deleted. He took the passage, looked at it, and said, "I can't read this; some words are left out." I suggested he try anyway. He looked at me as though I were foolish; then he began reading. When he'd finished, I asked him to tell me about what he'd done. With a look of astonishment on his face he said, "The words just came out of my head!"

10

Text Organization

Its Value for Literacy Development

Susan Church

It was as the result of considerable frustration while attempting to assist my junior high resource program students to understand and remember textbook material that I began exploring the analysis of text structure as an aid to the reader's construction of meaning. My process of discovery began with my students and their very real problems coping with their textbooks. We started by looking at overall organizational patterns commonly used by writers and constructing diagrams showing the relationships among ideas. After I had worked with my students for a time I observed that they seemed to be understanding and remembering material which had formerly defeated them. Believing, as does Frank Smith, that "there is nothing so practical as a good theory," I turned to the research literature to try to understand why text analysis seemed to be so effective. Through the research literature I have subsequently found that the analysis of text has a sound theoretical basis. My work with students has suggested that text analysis has potential for broad application.

Theoreticians in cognitive psychology have, in recent years, developed models for how the human brain stores information. Lindsay and Norman (1977) use the term "semantic network" to describe the representation of knowledge in memory. The huge number of concepts stored in memory, they argue, are interconnected by means of a number of different kinds of relationships. The result is a huge web of concepts in which all knowledge is related.

This semantic network expands as the learner interacts with the world and develops schemas or internal representations of experience. These schemas are constructed as the learner either assimilates new information which fits with an existing representation or accommodates conflicting information by altering schemas. These internal representations allow learners to make predictions regarding future events on the basis of past experience; they interpret new situations based on prior knowledge.

Applied to reading, this theory suggests that the nonvisual information stored in the reader's head, in the semantic network, is the basis for comprehension. Part of this nonvisual information is the knowledge of structure of text. As Smith (1982, pp. 63–64) points out, each type of text has a genre scheme, or characteristic organizational presentation of content, which distinguishes it from other types of text. Texts also have discourse structures or internal relationships, such as the organization of paragraphs and chapters. Narratives have frameworks called story grammars. All of these various kinds of organizational structure are internalized as readers interact with a variety of written materials either through listening to text or through reading and writing themselves.

A number of theorists have developed models for analyzing the structure of text. Tierney and Mosenthal (1982) provide a good introduction for teachers wishing to understand more about text analysis. They group text-analytic models into six categories. They give brief descriptions of the procedures individual theorists have developed for examining the organization of text. One type of analysis has been called *propositional analysis*. With propositional analysis the emphasis is on propositions (idea units) and propositional structures (the connected propositions which constitute a text). The diagrams of structure generated from this type of analysis show the concepts and the relations among concepts predominantly within sentences. *Cohesion analyses* look at those elements of text which tie it together and make it more than a series of unrelated sentences. An example of a cohesive tie is pronoun reference. Such ties operate both within and across sentences and must be clear if the text is to be coherent and be meaningful to the reader. A *story grammar* is an internalized structure for stories. It consists of hierarchical categories such as setting, event structure, initiating event, reaction to initiating event, attempts and consequent components, and a final resolution. Tree diagrams showing the hierarchical relationships among these categories have been generated from an analysis of single-protagonist stories. *Event chain formulations* have been diagrammed for narratives with more than one protagonist. The structure of such narratives is usually depicted as a series of events for each protagonist, interconnected with arrows.

Expository prose predicate structures have been used to analyze expository text. Meyer's analysis (1975) shows the relationships among the concepts presented in a passage. These relationships are diagrammed to show the hierarchical structure of the content of the text. *Semantic mapping* has been another way of analyzing expository text. The organizational pattern of the text is shown in a map, which depicts such relationships as concept and example, concept and properties, concept and definition, temporal succession, cause and effect, conditional, and comparison.

The text analytic procedures I've just outlined have proved a useful tool for researchers wishing to investigate the influence of text organization on readers' understanding. A number of studies have demonstrated children's use of text structure to organize recall (Baker and Stein, 1981). Taylor (1980) found that both good and poor sixth-grade readers who used top-level structure to organize their recall remembered more than readers who did not. She also found developmental differences in the use of hierarchical structure; more sixth-graders used such organizational information in their recalls than fourth grade students did. Meyer, Brandt, and Bluth (1980) reported that "the structure strategy appeared to be a particularly effective retrieval mnemonic" for ninth-grade students. Tierney, Bridge, and Cera (1979) used a form of propositional analysis to compare good and poor readers' memory of text to the content and structure of the text. One of their conclusions was that the child's schematic expectations influence memory for text. In their study some subjects attempted to develop a meaningful interpretation of non-narrative text within their schemas for narrative structure. Results of this research and of other studies seem to be fairly consistent. They demonstrate that not only do readers have knowledge of text structure, they use this knowledge to help them understand and remember what they are reading.

While Tierney, Bridge, and Cera (1979) argue that text analysis can provide teachers insight regarding the role of the text in the reading process, Tierney and Mosenthal (1982) caution that reading involves "a complex interaction among the cognitive structures of the author, the text, the cognitive structures of the reader, and the communicative situation" (p. 55). In other words, the text is only one component in the complex process of constructing meaning.

After reading this literature I had several questions. What does this research on the organization of text mean for instruction? Does it mean I should be teaching text structure? If so, how should I be going about it?

My reading has provided no conclusive answer to whether I should be teaching text organization formally or not. Some studies support the position that instruction is helpful. Meyer et al. (1980) report on two doctoral dissertations in which students, taught to use top-level structure (for expository text), greatly increased the amount of information they remembered. On the other hand, Dreher and Singer (1980) found that teaching fifth-grade students to identify story structure did not improve their recall. (They point out the students in the study may already have developed the structures which were the focus of instruction and so could not be expected to improve.)

Assuming that helping students develop an awareness of text organization is useful, the answer to the question "How should I be going about it?" seems to be "Not directly." Most researchers are arguing that instruction should be designed to provide students many experiences with a variety of genres to allow for the natural development of schemas for text. The teacher can assist, they contend, by structuring activities which will bring to conscious awareness these internalized structures and by allowing children to do something interesting and purposeful with their knowledge. A number of writers (Whaley, 1981; McConaughty, 1980), for example, suggest fostering the development of the concept of story, first by providing children a wide experience with reading, then using this experience to draw students' attention to the various aspects of story structure, using summaries and diagrams.

Various means of diagramming or mapping of text have been

suggested (Hanf, 1971; Thielen, 1982; Vaughn, 1982; Alverman, 1982). The diagramming or mapping is intended to show the interrelationships among the ideas occurring in the text, making them easier to remember. One way of mapping (Cleland, 1981; Freeman and Reynolds, 1980) places focusing questions at the center of a map or "web" with branches containing answers and supporting detail radiating from the central concept. Maps or webs have also been used to depict plot, or comparison of emotions (Cleland, 1981), or to organize information units around a central theme (Norton, 1977, 1982). One caution which pervades the literature (King and Rentel, 1981) is that for students to progress in their development of schemas for text they must be engaged in reading a variety of genres and in generating a variety of texts through their own writing. It appears essential that students have an opportunity to experiment with text organizational structures both as readers and writers.

How have I incorporated all of this information into my teaching? I have introduced text analysis to my students as a strategy they can use to help them both understand and remember what they read as well as to help them organize their writing. I want them to become active, independent readers who look for organizational patterns as they read and use them as a framework for understanding. I use group reading and writing activities to help students become familiar with a variety of text structures. During these activities, I try and demonstrate the kinds of questions they should be asking themselves as they read and write. It is important the diagrams we create reflect the students' understanding of what they've read (not mine) so extensive student input is essential.

I want to illustrate my understanding and application of text organization with the following transcript of a lesson with some eighth-grade students. Before I began the lesson, I chose a selection from their geography textbook which they were having considerable difficulty reading. I read it through and diagrammed it for myself so that I would know where the students might run into difficulty and I began formulating questions which might help them to diagram the concepts and relationships in the passage.

The text we were examining (Figure 10–1) was taken from *The United States* by Robin E. Crickmer and William Hildebrand (Holt, Rinehart and Winston of Canada, 1972, p. 229; reprinted by permission).

I began by asking the students to look at the title of the section: "The Pacific Coastlands."

T: What is this section about?
S1: The Pacific Coastlands.
T: Where does that suggest this geographical area is located?
S1: Along the coast of the Pacific Ocean.
T: Does anyone know what states are along the Pacific Coast?
S2: I think California.
T: And?

(Silence)

T: Look at the page. Anywhere you can find out which states?

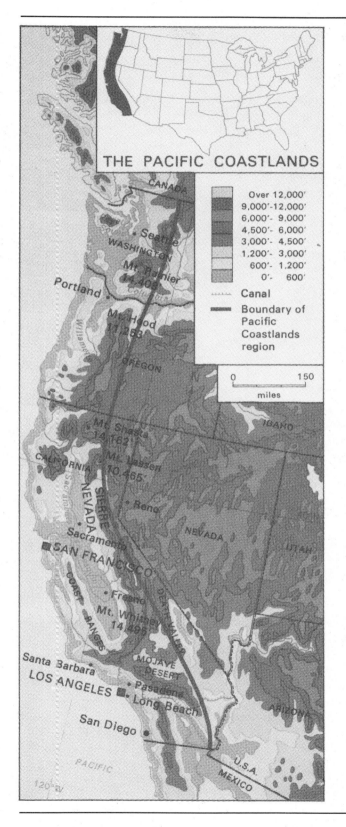

THE PACIFIC COASTLANDS

Over 12,000'
9,000'-12,000'
6,000'- 9,000'
4,500'- 6,000'
3,000'- 4,500'
1,200'- 3,000'
600'- 1,200'
0'- 600'

········· Canal

━━━ Boundary of
Pacific
Coastlands
region

0   150
miles

THE PACIFIC COASTLANDS

Within the three western states that border the mighty Pacific Ocean are some of the most spectacular contrasts that nature has created. Astoria, on the Pacific coast of Oregon, averages 80 inches of precipitation a year, while much of California's southern interior seldom gets any rain whatever. In the northern coastal areas of California, Washington and Oregon are found the greatest forests in the country; much of the south of this region is a desert. In the Sierra Nevadas is Mount Whitney, at 14,495 feet above sea level, the highest mountain in the continental U.S.; about a hundred miles away is Death Valley, 279 feet below sea level–the lowest spot on the continent. High in the Sierras, a climber could find snowfields in mid-summer; at the same time the Imperial Valley could be experiencing temperatures of 120°F. Large areas of these states are uninhabited; elsewhere, as in Los Angeles, people have crowded together into one of the country's largest urban centres.

What chiefly sets this region apart from the rest of the West is its nearness to the great Pacific Ocean. This largest of the world's oceans brings the life-giving moisture that makes possible some of the world's most productive forests and farmlands; its waters teem with valuable fish; it provides the region with water highways along the coast and with trade routes to the Far East, as well as to the Atlantic via the Panama Canal. In this region are concentrated more people than anywhere else in the West, California alone having a population of over 21 million, more than any other state.

Figure 10 – 1

S3: From the map ... Washington, Oregon, California. Oh, yes ... Los Angeles ... lots of TV shows come from there ... the coast.

(At this point we started to discuss the information we had so far.)

T: What do we know so far?
S1: It is the area along the Pacific Coast.
T: What shall I call that on the diagram?
S1: Where it is.
T: Is that OK?
S2: It should be location.
T: How do you feel about that?
S3: That's good.
T: What else do we know?
S4: Three states ... Washington, Oregon, California.
T: What shall I write?
S4: Put states and lines for Washington, Oregon, California.

(See Figure 10–2.)

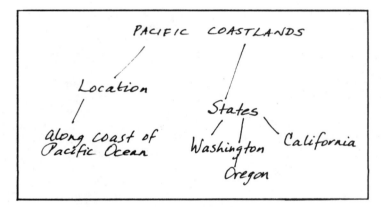

Figure 10 – 2

T: Let's read through this section quickly before we start pulling out the information for the diagram.

(Students read silently.)

T: Is any of our information on the diagram repeated in the text?
S1: Yes. It says, "The three western states that border the mighty Pacific Ocean": that is the same as what we have. Then, it gives the names: "California, Washington and Oregon."
T: So what does the author tell you in that first paragraph?
S2: (Reads first sentence) "Within the three western states that border the mighty Pacific Ocean are some of the most spectacular contrasts that nature has created."
T: What does that mean?
S2: I'm not really sure.
T: Can anyone help? (No reply) Well, read on through that paragraph and see if you can figure it out.
S3: Well ... it talks about lots of pre- ... pre- ... pre- ... what is that?

S4: Precipitation. I've seen that on the weather. It means rain and snow and stuff.

S3: Oh well, anyway, it talks about 80 inches in one place and hardly any in another and then it talks about forests and deserts, and 14,495 feet above sea level and 279 feet below sea level ... so, I think it's showing opposites or something.

T: How were you able to figure that out?

S3: Well, I looked at those examples and they all seemed to be the same kind of thing.

T: What does that tell you about reading?

S3: Sometimes, if you read more you can get it.

T: Let's see if we can pick out these opposites or contrasts for our diagram. What is the first one?

S3: I said already.

T: So what should I write?

S3: "Pacific Coast region 80 inches precipitation. California's southern interior seldom any rain."

T: Where would the southern interior be?

S4: Inside. You use interior paint inside, so it would be inside the state.

T: Can you show us where it might be on the map?

(The rest of the contrasts are outlined until that section of the diagram looks like Figure 10–3.)

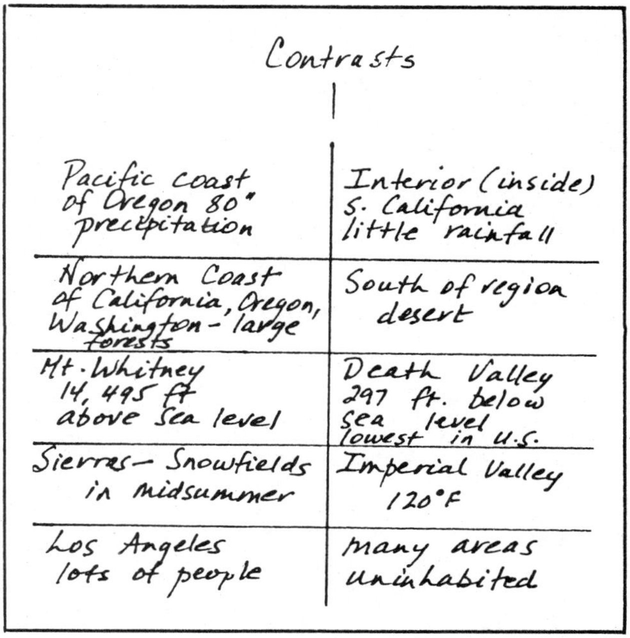

Figure 10 – 3

Contrasts	
Pacific coast of Oregon 80° precipitation	Interior (inside) S. California little rainfall
Northern Coast of California, Oregon, Washington - large forests	South of region desert
Mt. Whitney 14,495 ft above sea level	Death Valley 297 ft. below sea level lowest in U.S.
Sierras— Snowfields in midsummer	Imperial Valley 120°F
Los Angeles lots of people	many areas uninhabited

T: What does this mean? (Writes "uninhabited" on the board.)

S4: No people.

T: How did you know that?

S4: Well, Los Angeles has lots of people so the other side must be no people.

T: Let's add another column to our chart. What are we contrasting in the first one?

S2: Precipitation.

T: And what did we say that was?

S2: Snow and rain and stuff.

T: What other stuff might it be?

S2: Oh let's see . . . hail, sleet, anything out of the sky that's wet.

T: What about the second one?

S1: How about amount of forests?

S4: No, a desert doesn't have anything on it. How about growth?

T: What should I write?

Ss: Growth.

T: Does anyone know another name for growth? (Writes "vegetation.")

S4: Oh yes. Vegetation. I heard about that in science.

T: What about the third one?

S2: How about height?

T: Alright with everyone? Does anyone know another name for height? (Writes "elevation.")

S3: Oh, that's elevation. Does that mean height?

T: Yes, elevation means how far above or below sea level.

S3: It's on maps, isn't it?

T: Yes; look at the map in your book.

S3: Yes, the colors show different heights.

T: What about the fourth one?

S4: Temperature.

T: And the fifth?

S1: Amount of people.

T: What do we call that?

S2: Population.

(In this way categories for each of the contrasts are generated and the vocabulary used in geography introduced and associated with these specific examples. See Figure 10–4.)

	CONTRASTS	
Precipitation	Pacific Coast of Oregon 80° precipitation	Interior (inside) S. California little rainfall
Vegetation	Northern Coast of California Oregon Washington – 'large forests	South of region Desert
Elevation	Mt. Whitney 14,495 ft above Sea level	Death Valley 297 ft. below sea level lowest in U.S.
Temperature	Sierras — Snowfields in midsummer	Imperial Valley 120° F
Population	Los Angeles lots of people	many areas uninhabited

Figure 10 – 4

T: What does the next paragraph tell us about?

S1: It says it's near to the Pacific.

T: And what does the next sentence tell us?

S2: The moisture helps farms and forests grow.

T: Does it say how that happens?

S2: No, but it must rain a lot.

T: We're going to read about that later, so keep it in mind. What does the next bit, "Its waters teem with . . . fish," mean?

S4: There must be lots.

T: How did you figure it out?

S4: It just seemed like they were talking about things the Pacific Ocean does and that it probably would have lots of fish. It says they're valuable, too.

T: What else?

S2: It has water highways and trade routes.

T: What about that last sentence?

S3: That doesn't have anything to do with the rest.

T: So let's deal with this business about the Pacific Ocean first. What shall we call this section?

S1: What the Pacific Ocean does.

T: What does it do?

S3: Gives moisture for farms and forests.

S4: Has valuable fish.

S1: Has water highways and trade routes.

T: Where?

S1: Highways along the coast . . . trade routes to the far east and to the Atlantic.

(See Figure 10–5.)

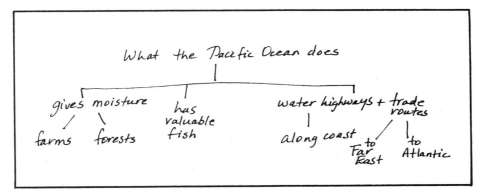

Figure 10 – 5

T: Would someone show us on the map of the world where those routes might be?
What am I going to do with that last sentence?

S4: Maybe make another line and put "many people . . . California more than any other state."

S2: Let's say, "More people than rest of the west . . . California more than any other state."

T: Can you think of a heading for this?

S1: Population.

(See Figure 10–6.)

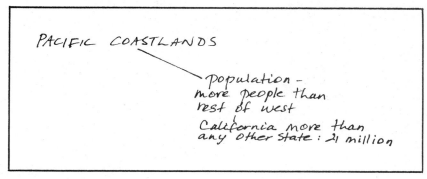

PACIFIC COASTLANDS

population –
more people than
rest of west
California more than
any other state : 21 million

Figure 10 – 6

T: Do you think that 21 million is accurate?
S2: No, this book is old.
T: Where would you check?
S3: Encyclopedia.
T: Maybe ... Where would the most up-to-date information be? Why don't you check with the librarian and find out what sources you could use and tell us tomorrow what the current figure is and if California is still the state with the largest population.

When the diagram was completed (Figure 10–7), the students wrote a summary using the information from it to structure their writing. In this case, I suggested they use the categories from the contrasts section to make general statements rather than repeating the specific examples given in the original passage. I wanted them to see that there are choices writers have to make.

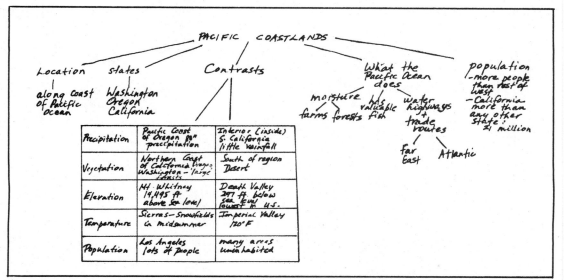

Figure 10 – 7

The diagram was saved and more information was added as we read about the Pacific Coast. The section of text about the coastal rainfall was mapped onto the diagram, providing further detail about moisture. The diagram thus provided a framework not only for this section of the text but for subsequent reading.

It seems, then, that text-structuring activities can be useful. My students appear to have profited from using diagrams for understanding text, for reorganizing and structuring information for tests, and for organizing their writing and class projects. I have given no formal instruction on "how to diagram a text." Instead, I have offered the students many opportunities to engage in text analysis. Each opportunity is a "demonstration" (Smith, 1982) of how a text may be organized.

It is possible to turn any instructional technique such as this text organizing activity into a skill by emphasizing the product (the diagram) rather than the process (understanding and remembering information). Therefore, I use these activities judiciously, always careful to have the students participate in generating the diagrams. I try to keep in mind that such activities must be used to facilitate the construction of meaning, not as an end in themselves.

Conferencing

Writing as a
Collaborative
Activity

Judith M. Newman

"What are you thinking of writing about?" I asked her.

"Well," she replied, "I've reread my journals and I suddenly realized that I no longer believe some of what I used to believe. I went back to the first article we read, the one where I disagreed with the author's argument, and reading it last night I could see that I didn't disagree anymore. And I wondered about what had made me change my mind about ideas like 'writing finding its own meaning,' 'reading and writing are social activities,' and 'thoughts are created in the process of writing.'"

"Have you any idea what made you change your mind?" one of the others prompted.

"I guess both the reading and writing experiences we've been having for the last couple of weeks have had their effect. I was encouraged to try free writing and I discovered I didn't need to have everything worked out before I started putting words on paper. I found that the writing sometimes went in unexpected directions; it was saying something new, something that was my own, not just borrowed from the research literature."

"What was your reaction when you realized that?"

"It suddenly made me think about the writing I've been doing with my students. I could see where I have been focusing on the products, having them plan what they were going to write first, so that their writing would be better organized. What I haven't appreciated is the fact that we all need to be able to set aside constraints and just write to see what might come out."

"What is the one insight you would want to share with other teachers?" someone asked.

"I'm not sure yet," she answered. "I think I have to write about what

A version of this article originally appeared in *Educational Perspectives*, Vol. 25 (Winter 1985).

I think I've learned, then I'll be able to stand back and decide what I think was most important."

"How do you think you'll proceed?"

"I planned on rereading my journals, seeing what I could find in each, and then noting the 'ah-ha's' on cards. I thought that would help me find out what I've learned; sort of like summing up the free writes."

"Are you able to start, then?"

"Yes," she said.

The above took place in a group conference like many which have occurred this past year among my graduate students, all teachers. We've been exploring the ways conferencing can assist our writing. We've conferenced through written responses to journals and free writings. We've conferenced as a way of taking a running start at a piece. We've shared works in progress. And we've discussed final drafts. We've discovered many ways in which to support one another through the difficult business of writing.

The most important thing we have learned is that writing is an intensely social activity. Contrary to popular belief, we have discovered writing is not something one struggles to do alone. Instead, we have found that it is more than helpful to have others assist with the massive amount of decision making involved in writing anything. That's where conferencing comes in. There are many different kinds of conference discussed in the research literature: informal conferences, teacher-student conferences, peer conferences, sharing meetings, the teacherless writing class. And while the guidelines for conducting these various sorts of conference may appear contra-dictory, all of them have a role to play in helping writers extend their control over the writing process.

What are these different kinds of conference like? Donald Graves (1983) offers useful suggestions for teacher-student conferences in *Writing: Teachers and Children at Work*. Teacher-student con-ferences can occur at any time during the working of a piece—before anything has been put on paper, while a work is in progress, and as it draws to completion. The purpose of the teacher-student conference is to sustain writers, to help them maintain a focus on the meaning of the piece. Only secondarily is the teacher-student conference concerned with the conventions or correctness of the writing and then only as the piece becomes ready for publication.

The teacher's role in these conferences is to *listen*, particularly with an ear for what the writers seem to want to convey. In fact, Graves insists, writers must talk first. They must be given an opportunity to explain where they are in the writing process and to let their audience (in this case the teacher) know what help they are looking for. To encourage writers to talk, Graves suggests some helpful opening questions: What ideas have you been considering? How have you come this far? Can you sum up what you're trying to do in a sen-tence or two? To help focus or expand a piece he offers some general questions which could be asked of almost any piece: What's the main thing you're trying to say? It all starts ... how? Do you think the stuff you're telling me now is important; should it go in? Tell me again just what happened. The essential characteristic of teacher-student conferences is that they are *brief*; each exchange is no more than a moment or two, only long enough to give writers a chance to request assistance or for teachers to reassure themselves that the writers are progressing.

Lucy Calkins in *Lessons from a Child* (1983) describes three functions for these formal teacher-student conferences. They are intended to help writers develop the specific content of a piece, to help them reflect on the writing process and the specific strategies they use for writing, and for helping them learn to judge their own efforts. It is interesting that these latter two functions were an outgrowth of the research process. Questions about the writing process itself were asked by Calkins so that she could come to some understanding of what the children were experiencing. However, it wasn't long before the children started asking process questions of one another: How's it coming? What are you going to do next? What difficulty are you having? What new problems have you run into? What help would you like? Similarly with the children's ability to make reasonable judgments about the quality of their work. Calkins was interested in the children's perception of what made a piece of writing "good." Her evaluative questions soon became a part of the children's repertoire. Someone might announce, "I like it" of something just completed, only to be asked by one of the others, "What do you like about it?" Calkins recognized that these questions were important for helping the children assess their work more critically and such discussion enabled them to develop criteria for judging writing.

Peer conferences are another kind of conference described in the research literature. Calkins distinguishes two types of peer conferences: formal "sharing meetings" and informal ones, which are going on all the time. The major difference between the two seems to be that the sharing meetings are group sessions set up by the teacher, while informal peer conferences are student initiated one-to-one interactions. She describes how it was not unusual for students to help one another with topic selection and to sustain one another as they wrote by offering advice about spelling and punctuation, volunteering suggestions for revision, and just being an interested audience. As Calkins comments, "These interactions were interwoven throughout the evolution of a piece, sustaining and extending its life-force." What becomes apparent from Calkins's description of these informal peer conferences is the importance of creating a classroom climate in which it is legitimate for children to share freely. For these informal conferences to be useful it is essential that children actually be able to talk to one another without fear of being censured; that means permitting real chitchat. They have to be allowed to make aside comments, or ask someone for their reaction to a bit of writing, or talk to themselves, as well as be permitted to move around the room. Also interesting is Calkins's observation that what went on in the informal peer interactions was a reflection of the teacher-student and researcher-student conferences. In other words, the students were incorporating the sharing and writing strategies offered during the more formal adult-child exchanges into their writing repertoire and using them to help one another as writers.

Calkins also describes the "sharing meetings," in which students presented work in progress as well as completed drafts at whole class sessions. She outlines a structure which evolved for these sessions:

1. Writers would begin by explaining where they were in the writing process, and what help they needed. . . .
2. Usually, but not always, the writer then would read the piece—or the pertinent section of the piece—out loud.
3. The writer would call on listeners. Usually listeners would begin by retelling what they'd heard . . . sometimes they'd begin by responding to or appreciating the content of the piece.
4. Questions or suggestions would then be offered, not about everything, but about the concern raised by the writer. Sometimes other things would come up as well, but not always [Calkins, 1983, p. 126].

These share meetings are very like the "teacherless writing class" described by Peter Elbow (1973) in his *Writing without Teachers*. While Elbow doesn't refer to the sharing sessions as "conferencing," that is what he is describing. He contends that an essential ingredient of becoming a writer involves learning what effect one's words have on others. He argues that it isn't until we can anticipate how readers are likely to respond to what we've written that we can make decisions about where to go with a piece and how to get there. He believes that learning to sense one's audience results from having real readers respond to our writing. Hence the writing group. In his teacherless writing class each member of the group (anywhere from six to ten participants) has a responsibility to be a writer and an opportunity to present his or her writing for the reactions of the others.

In his description of the writing group, Elbow deals with the responsibilities of both readers and writers. First of all, readers have a responsibility to read (or listen) well. That is, they have to give both time and attention to each piece as it is presented whether they think it "good" or not. "If," Elbow argues, "we expect our writing to receive attention from the others we have an obligation to give their writing our time and attention." Second, readers are required to share what the words made them experience. They may summarize what they have understood of the piece; they can tell how the words made them feel or what images were evoked as they listened or read, they may use metaphors to help the writer "see" what effect the writing had. What readers can't do is tell the writer what to do to "fix" the writing. (This latter isn't strictly true. Elbow does suggest there is no value in censoring advice—if readers have something to suggest they shouldn't waste time not saying it—however, the advice, in and of itself, is of little use except as a vehicle for leading readers back to their perceptions of the writing.) Third, Elbow argues, readers have a responsibility to be writers. Everyone in the conference group must be in a position of vulnerability. No one can be exempt from having to write and from having to share their writing.

Writers, on the other hand have to *listen*. Listen to what the readers have to say in order to find out how they have reacted. What writers mustn't do is respond. They mustn't be drawn into arguing about the reactions, mustn't become defensive about their writing, apologize for it, or attempt to justify it. These reactions only serve to censor what the readers will be willing to share. Writers have to accept that the readers' reactions are legitimate. They have to hear them out, then decide what can be done. Writers have to write. They have to write whether they feel like it or not. And they have to share, whether they think that what they have written is good or not.

Here, then, we have two rather different views on conferencing. Graves argues that the conference should be used to help the writer talk about his or her piece; Elbow, on the other hand, is insistent that the conference is a time for the writer to listen. Graves is describing teacher-initiated one-to-one interactions; Elbow believes that writer-initiated sharing should occur in a group context.

Both, as my graduate students and I discovered, have merit. Listening to authors is important; so is having authors listen to readers. The distinction between Graves's and Elbow's sense of what constitutes a writing conference stems from their different focuses. Graves is writing from an instructional point of view. He is concerned with teachers learning to help students. In his view, teachers must learn to listen to writers before rushing in and telling. Elbow, on the other hand, is writing from a writer's perspective. He wants to make sure writers have an opportunity to discover what effect their words have on readers. Consequently, much is to be gained by having writers doing the listening.

Clearly, then, there are two ways in which conferences can assist writers. One way is by providing opportunities, both with individuals and in groups, for talking about their intentions and the difficulties they are having realizing them so that they can focus on what might not be working and consider alternatives. A second way is by letting them discover what effect their writing has on readers as a means of helping them decide what to do with it. Both types of conference have one goal in common; that is, to ensure that writers retain ownership of their texts.

How did the graduate students and I apply what we learned from Graves, Calkins, Elbow, and others? First, we discovered the value of conferencing even before putting pen to paper. We discovered that the opportunity to bounce around our ideas as they were just be-ginning to take shape in our heads helped us get under way. As illustrated by the conference with which I began this chapter, those starting conferences were often conducted in groups where each member had an opportunity to air his or her ideas. In these sessions writers talked, first laying out their ideas, then responding to queries from the others. While these initial sharing sessions were often undertaken at my invitation, on a couple of occasions students initiated such conferences themselves.

We also learned to conference with pieces in progress. We found it helpful to have someone else's reactions when faced with decisions—should the writing go this way or that? We found that another writer's opinion at such a juncture saved us struggle and time. It's true that on occasion we did find ourselves being led down some garden paths; nevertheless, the overall support was invaluable. We also found that talking out stuck points was advantageous. In neither of these instances was it necessary that readers actually have the piece in their hands. In fact, we found it easier to listen to writers discuss the options they were considering or what seemed to be problematic and react to what they had to say.

We used conferences at the end of drafts. In this case we tried a number of tactics. We tried reading quickly while the writer was present—making no written comments but just receiving the piece, then responding to it. That worked well if a piece was short, but if the writing was more than a couple of pages long we found it easier to read it beforehand, jotting a few comments on a separate piece of paper. We also tried giving written synopses of what it was we thought the writer was saying. One of our most useful strategies was to present the writing accompanied by specific questions to which feedback was requested. This left the writer firmly in control of the conference. The invitation extended by the writer was explicit: you can read for these aspects of the piece but don't comment on the rest; I can't handle it yet. Then as readers we learned to make judgments about that contract. We learned to answer the writer's questions, but then, depending on how fragile we thought the writer actually was, we might react to other aspects of the writing as well. We learned the hard way that a good deal of trust must be established before such license could be taken.

We learned to conference by having authors talk first, letting them sum up what the piece was about in a sentence or two or by having them explain briefly what they were trying to accomplish with it. We found that we could then direct our reactions to the writer's specific intentions. We were also able to react to one another's reactions. Authors learned from the dialoguing and often were able to come to a decision about what they might do next.

The group conferencing let us share our writing process strategies both explicitly and vicariously. Sometimes we talked about how we worked. Often, however, what became apparent was that many of our writing difficulties were solved by seeing how someone else solved his or hers. We were only beginning to appreciate how much could be learned from seeing other people's work in progress. This aspect of sharing had been unexpected. Yet it proved to be one of the most powerful features of the group conferencing. This vicarious learning, this inadvertent collaboration, this "living off the land," as Graves calls it, was a vital component of becoming writers. That is not to suggest that soliciting individual help from other students or from the teacher wasn't useful, or that the teacher's offer of assistance or expression of interest wasn't supportive, but a fundamental ingredient of learning to write, we discovered, was seeing how others handled writing problems.

It was only after authors let us know a piece was well under control that we helped them explore the more technical aspects of writing. We tended to focus on large organizational difficulties first. Subsequent conferences seemed to deal with specific wording of sentences, word choices; typographical errors might be pointed out; spelling and punctuation were occasionally discussed. It wasn't uncommon, for example, for someone to query a particular punctuation usage, which would send us to a reference source to help with a decision. That was when we learned a great deal about how punctuation could be used. Finally, formatting and layout decisions were considered. On a number of occasions we would think a piece was done only to find that a few more small changes might be desirable. But there clearly came a point when the author called a halt. That point, we learned, was determined by the publishing intentions. If a piece was being readied for submission to a journal, then finicky attention to detail was appropriate. If the piece was being set aside for the time being, then further attention to detail was no longer useful.

How were our personal experiences with writing and conferencing useful for our students? We found, perhaps with some measure of surprise, that what we were learning about writing ourselves was immediately of value. We found that our first grade students could participate in sharing meetings and discuss their reactions to someone's writing. The children quickly learned to ask both the teacher and other students for specific kinds of help and to decide which of the suggestions offered they might try. As Graves and Calkins have described, the teacher had an important role to play in initiating these kinds of interactions but it wasn't long before the children were in control themselves. More difficult, perhaps, were the junior high school students with whom some of the teachers worked. These students needed considerable encouragement before they were willing to risk writing and sharing what they wrote. But they, too, learned to assume control of the writing process.

Because writing requires social interaction, much of what we have done in the guise of writing instruction has actually led students away from writing proficiency, not toward it. We have been teaching that writing is something writers struggle to do on their own. Our most valuable insight was that writing and learning to be a writer involve collaboration. Discovering that writing is a social, not a solitary, activity was an important consequence of our experiences with conferencing. It was through engagement with others, by talking about our ideas and problems, by listening to their reactions and suggestions, by experiencing the effect of our writing, by seeing how others were going about solving their writing problems, that we learned how writing could be done.

12

It Makes You Feel Needed

Students as Teachers

Judy Mossip

A fifth grader opens the door of the primary class, enters, and stands watching the children working. A signal from the primary teacher sends two five-year-olds off to read with the visitor in a comfortable corner of the room. The two little ones are quickly drawn into the book. They sit close to the older child, comment on the story as it unfolds, point to things that interest them, turn the pages and join in the reading whenever they want. The reader knows how to keep them interested in the book. He points, laughs, asks questions, and always reads with enthusiasm. For five wonderful minutes these three are partners in learning. Then the shared reading session ends and the young ones are led back to the group sitting around the class-room teacher. The young visitor slips out quietly and heads for his classroom, where he will let the next student know it is her turn to visit the primary room.

Shared reading is a powerful activity. It is filled with the joy of sharing and of success. Its most obvious purpose is to help the grade fives and the primaries read fluently and enjoy books. Shared reading does much more, however; it demonstrates some important things about kids and how they learn.

I didn't anticipate the things that shared reading has shown me when I first started doing it with my class four years ago. I believed then, as I do now, that making reading easy and purposeful would help children become better readers. Through shared reading the reader and the listener would share the author's message. The younger child would become familiar with print and how books "work." Shared reading would give the grade fives and the primaries an audience for their reading. The books would be primary level, easy for all of the grade five children to read. They would have a purpose for reading a book that was easy for them, and the primary children wouldn't know that some of the older students struggled to read harder books.

Shared reading was first introduced to supplement what the primary teacher taught her students about reading and to encourage and improve the nonfluent and reluctant readers in my class. Over the next four years the emphasis changed, however. The relationship between the older and younger children became important. The conversations that I at first discouraged became an integral part of the learning. We collaborated with the primaries in other ways— interviewing them, writing for them and with them, and helping them with activities that were just a bit hard for them to do on their own (making cookies and masks).

The sense of responsibility for these young learners grew, and each older student was delighted when the young child learned something new. The sense of caring extended to the school year and probably the neighborhood, where the older students had an increased desire to protect and nurture the younger children. For example, one cold morning this year, several of my students arrived talking about a primary child who had fallen in a puddle and was afraid to come to school. We delegated one of the class to go back for him, and ten minutes later I saw the little boy being slowly led to the school. The older student was comforting the child as she took him to his teacher.

Shared reading has become one of the most important things we do each year. From the beginning there has been a feeling of trust and a sense of purpose. My students know that I am confident about their abilities to work with the young learners. In our class we are partners in learning, and they carry this feeling of collaboration to shared reading. I really don't think that they have ever thought that shared reading was set up to teach them anything, but of course it has taught them many things. Although they can't always explain what it is they do as teachers, it is very similar to what I do with them. I try responding to what the learner is doing. I believe the teacher's role is to provide the support that enables the learner to take risks. The teacher demonstrates what is to be done and praises the child who makes the attempt. According to one of my students, "a good teacher makes hard things easy."

The students in my grade five class make learning easy for the primary children. These grade five teachers learn as much as they teach, however. Shared reading is an opportunity for the older students to learn about responsibility, about patience—about them-selves. They can relate to the struggles of the primaries because they remember being that young and still know what it is like to try to learn. A feeling of togetherness and hopefulness develops in even the most negative child when he or she has a chance to interact with a younger child.

Shared reading is for all older students. Every child is capable of making a contribution to shared reading. Some children carry on the most interesting conversations about the books and other topics. Others find the task of entering the primary class and keeping the attention of two young ones to be quite challenging enough. The students in my class didn't need to be taught too much about how to work with a younger child. Most of them have experience relating to these children on the school grounds and in the neighborhood. My role is to give them a specific reason to be together and to give them the support they need in this new setting. They seem to know about shared reading before I introduce the idea and they volunteer with enthusiasm each September. They ask questions about how we will do it and hint at their nervousness. Within a few weeks they are confident and competent language teachers. An observer in the primary or grade five class might ask how shared reading becomes a natural part of the busy day. Explaining what I did this year may partially answer that question.

Shared reading is demonstrated in our class every day. I enjoy reading to my students and try to share my enthusiasm and involvement in literature. We talk about aspects of the book that interest us. I know they like books read to them that way because they say so many times through the year. The older children try to do with the primaries what I do with them.

The children are given more support than just me reading to them, however. I began the school year with a demonstration lesson. The primary teacher knew the young ones who were confident enough to come to our class. I demonstrated in this session what I wanted my students to do. I made the young ones feel comfortable on either side of me where they could easily see the book. Two seems to be the best number for this. I read the title and mentioned the author. I followed the print with my fingers and talked about the story and the pictures that helped tell it. I read it once and invited them to join in as I read it a second time. I asked them questions about the story and the pictures, trying to get them to be active participants. My students could see that the two primary students were involved in the book and after they were escorted back to their room we talked about what I had done to create that involvement.

The primary students showed from the start that they enjoyed the reading session and loved talking about the book. My students were eager to try to please them. Several more visits were made by the primaries, but on those visits the readers were the grade five students who felt confident enough to read in front of us all. After each session we talked about what worked and what hadn't. One of the last observation sessions was videotaped, which gave us a chance to discuss the interaction as we watched it.

My class went to visit the primary teacher, who explained how valuable shared reading is to her and her students. She explained how she wanted them to enter the classroom and get her attention, where they would sit to read, and how to help the primary children rejoin the whole class activity. This short talk made the children feel welcome and appreciated. They were anxious to begin reading to the primaries, and I was confident that they could.

Shared reading was begun, and it really became self-managing. The children always keep track of who is reading and when. They take a look at their book before they go over to read, and they are good about reminding each other about the time. I try to make time every week to ask about their experiences and solve the problems that come up.

What books are used?

We use books that we know the primaries will enjoy and find easy. They are most often predictable books because they meet those two criteria. The books are chosen by the two adult teachers, the primary children, and the grade fives. The older students enjoy bringing books from home that helped them learn to read. They also write books for the young ones to enjoy. There are about thirty books from which to choose, and we get new books when the primary children want a change.

Where are the books kept?

To allow the older students time to practice the book, the books are kept in a special box in our classroom. We used to leave the books in the primary classroom after they were read, but that became too confusing. Since we use books from the school and public libraries, the students can easily find them to read for themselves when they are ready.

How is shared reading scheduled?

The fifth grade children go one at a time in alphabetical order. A class list is posted to keep them organized. Three children read per day, which means that within twenty minutes or so it's over for the day. I used to do it during silent reading but most recently have done it while I am reading out loud. This has created problems because the children naturally don't want to miss part of the book we are reading. Discussions with the primary teacher have allowed us to change the time. They now go out just after I read and everyone is doing individual or group work. Since each child is not out of the class long, they easily fit back into the class activities.

How many of the class takes part in shared reading?

Since shared reading is a voluntary activity, I take whomever I get each year. Some years three-quarters of the class reads and other years more do. This year every one of the children volunteered and not one has dropped out. Some children who are reluctant at first end up volunteering after they know more about it and have a chance to see how it is done.

What do the young teachers do about the primaries who want to read?

From the beginning of the shared reading experience the primaries are encouraged to join in. The fifth graders make the young ones feel good about their ability and potential to read well and never correct a child who doesn't read the print exactly. The primaries are encouraged to take risks just as the children in my room are.

How are the reading trios formed?

Because the ratio is two to one, the children are randomly matched each time they work together. The matching is quite flexible, though. If a long book is started with two children, the older student would ask for the same two children on the next visit. For special projects, the children at both grade levels choose a partner, and at times the adult teachers arrange the most suitable matches.

How do you know how the students are doing as readers?

The primary teacher usually notices if there are any significant behavior problems and informs me. I try to have another teacher come in for ten minutes every few months so I can observe the shared reading session. The easiest way to keep track is to ask the students at both grade levels.

How do you establish a relationship with another class?

I have looked for a teacher in the lower grades who has a philosophy of learning and teaching similar to mine. A belief in children teaching children is important. I have been fortunate to have a cooperative teacher at the primary level for each year that my class has done shared reading. There have been three different teachers over the years, but each has been glad to work with us.

What problems have you had?

One year I discovered that an older student was making every page a "test" for the younger child by asking too many questions. Every year the older students need advice about how to handle the badly behaved or restless child. When my students are paired with a young one for a special project, they need to talk about the problems that they are having with that particular child and are encouraged to be especially patient. Sometimes I notice enthusiasm waning in my class, and I usually change the books and provide a few encouraging words. Some days a child just doesn't feel like going to read, and they always know they can skip a turn. Sometimes in the year the young children require more discipline or patience and we talk about that then.

What effect has shared reading had on the fifth graders?

My ideas about the benefits of shared reading have changed as I have observed my students over the past four years. The activity has certainly done much more than improve their reading ability. I am convinced that it also affects how they learn, how they feel about themselves, and how they see themselves as members of society. They feel needed and enjoy helping someone else learn. Their comments about shared reading indicate real insight into learning and teaching.

- "Primaries are small but smarter than you think."
- "I am just as foolish as they are."
- "Liked it because of the things that 'slip out.' "
- "I'd make a crummy parent."
- "Made me feel a lot older."
- "Go one step at a time and you can't just tell them."
- "It helped me read better."
- "They remind you about yourself."
- "They have to talk to know."
- "Learn spelling by reading like we do."
- "They have different ways of looking at things, mostly just imagine."
- "I ask them a word just before I go and if they don't know it I tell them."
- "When you do something they look at you and then they do the same."
- "I like to take the time to explain. Some other teachers can't take the time to explain things to one individual child. I'd like to give each child a chance."
- "Sometimes they interrupt when they like a part or they like a picture, but that might be part of it all."

Shared reading is important to all of the students involved. At times it is inconvenient, and the grade fives often work harder than they probably thought they would have to when they first volunteered. Shared reading develops social relationships; it also helps foster the risk taking and meaningful involvement so necessary for learning. Shared reading helps the grade fives realize they have come a long way and can be proud of their continuing journey on the literacy road.

13

Activity Cards
Winniefred Kwak
and
Judith M. Newman

The most common view of instruction sees it predominantly as a one-way transmission of information: where the classroom is a place for receiving knowledge, where children are busy reproducing what we present them. The whole language view of learning, on the other hand, argues that we need to see knowledge as something which children must create for themselves. From a whole language perspective the classroom becomes an environment where children, through talking, reading, and writing, build understanding.

In a whole language classroom an emphasis on learning facts is replaced with opportunities for solving problems and making links between school learning and the children's everyday lives. Student investigations take the place of teacher presentations. Whole-class activities, with everyone doing the same thing at the same time, in the same way, give way to small-group discussions and individual projects. Talking, reading, and writing become vehicles for constructing new ideas. In such environments the teacher is no longer in sole possession of knowledge; instead, children are helped to take responsibility for their own learning.

In order to encourage children to become active, independent learners we need to create activities in which their efforts and initiative lead to understanding. Activity cards are useful for providing such learning experiences. They are invitations to engage in learning activities through which children can develop as readers and writers.

How activity cards can be helpful for letting children become more active learners may be clearer from the following lesson with a group of eight- to eleven-year-old children engaged in trying their first activity card.

Each child received a copy of the activity card (Figure 13–1).

Cs: What are we supposed to do? What is this all about?
T: What can you do to answer your own questions?

137

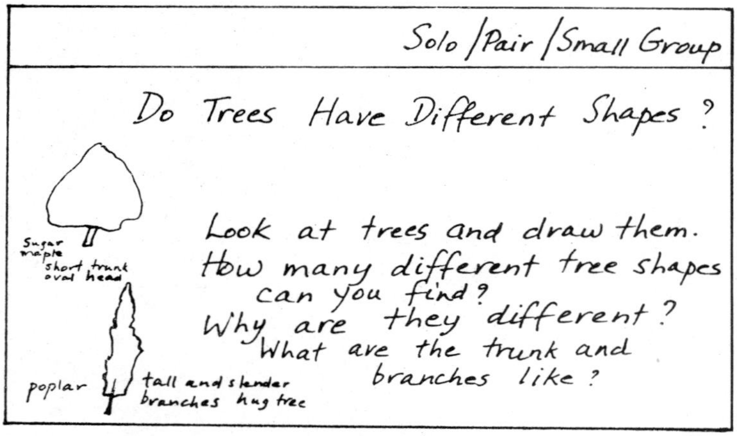

Solo /Pair /Small Group

Do Trees Have Different Shapes?

Sugar maple
short trunk
oval head

poplar
tall and slender
branches hug tree

Look at trees and draw them.
How many different tree shapes
can you find?
Why are they different?
What are the trunk and
branches like?

Figure 13 – 1

C-1: Read the card?

(Several children read or glance over the card, then wait to see what will happen next.)

T: (waits, then asks) What did you find out?
(A few hands are raised.)
What can you do if you don't understand?

C-2: Ask the teacher.

T: Is there anything else you can do?

C-3: Read it again.

T: What else can you do?

(The children are silent.)

C-1: (Hesitantly) Ask someone else?

T: Fine, you have some good ideas. Now try and discover what the card is about.

(Some children read the card again; a few discuss the problem among themselves.)

C-4: The card is about trees having shapes.

T: Do you think trees have different shapes?

C-3: Well, the shape of a Christmas tree is different from a maple tree.

T: Yes, that's true. Are there other differences?

(The children glance over the card again.)

C-5: You're supposed to draw tree shapes.

C-2: You have to write about trees.

T: What will you write?

C-5: The name and how big it is.

C-1: And something about the branches and the trunk.

T: Where will you find that information?

C-1: From the writing near the pictures?

T: What will you write about the trunk and branches?

C-4: How they're holding up the tree.

T: Those are good ideas. Carry on, then.

(The children silently look at one another.)

C-3: But there aren't any trees here. How're we supposed to do it?

  T: Have you any suggestions?

C-1: Can we go outside?

C-4: We could look them up in books.

  T: Both of those are good ideas. Decide what you'd like to do.

(The children decide to go outside.)

  T: (as the children are getting ready to go out) Do we just go and look at trees?

(The children are silent for a moment, then they decide they will need paper, pencils, erasers, crayons, something stiff to write on, and sweaters. They get what they need and leave. Once outside, the children have several questions.)

C-3: I forget what I'm supposed to do.

  T: What can you do about that?

C-4: Look at the card again?

  T: OK. See if someone has brought a copy of the card along.

C-2: I don't know what to write.

  T: How can you find out?

(The child leaves and asks a friend.)

C-1: I read the card again, but there's nothing special about this tree.

  T: Does it have to be a special tree?

C-5: I don't know what to write if it's not special.

  T: What are you going to do, then?

C-5: Could I do another tree?

  T: You decide how you're going to do the activity.

C-4: How much do I have to write?

  T: You decide how much is enough.

C-5: How many trees do I have to do?

  T: Does the card say anything about that?

C-4: There's nothing about how many trees you're supposed to do.

  T: Then you decide.

C-4: Would two be enough?

  T: You have to make your own decision.

C-5: Do you have to write sentences?

  T: You decide what's best. Just think about what you will do with your work when you're finished and who will read it.

C-1: Only you will read it.

  T: Is that so?

C-2: Well, when we're finished we give our work to you.

  T: But think about what usually happens to your work then.

C-2: You check it.

  T: Yes, but I also put it up for others to see.

C-2: So I have to write in sentences?

  T: You decide.

Some children wanted advice about how to draw particular trees; the teacher suggested they make their own decisions. Others asked for help with spelling; the teacher suggested they do the best they could. Back in the classroom the children's efforts were displayed and the activity discussed. They talked about what they'd learned about trees. Then they considered the activity itself.

> T: Tell me something about how you were learning.
> C-3: You didn't help. We had to do it by ourselves.
> T: I don't think you worked all alone. You talked with each other.
> C-1: You told us to.
> T: I agreed it was a good idea to help each other. Did it help?
> C-4: It was OK. It was faster than waiting your turn when you go to the teacher.
> T: Did working together help in any other way?
> C-2: If you don't know, you can ask anybody for help. Some of the others usually know what to do.

Several observations can be made about the experience. At first, the children saw the activity as an assignment. They expected the teacher to explain the task to them. When that information was not given, they realized they had to make some decisions themselves. That created two problems. The text of the card was more concise than the stories the children were used to reading. Consequently, some of them had difficulty understanding it. Another problem was that asking a friend, instead of the teacher, for help did not seem to be a legitimate way of finding out what to do. These difficulties were discussed. The children became aware of the fact that in order to carry out the activity they had to make their own decisions; they needed to decide on an appropriate location and what tools were needed, for example.

Once the children arrived at the work site, new problems had to be solved. The assignment, which seemed circumscribed in the classroom, now proved to be open to various interpretations (what to write, how much to write, how many trees, which trees, etc.). In each case, the children had to make their own decisions rather than following teacher directions. This implied they had to interact with the card, with the environment, and with each other in order to be able to carry on. Throughout, the teacher supported the children by making encouraging comments and raising open questions which would lead the children to make some decisions on their own.

Upon their return to the classroom, the children were helped to discuss the activity and the work they had produced. They talked about what they'd learned about trees, and shared the questions they had. Not only did they learn that taking their own initiatives and working cooperatively led to better understanding, they also saw that each answer leads to new questions.

The use of activity cards may invoke images of "everyone doing his or her own thing" in an "unstructured" classroom where children "learn all by themselves." Such a view misinterprets what is actually involved in creating a student-centered learning environment. Student-centered learning does not imply *no* teacher intervention. In the first place, the activities are created by the teacher. They are planned to include specific learning experiences, to raise particular problems for the children to solve. The physical setting itself has been laid out to encourage interaction among the children. The furniture is arranged to form areas for small-group activity. The materials the children will need (books, newspapers, magazines, copies of articles, brochures, tapes, filmstrips, etc.) have been carefully selected to provide information on many different topics. These materials are well labeled and conspicuously located for easy access. Texts of varying degrees of difficulty are included. Since the activity cards do not specify the number of sources to be consulted, the children are encouraged to browse through several selections. They soon discover that the more "difficult" material usually offers more information. In this way the children are encouraged to try more difficult texts, but support is available in the form of material written more simply should the children require it.

Throughout the activity the teacher monitors carefully what the children are doing, helping them articulate whatever difficulties they are having, helping them consider what is involved in solving the problems with which they are faced, and suggesting where they might look for further information. The teacher must be both perceptive and flexible, able to gauge the children's educational needs as well as encouraging them to follow their interests within the framework of an activity.

The use of activity cards assumes children learn best when the activities in which they are involved interest them. The cards, designed around a theme or topic, allow children choice. The children's interests as well as the changing circumstances through the school year can be accommodated quite easily. For example, a new activity card, "This is really lousy!," was created in response to the appearance of head lice in the school. The children observed lice, studied their biology, and read about the role lice have played in human history. The declaration of the Year of the Handicapped led to the study of "spare parts for people," with the children investigating what can be done for the handicapped.

Not only do the activity cards encompass a broad range of topics, they are also designed to be carried out by children of widely differing ability. The cards do not convey expectations about the level of competence at which the tasks are to be performed. The children are simply encouraged to do the best they can with each activity they undertake. Some activity cards can be designed to provide more support than others. Some may provide specific step-by-step instructions, while others require the children to decide how they will carry out their investigation. In either case, the cards are designed to lead the children to a delineation of the problem and to increase the amount of reading and writing they do.

The activity cards are a useful way for encouraging the development of literacy. In the process of carrying out the various activities the children have to do a great deal of reading and writing. The activity cards have to be read; most of the information collected comes from print sources; notes from text sources, observations, interviews have to be written. Whatever the task, the children gain valuable experience engaging with reading and writing. Literacy becomes an indispensable part of learning in general.

Figures 13–2 and 13–3 should serve to illustrate what we've been saying.

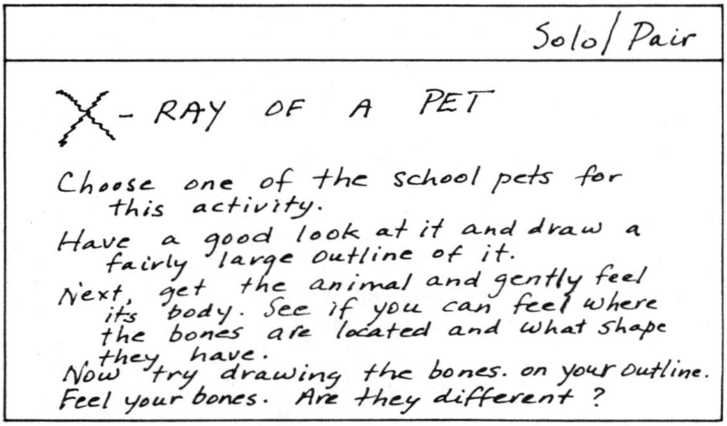

X - RAY OF A PET

Choose one of the school pets for this activity.

Have a good look at it and draw a fairly large outline of it.

Next, get the animal and gently feel its body. See if you can feel where the bones are located and what shape they have.

Now try drawing the bones on your outline.

Feel your bones. Are they different?

Figure 13 – 2

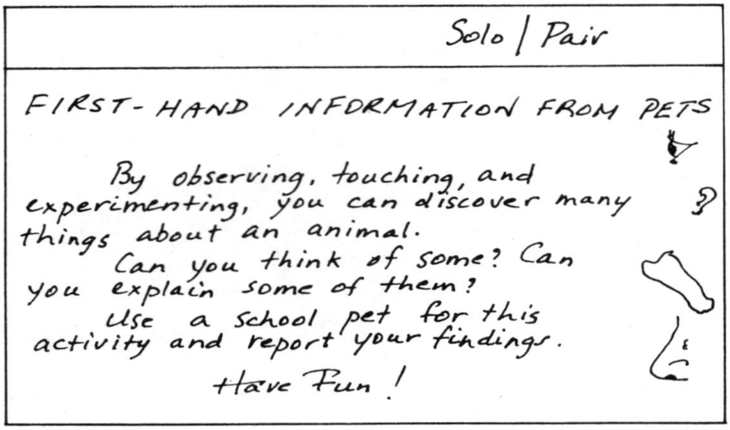

FIRST-HAND INFORMATION FROM PETS

By observing, touching, and experimenting, you can discover many things about an animal.

Can you think of some? Can you explain some of them?

Use a school pet for this activity and report your findings.

Have Fun!

Figure 13 – 3

"X-Ray of a Pet" (Figure 13–2) and "First-Hand Information from Pets" (Figure 13–3) were used at the beginning of a thematic unit on animals. The first card invites the children to start with some personal observation—feeling the bones of a pet—and to record their observations in the form of drawings as well as write about what they have learned. The card provides support with fairly concise instructions. Nevertheless, the activity is still open-ended. The children need to decide which school pet to observe. Since the proficiency with which the recording has to be carried out has not been specified, the children are free to interpret what is required and to do the best they can with the activity.

The second card also refers to various familiar aspects of animals but includes the suggestion that the children develop and conduct their own observations and experiments as well as the invitation to explain their findings. This second card asks the children to take greater initiative in defining the activity itself and carrying it out.

Let's compare the work produced by two children in response to these cards. These reports—Figure 13–4 (p. 143), by an eight-year-old; Figure 13–5 (p. 143), by an eleven-year-old—were produced after a half an hour's work.

Guinea Pig

Julian

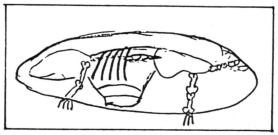

a Guinea pig can go truw an hole $4\frac{1}{2}$ cm long that mens that a quinea pig furr makes him look a lot fatter then he relly is and I think he use is it to trick of animals that cat him. So he exScaps thur Small hole.

Figure 13 – 4

All about a Guinea Pig

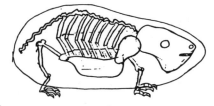

The giunea pig's heart beat is 200 beats a minute. He weighs about 113g. He can run about 2 miles an hour. The guinea can fit through this " " and the guinea pig is 8 by 4 in. No the guinea pig does not have good eyesight. They can only see about a fool away from themselves.

Yes the giunea pig has very good hearing because he can not see very well. He is alway sniffing cause hes breathing. He has choppers and grinders so he can chop his food and grind his food. Choppers cut the food so it is easyer to chew the food. Grinders grind up the food so the giunea can Sallow their food.

We thought the baby giunea pigs would be born about the first week of may. But we were wrong she wasn't even pregnt.

Figure 13 – 5

Differences in observational skills between the two children are apparent as well as differences in the amount of experimentation and research which was conducted. Each report, however, represents a good effort on the part of the student who wrote it. An evaluation of what children have learned from the experience must, therefore, take into account such differences as how well they can read, how comfortable they are as writers, how much experience they have had with defining activities and carrying them out.

In fact, the children's learning cannot be assessed on the basis of a single assignment. What they are learning, the control they are gaining as readers and writers, is only apparent when we look at their work over a period of time. Therefore, it is necessary to keep samples of the work the children do in order to be able to appraise their development. Note is made of the activities the children select, the resources they use (other people, books, personal observation), the presentation itself. We look for evidence that the children are able to take greater responsibility for organizing the learning activity on their own. We watch for signs that they have consulted reference materials and used what they have learned from them appropriately. We observe the ways in which the children organize what they have learned.

Our experience has been that activity cards offer children exciting and meaningful learning experiences through which they become more fluent readers and writers. The activity cards are a way of creating learning experiences which encourage children to deal with increasingly complex tasks involving the gathering of information, the organizing and presenting of it. The environment is inundated with written material, and the activities invite the children to read and write.

14

Mealworms

Learning about Written Language through Science Activities

Judith M. Newman

I have just sat down with J.P., an eight-year-old having some difficulty in school, and on the table in front of us is a glass dish with some mealworm larvae crawling around. J.P.'s eyes light up as he bends over the dish to watch these creatures move.

"Can I pick one up?" he asks me.

"Certainly," I answer.

"Look at it wiggle," he comments. "I can hardly feel it moving, though."

"What can you tell me about this creature?" I ask him.

With that query we began an exploration which finished with J.P. authoring his first book.

For some reason which I have never understood, we have thought that learning about written language was best done in the context of what we call "language arts" instruction: through the reading and writing of stories and poems. We've offered children narrative, fictional texts (as well as a few poetic and dramatic ones), in the belief that these are the most appropriate materials to use for teaching children about written language. By compartmentalizing curriculum as we have, we've come to assume that learning in each "subject" is discrete. Consequently, we have generally neglected the wealth of opportunity for learning about language, both written and spoken, provided by those activities we call "science," believing that these activities have little or nothing to do with language learning in the first place and are probably too difficult for language learning purposes in the second. But for J.P., and every other child with whom I have worked, learning about written language through science activities has been both exciting and effortless.

Let's return to J.P. and the mealworms. We spent most of our first

A version of this article appeared originally as "J.P. becomes an Eight-Year-Old Scientific Writer" in *Highway One*, Vol. 6, No. 3 (Fall 1983).

hour together talking about what was happening. We let the meal-worms walk on our hands, we tried them on the table, on pieces of paper. We lifted the paper to see what would happen when the mealworms reached the edge. We laid a book on top of two pencils, then placed the mealworms underneath and, crouching down, we watched to see what they did when they came into the light. We put a small amount of bran on the table with the mealworms nearby and watched to see if they could find it. We did the same with a few drops of water and with some apple. An hour was quickly over and we'd seen so much we wanted to remember that we decided to make some rough notes in a notebook for next time before we stopped. I say "we" because both J.P. and I wrote our own separate notes. J.P. was uncomfortable at first because he wasn't sure how to spell the words he wanted to use, but I assured him these notes were only to help us remember what we'd seen and done so we could plan what to try next time. For "homework" I asked him to think about what else we could find out about these creatures.

Investigating mealworms is a wonderful science and language activity, because very little is actually known about these creatures and there is practically nothing written about them for nonscientific readers. Even though I am "the teacher," I'm as much a learner as J.P. in this situation. That means that the note-taking is as necessary for me as it is for him. I also know that while I'll try to find some reading material about *Tenebrio* (mealworms' scientific name), I haven't found much yet. So even if J.P. mentions his "project" to his parents and should they investigate the encyclopedia, they won't find a great deal there. The books we are going to write and publish will be based on our original research and will be useful additions to my library as a source of reading material for other children.

A week later J.P. was back with some ideas for investigating mealworms. I had brought along some magnifying lenses and a dissecting microscope so we would be able to have a close look at these larvae. We counted the legs and the antennae. We estimated the number of body segments, then counted them on several mealworms and discovered this to be a constant number. We examined the head region under the microscope to see if we could locate eyes and mouth parts. We compared the top of the meal-worm's body with the underside of the larva. Then we returned to our notes. J.P. was a little less hesitant about recording his observations this time.

Next we tried some experiments. We'd noticed the mealworms seemed to move forward most of the time. J.P. wondered whether they could move backward. We discussed what he might try in order to find out. He decided that tapping the animals lightly on the head would probably work. He tried it several times—sure enough, the mealworms went into reverse. What if he just placed a barrier in front of them? That didn't have the effect he'd expected. Instead of moving backward, the mealworm made a ninety-degree turn and continued along the side of the barrier. This raised another question. Did mealworms always turn in the same direction or was the direction in which they turned random? With some prompting, J.P. decided he would give each of three mealworms several trials. He placed his mealworms (one at a time) a couple of inches and at a right angle from a glass microscope slide held on edge and watched what happened. Sometimes the larva turned to the right, sometimes to the left. The mealworms didn't seem to have any directional preference.

After watching the mealworms in this situation for a while, it occurred to me to wonder how they guide themselves along the "wall." Did they need to feel the wall with the side of their bodies, only with their legs, with their antennae? J.P. and I discussed what we could do to find out. We considered how we might try to set up different kinds of walls—short ones to touch only the legs, over-hanging ones to touch only the back, angled ones so that the mealworms would have to decide to turn. We didn't actually conduct these experiments, but we had an animated discussion about them.

The container in which the mealworms were living had what appeared to be other kinds of creatures living in it. To start our third session I placed a small plastic container with some of these "other" animals in it in front of J.P. Some of these creatures he recognized as "bugs" (beetles, actually). We counted the legs—six—the same as the mealworms. It was difficult getting a good look at these beetles because they moved quickly and they tickled when they walked on our hands. The other creature was a whitish color and didn't move much at all. It had no legs that we could see. Its head seemed not to be separated from its body.

"Why," I asked J.P., "do you suppose the mealworms are living with these other creatures?" He screwed up his face as he thought about it. Did he recognize any similarities among these three "different" animals? I happened to know J.P. had "studied" the life cycle of butterflies in school in the fall. I also knew he hadn't actually seen specimens of the various stages. I was curious, then, to see whether he would come to the conclusion that he had a larva, a pupa, and an adult of one kind of animal in front of him. It took some questioning on my part to help him make that connection. Once more we made notes about what we had learned (Figure 14–1).

At this point we shifted our focus from observing to writing about our observations. We took J.P.'s page of notes and read it together. At this point we did two things. First, I asked him to reread his notes on his own and to circle whatever words he was unsure about. I then wrote the conventional spelling for the words J.P. had circled, pointing out to him how close his functional spelling was. Next, I asked him to tell me what topics he had written about. I wrote the four headings he mentioned (live where, legs, head, joints: i.e., body segments) in the upper right corner (Figure 14–2).

Now we were ready to begin producing our books. I had prepared two books in advance. I had taken four sheets of 8½ by 11-inch paper, added a sheet of colored construction paper, and sewed them down the center. I had taken several other sheets of paper and cut them into small rectangles. To make a book, we would write our text out on the small pieces of paper, and when we were satisfied with what we'd written we would glue these pieces of text into our book. That way, misprintings would be no problem since we could easily discard the small piece of paper on which we were writing and quickly rewrite on another without affecting what we'd already transcribed. I

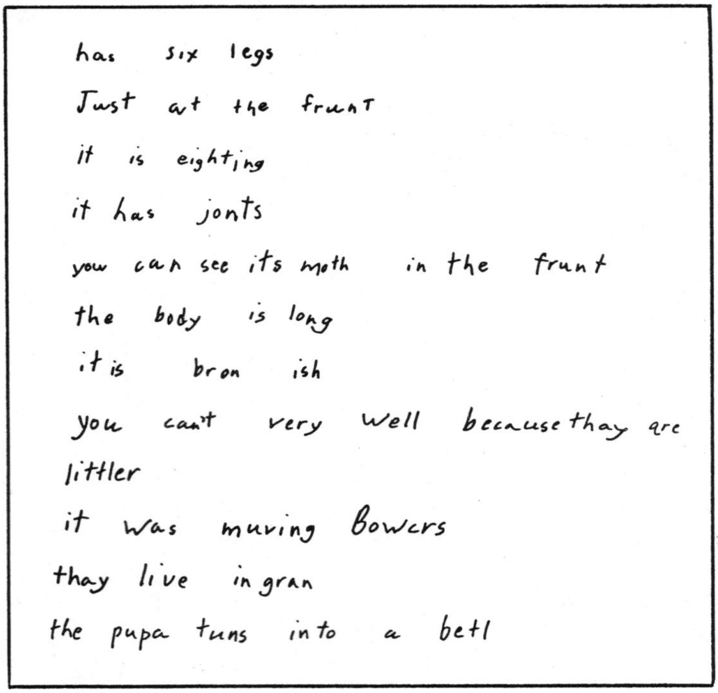

has six legs
Just at the frunT
it is eighting
it has jonts
you can see its moth in the frunt
the body is long
it is bron ish
you can't very well because thay are littler
it was muving Bowers
thay live in gran
the pupa tuns into a betl

Figure 14 – 1

Mealworms

1) live where
2) legs
3) ~~eye~~ head
4) joints

has six legs
legs/Just at the frunT front
it is eighting eating
it has jonts joints
you can see its moth (mouth) in the frunt (front)
the body is long
it is bron ish brownish
you can't ^ (see the eyes) very well because thay an littler
it was muving (moving) Bowers (Backwards)
thay live in gran grain
the pupa tuns into a betl
pupa turns beetle

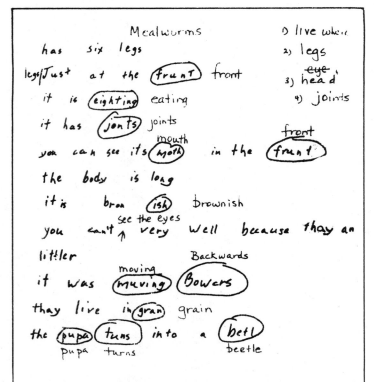

Figure 14 – 2

decided to help J.P. with one last bit of organizing; I asked him to number his topic headings. We were set, then, to begin creating the books. In order to resist the temptation to interfere with J.P.'s efforts, I kept myself out of his way by working on my own book.

Figure 14–3 is the first page of J.P.'s mealworm book. Notice how he extended the information he'd had in his notes by a full sentence. Observe, too, how he correctly copied from his notes and spelled functionally when he had to.

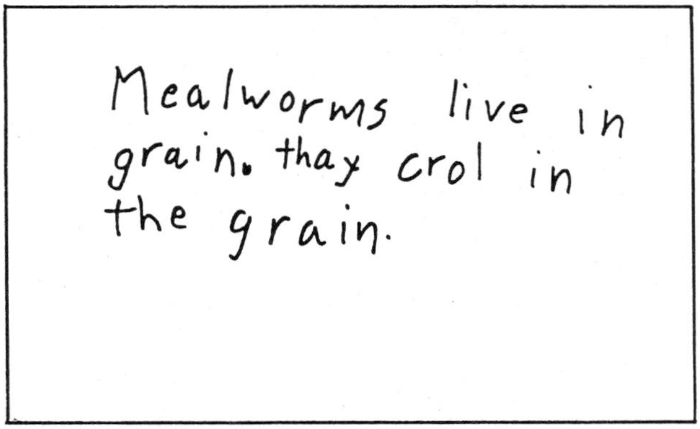

Mealworms live in grain. thay crol in the grain.

Figure 14 – 3

Figure 14–4 (a) and (b) shows the second and third pages of his book. Again he extends his writing well beyond the limited amount of information he had written in his notes. He uses appropriate

Mealworms have six legs. thay Wigel whith the dack and crol with the front.

(a)

Their legs are in the front of the boby. Wen they walk their legs arnt stif.

(b)

Figure 14 – 4

punctuation, some capitalization. His printing is reasonably legible. He even spells "*they*" conventionally on the right-hand page.

J.P. decided to combine topics three and four (head and joints) in the pages shown in Figure 14–5 (a) and (b). Observe the functional spelling for "*front*" in his diagram, although he spelled it conventionally (copied from his page of notes) in the text. Notice as well the correct use of "*B*" for "back" in the diagram and the reversal in the text. J.P. does know the difference between *B*'s and *D*'s but isn't always attending to which he wants to use. If we were to examine both his notes and his text we would discover J.P. makes the appropriate decision in the majority of cases: not once in the notes does a reversal appear; only three occur in the book—could they be caused by the extra care he is taking while writing his good copy?

you can see the mouth in the front. you can't see the eyes very well because they are little

(a)

frunt   Back

most of them have 12 or 13 Jonts. It has jonts on the front and dack to.

(b)

Figure 14 – 5

The last page of J.P.'s book (Figure 14–6) includes a topic not on his list. It was prompted by the last sentence in his notes and by the fact that he had a couple of blank pages left in his book. The description of the life cycle of mealworms he gives us here goes well beyond the minimal information contained in his notes.

It was a proud eight-year-old beside me as he closed his book with a flourish. He handed it to me to read. He read it along with me. I handed it back. Then I asked if he would like to read mine. J.P. opened the book and began reading aloud:

Mealworms are the larvae of grain beetles. Like all insects their legs and their bodies have joints. Their legs have three joints. Their bodies have thirteen joints. The bodies are jointed on the top and on the bottom as well.

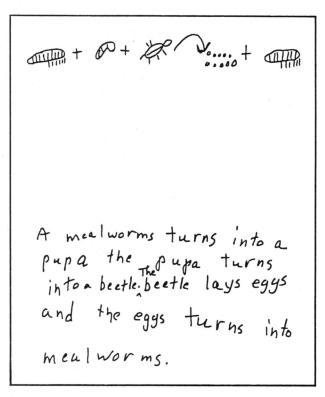

A mealworms turns into a pupa the The pupa turns into a beetle. the beetle lays eggs and the eggs turns into mealworms.

Figure 14 – 6

J.P. paused for a moment, then exclaimed: "My joints are all wrong!" He had noticed the difference between my conventional spelling for that word and his functional one. I had decided, as we were writing, that rather than point out his "error" to him, I would use the word a number of times in my book to see what would happen. While he elected not to change his own book, the difference hadn't gone unnoticed. In this instance J.P., reading "like a writer," made note of something about which he still was uncertain.

Learning language is an inexorable part of learning about the world:

Children learn language because it is there, part of the world around them, and because it makes sense in that world. Language and the rest of the world are inseparable. . . . Children will neither attend to nor willingly practice language that does not seem to have a point. They are only interested in language that is an integral part of the world; language cannot be something different (Smith, 1979).

Language serves practical purposes. It is not something to be learned as an abstraction, divorced from the real world. Language learning involves the same problem-solving strategies and processes that are involved in learning anything else.

Investigating mealworms is a terrific example of the kind of learning activity which can support students' efforts to develop as readers and writers. Fluent readers and writers gain experience with written and oral language as they discuss, read, and write about whatever they are investigating. Less fluent readers and writers are helped to use what prior knowledge they have as well as whatever new information they obtain from their investigations to make writing and reading easier. Such language/science activities encourage students to become writers in order to consolidate what it is they have learned as well as to share with others their discoveries.

Some of us have adopted the phrase "whole language" to describe how we believe language instruction needs to be conceptualized. That is, we have come to recognize that language learning cannot be fragmented into tidy packages to be delivered in some prearranged sequence. Language learning is holistic and unpredictable. In order to learn about language we need to be participants in real language experiences where it is possible to "borrow" what one needs at the moment from what may be available in the environment.

Yet, by referring to our theoretical framework as "whole language" we are doing language learning and language instruction a disservice. The term is still too narrow; it implies that we learn about language only in the context of language, when in reality we learn about language in the context of learning about the world. It is true that literature is a part of that world, but it isn't the whole world. An important source of experiences for learning both oral and written language is to be found in that domain of knowledge we call "science." To exclude the world of science from what we do in the name of "language learning" is to miss the wealth of opportunity science activities offer for helping students develop as language users.

J.P. came to me for help because his parents were concerned about his reading development. During the course of "instruction" J.P. investigated frogs, mealworms, magnets, and batteries and bulbs. Each investigation involved recording his observations, reading what appropriate material we could find on the topic, and writing his own book. By the end of our sessions, J.P. had authored four books, each succeeding book longer and more detailed than the previous one. At the end of his first book J.P. was starting to consider himself an author, able to engage in the process as any other author would. By the end of his fourth, he was well on his way to being able to sustain his own learning about written language.

Why did J.P. engage in these learning activities so enthusiastically? Because he could see that language was serving some real, practical purpose. He wasn't engaged in learning language abstractions; he was actively using written and oral language to get something done.

Note

A useful source for science activities for elementary school children is the *Elementary Science Study* (ESS) series of science modules published by McGraw-Hill. *Behavior of Mealworms* provided the initial information which allowed me and J.P. to get under way.

15

The War of
the Words

Susan Church

"That Curtis is so stupid!" Carla said in disgust as she came into my room one morning. Karen and Beth, the other girls in the small group who work together in my Resource room, just rolled their eyes and nodded in agreement.

Carla proceeded to tell me about the history class she and Karen had just attended, where the topic had been the changing role of women in Canadian society. The discussion had been related to a comparison of women in the nineteenth century and today. A number of the boys had angered the girls with their chauvinistic comments. Curtis had said, "Things really were better in the nineteenth century when women knew their place and stayed in the kitchen. They really can't do things as well as men."

The girls were frustrated that they hadn't been able to argue their position more forcefully. They felt they had been bested in the verbal battle and were upset. I could see how they might have felt over-whelmed in this situation; all three had experienced problems in learning to read and write and were not confident learners. Even in the relatively safe small-group situation they were reluctant to take risks. Classroom teachers had observed that they were usually quiet and rather passive, ordinarily not likely to be active participants in this sort of lively discussion.

I was delighted to see that they had become so agitated about something which had occurred in the classroom. In the six months I had been working with them I had been trying to help them to develop language competency, to assume more control over their own learning, and to feel more positive about themselves. In addition, I wanted them to make more sense of the content of the classroom curriculum. Their primary objective was to earn passing marks. Until this day they had been noticeably unenthusiastic about their classroom programs and about our activities in the Resource program despite my efforts to use classroom and related materials in

153

interesting ways. I was asking myself, "What in the world do I have to do to get these girls excited about learning? How can I activate them?"

This looked like an opportunity I couldn't let pass. I was interested in the issue and more than a little annoyed at Curtis and his macho friends as well. So, I decided it would be worthwhile to explore the topic a bit further. The history teacher had decided to do the same thing in class; he was concerned about the narrow-minded attitudes he had heard expressed and thought the class, especially the boys, would benefit from further reading and discussion. His focus was to be women in Canadian history. I decided that I would develop some activities for the girls which would complement this classroom program.

Because of my interest in women's issues I had been clipping articles regarding women as I ran across them in my reading. I added other selections to this collection in an effort to provide a range of reading materials through which the girls could develop a broader understanding of the topic. By the time we were ready to begin our exploration, the file included the following:

- an excerpt from their history text
- short biographies of famous Canadian women (Lucy Maud Montgomery, Nellie McClung, Emily Stowe, Emily Murphy)
- short, relatively simple articles from easy texts (one about women mathematicians, one about a labor leader)
- an article on the Billie Jean King—Bobby Riggs tennis match
- a short story
- newspaper articles (description of an organization formed to increase the involvement of women in science, a statement of women writers in Canada regarding inequalities, report on sex discrimination in the workplace)
- an article from a general-interest science magazine describing sex differences in the brain
- an article from *Ms.* magazine refuting the evidence in the above article
- a magazine article on women and computers
- an article from a student magazine describing the problems a female engineer encountered in a predominately male profession

We spent the next few classes sampling this material. During the session each of us selected one or two articles to read. As we read, we took notes so that we could share the information with the others. I found that the girls had not developed efficient methods of taking notes. They resorted to copying whole sentences from the text or to jotting words and phrases with no system for organizing them. As I read my articles, I showed them ways of taking notes that I had found useful. They had had some experience with diagramming or mapping text, so I suggested that they try applying that strategy in this situation. I showed them how I was making a tree diagram in which I wrote down a central point and then showed subsidiary ideas as branches connected with lines and arrows. I asked them each to try that with a section of their articles. I encouraged each of them to experiment and find workable methods of her own. I found that they needed a great deal of support in this process because they had little experience with making their own notes in this way. However, the activity had the advantage of giving them a reason for making usable notes; each reader was responsible for explaining her article to the rest of us. The note making became somewhat easier as we went, but learning to do it well, independently, takes time and lots of practice with teacher support.

They had free choice in their selection of articles. I chose the more complex texts, which had information which was relevant but might have proved too frustrating for them to try to read independently. One girl was a very reluctant reader; she grabbed all the shortest articles. This did not concern me because I judged she would shift to longer ones as she gained confidence. In fact, I encouraged them to try the shorter, easier texts first. I included two versions of each of the biographies of the Canadian women, one simpler than the other. I suggested that each of them choose one woman, read the easier text first and then the more difficult. They were quite surprised at how well they understood the second text after they had read and discussed the first. I told them that I often use that strategy when I have something difficult to read. They seemed to feel it might also help them. Later they were able to use these articles for a project assigned by the history teacher.

Toward the end of each class we shared our information, each reader using her notes as a guide. These notes were private, intended to be used only by the writer, so the students were free to write without being too concerned about surface structure conventions. We talked about the content of the articles, and also about the social and historical factors which have contributed to the inequities that exist for today's women. They began to understand the social and cultural context which fostered the attitudes reflected in the comments of the boys in the class. One of them observed, "Women aren't as capable at some things because they haven't been given a chance."

We spent four class periods reading and discussing articles. When we finished, we attempted to generate a chart of the information we had gathered. We found this fairly difficult because we had explored so many facets of the topic. We started with a brainstorm, in which we put the topic in the center of a sheet of paper and then added the various bits of information around it like the spokes of a wheel. Then we reorganized the bits, grouping them under subtopics which the girls generated. Finally we transferred the reorganized information to a chart. The process of organizing the information gave us an appreciation of the complexity of the issue and enabled us to see the interrelationships among ideas. By the time we completed the series of activities, the girls understood the content and were able to articulate what they knew; they were able to handle their history projects with no difficulty and were more confident about engaging in class discussion.

At that point I decided that it might be very interesting to see how some boys would react a similar experience. I chose Tom and Grant, students who are fairly confident readers and speakers but reluctant writers. Fond of hearing themselves talk and masters at using conversation to avoid writing, they both had been known to make sweeping generalizations based on little or no evidence. I had reason to suspect that they would assume a chauvinistic stance, if only to stir up a bit of excitement. I thought I might possibly draw them into writing if the issue generated enough feeling.

We shared the articles in the same way the girls and I had. The boys were more willing to take risks with reading; both tackled the longer articles with more confidence than the girls had at the start. However, they balked at taking notes, claiming they could remember everything important without writing. When articles were read and discussed during the same session, this was true. However, when a few days elapsed between reading and discussion, they found that they retained only a general sense of the meaning and could not provide supporting details. Since the activity extended over several sessions, they soon conceded that they would have to write a few notes to provide continuity. They were even less skilled than the girls and were less willing to take suggestions or to try to improve. They were satisfied to write words and phrases at random on their papers. I demonstrated other ways of organizing information through my note taking and served as recorder when we generated a collective diagram of the information. However, I judged that these boys would need to experience many more situations in which they made notes for a real purpose before they would be convinced of the value of the skill.

I was definitely outnumbered in the discussions related to the articles. Both of the boys defended male superiority; I tried to get them to consider with open minds the issues raised in the articles. I saw no shifts in attitude as a result either of the reading or the discussion. Our sessions were almost a repetition of the history class the girls had described. Initially I was quite discouraged, but then I realized that this might provide an opportunity for the girls to use what they had learned through their reading and discussion.

I told the boys that I felt the need to bring in reinforcements to support my side of the argument. I asked them each to write a short reaction statement, which I passed along to the girls at our next session. The first exchange was as follows:

TOM

Most men with an exception of a few wimps are bigger and stronger than wimon further more how many CWFL (Canadian Wimon fottball leauge) do you see

how many women do you see at the top of Mt. Everest and if you do see any they are probly dead hay!!! don't get me wrong I think should be able to do it but the thing is they didnt

I think women are more intelligent than man but thier nt as capibel I don't think they are lowlife or any thing but I dont think they are equal

CARLA, KARYN, BETH

What's so important about football?!!! It's just a sport that everyone gets hurt. What does it prove to play football just that your big enough to run into people!! I'd like to know how many men are at the top of Mt. Everest. Women arn't cpable of what?!! Women that work really hold down two jobs their working job plus the role at home.

This reply sent Tom off to the library to get more ammunition to back up his arguments. His reply was the longest piece of writing I had ever seen him compose. It was completely voluntary; in fact, he asked to stay for an extra class to finish writing it.

football isn't very important actually it's at the bottom of the list and women didnt even make it to the bottom yet and never will at least not in our gereration and "ooooooooooooooo" everyone gets hurt and they might even break a finger nail or stub their toe ooooooooooooooooow What a shame. and Ill have you know that 17 men have climed Mt. everest and also the largest moutain in the world was named after a man sir gorge Everestis and so far in my reserch I have herd of no women climing Mt Everest by the looks of things women arent capable of climing a mole hil let alone a moutain quote "women that work realy hold down two jobs their WORKING job and thire house work" end of quot so what you said your self is that work out side the home is work but stuff you do in the home is not classed as work. *You said it not me*

P.S. I challage you to find out how many women who helped canadian and U.S. history in the field of medicine or the field of polatics and compare them with the amounts of men me and grant find plus you should give the name what she did and what resultited became of it good and bad

The girls were not buying that!

We are not accepting you challange because we know the numbers are less because women have not been given a chance!!! You are a victim of believes everything you see on T.V. Not all women are concerned about their firgernails. We are giving new challege on next letter (other)

By this time Grant had gotten into the act. At some point women's role in the economy had been mentioned. Grant discussed this with his father at the dinner table and came back with this:

Hello, how are you today. in reply of your statement "half the money in Canada is handled by women" so that is why the economy is in such a bad state [Grant told me his father had said this.] I myself took a survay that men didn't like wemon in the work place and wemon don't care. So do you have any more bright ideas about wemon.

HA,HA,HA

Grant's survey had a sample size of four, selected from the women in the neighborhood who were at home when he passed through at three in the afternoon. The girls did not have to be told that his survey lacked validity.

Yes we do have a lot more to say! The people handling the money are all right it's just the polititcian which are mostly men!!!! The reason women arn't polititcian is because they haven't been given a chance. Your survey was not very convincing! P.S. We chalange you to a survey. Which is to you ask all the grade 7 teachers questions we agree upon. We will ask the same questions to the grade 8 teachers.

Had I taken out my red pen I would have found plenty of problems with the writing these students produced. However, it was clear that the messages were coming through despite the functional spellings, lack of punctuation and capitalization, and awkward sentence structure. I chose not to focus upon editing for surface structure conventions because the writing was so obviously serving the purposes of the writers; communication was taking place. The students were excited and involved and wanted to write.

The next writing task demanded a bit more attention to surface features because the audience was widening. The students decided to survey all the teachers in the school, so they needed to draft a set of questions. The boys produced a first draft, tried it out on a couple of teachers, changed some questions which weren't clear, and then passed the draft over to the girls for editing. They made some further changes; they were concerned about the wording of one or two questions so collaborated on a rewrite and then added one or two questions of their own. The boys, eager to get on with it, approved this with no further changes (see Figure 15–1).

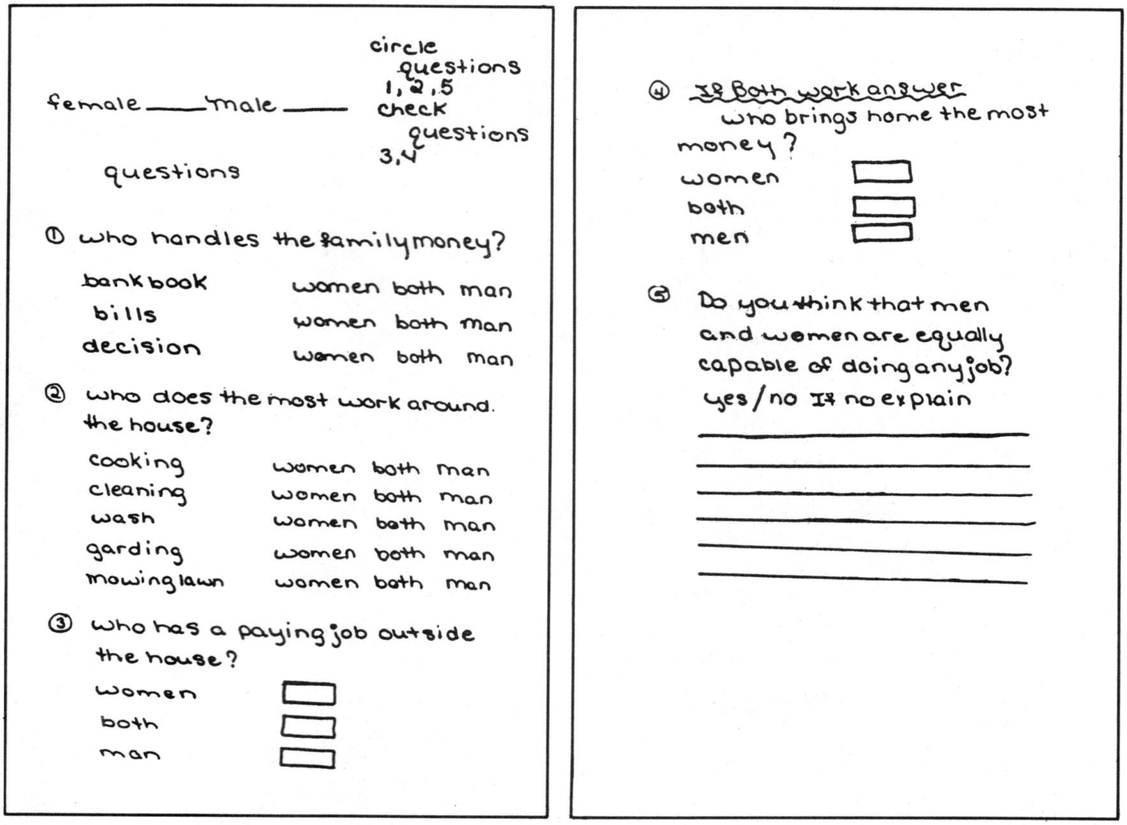

(a)

(b)

Figure 15 – 1

Then, for the first time, I brought the two groups together to make plans for carrying out the survey. I provided a list of all the teachers and left it to the students to figure out how to organize themselves. They had decided to publish the results in the school newspaper, so were working within time constraints. With surprisingly little difficulty they drew up a plan and a time frame.

For the next few days the five students popped in and out of my room giving progress reports. I couldn't believe this was the same Tom who never met deadlines and who had a thousand excuses for not getting his homework done. Teachers commented favorably upon his energetic approach to the task and asked what had caused the change. A couple of teachers felt things had gone a bit far when they were severely reprimanded for losing their forms. One of the students commented, "Teachers get real angry when students lose things and then they do it themselves." The staff room was the scene of some heated discussions as the teachers filled out the surveys; the male/female lines were drawn fairly clearly in some instances.

On the day all the forms were due, Tom came into my room shaking his head. "I never realized . . . I never would have believed it," he said. He had been astounded to learn that the physical education teacher, a "real man," assumed responsibility for most of the child care, cooking, and cleaning because his wife worked longer hours than he. I sensed that this real-world evidence had given Tom more reason to question his beliefs than had all the reading, writing, and discussing.

The next task was to analyze the information. I put the pile of forms in the middle of the table and said, "Now, what are you going to do with all this?" They looked at each other as if to say, "Isn't she going to give us any directions?" The first decision they made was to disregard the first four questions and deal only with question 5, "Do you think that men and women are equally capable of doing any job?" They had run into some difficulties when gathering the data because the first four questions applied only to married people. They had decided to have the single teachers answer only question 5. This made the questionnaires a bit more manageable.

I waited as they discussed some possibilities. Then Tom assumed a leadership role, saying, "We need to do a frequency count; that's how surveys are done. My mother used to do them when we lived in Cape Breton." Under his direction the students separated the forms on the basis of the sex of the respondent and further divided each of these piles into "yes" and "no." Then I recorded the frequency counts as they called them off. I asked, "Now you have the numbers, how do you make them a bit more meaningful?" One of the students suggested that we figure out percentages for the total staff, for the females, and for the males.

Grant, who had been assigned the total-staff computations, groaned, "Oh no, it comes out fifty–fifty! We didn't solve anything!" The percentages for the male teachers were 40 percent yes, 60 percent no, and for the female teachers 63 percent yes, 37 percent no. By this time all five students had come to realize that they were not dealing with a black-and-white issue with simplistic answers. They were even more interested in the comments teachers had added than in the actual numbers.

Their final task was to draft an article for the school newspaper. This was a collective effort. Carla was unanimously chosen as recorder because her spelling and handwriting were the most legible. The writing went surprisingly well; by this time the students had something they wanted to say. They wanted the staff to know the results and they wanted to convey their feelings about the outcome. The title and their last paragaph did that quite well, I think (see Figure 15–2).

```
        50/50, Still!

   This spring two classes of Mrs.
Church's studied about women's
rights.  A group of boys and a
group of girls were arguing a-
bout this subject.  We decided
to do a survey among the tea-
chers.  The survey was to figure
out what the staff thought about
the question:
"Do you think men and women are
equally capable of doing any
job?"
   Thirty-five of forty-one sur-
veys were returned.  The re-
sults were:
                  Yes     No
   Total Staff   50%      50%
   Men           40%      60%
   Women         62.5%    37.5%
   The main reason for saying no
was that some jobs required
more physical strength.  For
example, one person said: "No,
some jobs are too physically
demanding such as labour type
jobs."  The percentage of peo-
ple that answered like this
was 76.5%.  The other reason
for saying no was each sex
has special qualities that make
them better suited to certain
tasks."  The percentage of peo-
ple who answered like this was
23.5%
   The survey didn't help to
settle our problems.  We found
out that the disagreement exists
among other people as well.
```

Figure 15 – 2

Why did these reluctant learners become so actively engaged in learning? What had been different about this learning situation from those the students usually experienced in the classroom and from those I had previously tried to create in the Resource room?

I think a complex of factors interacted to create excitement and commitment to the task and to foster learning. First, the content was socially and personally relevant to the students. Like many contemporary men and women, these adolescents are engaged in a process of figuring out what it means to be female or male in modern society. There was no need to "motivate" these students; they cared deeply about the issues we raised and had strong opinions which they were willing to defend in talk and writing. However, had I used the relevant content in traditional ways, I suspect the students would not have changed very much. A second, essential element was a change in the process through which the learners came to understand that content. Through social interaction with peers and with adults they each began to make some sense of this complex issue, even though that sense meant only that they recognized the shades of gray between the black and white extremes of their initial stances. This process of creating meaning together was instrumental in the learning. As Barnes (1975) has said,

To become meaningful a curriculum has to be enacted by pupils as well as teachers, all of whom have their private lives outside school. By "enact" I mean come together in a meaningful communication—talk, write, read books, collaborate, become angry with one another, learn what to say and do, and how to interpret what others say and do [p. 14].

A third factor was a shift of some of the control over the learning process from the teacher to the students. I created the initial experience by providing the articles and structuring the first language activity. After that, the students themselves generated as many extensions of the original task as I did; we collaborated in developing a curriculum. Because the learners felt in control and were working with a self-generated purpose, they became much more willing to take risks. In other situations all of them had been conscious of their inadequacies as language users and thus had been unwilling to read or write. They forgot about all these negative self-evaluations when they became caught up in the controversy generated by the women's rights issue; they talked and wrote with a stronger voice. I think this greater willingness to take risks was a fourth significant factor.

A fifth factor, which was really part of the shift in control and the increase in risk taking, was a change in the nature of the evaluation the students experienced. Their feedback came from a real audience rather than from a teacher's red pen. The learners knew whether or not they were using language effectively; their listeners and readers told them through their reactions. In the exchange of letters the writers showed great concern for creating a message the readers would understand. They found the meaning was clear even though they had not achieved 100 percent accuracy in the surface-level convertions. However, when they drafted the survey and wrote the article to be published, the learners themselves requested help with a closer editing, realizing that conventions are important in public writing An appropriate level of self-monitoring evolved within the context of the situation. Red corrective marks were unnecessary.

I was able to make my evaluations of the students without the marks, too. It would have been difficult to quantify this learning, but I could easily describe changes in my learners. I was able to see an increase in the amount of language they used and in their degree of effectiveness in using language to achieve their purposes. It was unnecessary for me to test their mastery of the content; I was able to observe that they could use prior knowledge and new information in the discussion and in their writing. They also showed me that they could use many of the conventions of writing.

How did the learners feel about this experience? When asked what they thought they had learned, students said:

The group discussion got my brain going. They started discussing it . . . people saying things gets your brain going. One thing leads to another and you just keep on talking.

I learned a lot about Women's Lib. We had both sides. When you have fun learning something you usually remember it. I learned about the people involved. I pretended to take a side I didn't really agree with to see if they really knew what they were talking about. . . .

It helped me to understand the article I read.

When asked if they enjoyed the activity, they replied as follows:

Yes, definitely. It's fun. You get to argue without getting yelled at. We got to do a lot of things we don't get to do in class, like talk about things. We got to read what we wanted to read. We could choose an article. The teacher usually says, "Read this or read that."

It would be a good idea to have it in class (regular classroom). It's more interesting than writing it out, handing it in, writing it out, handing it in all the time.

I learned as least as much as my students from this experience. After reflecting upon it, I concluded that in order to recreate the enthusiasm and engagement in future activities I would have to ensure that similar factors were operating in the situation. I would have to provide student choice within a range of relevant content, to encourage learner interaction, to share control over learning with the learners, to foster risk taking, to evaluate student progress within the situational context, and to encourage student self-evaluation. By keeping these principles of learning in mind, I have been able to generate similar positive learning experiences and have seen many other teachers do the same with learners of all ages in a variety of settings.

It seems to me that what happens is an example of Barnes's "enactment of the curriculum." By creating these sorts of learning experiences, teachers can help students to understand and remember the content in all areas of the school program and at the same time become competent users of language. It is not "language across the curriculum," but language and curriculum inseparable from each other.

16

Yes, They
Can Learn

James Boyer

A thousand arrows darkened the sky as they hurtled toward the dragon, which looked more like a craggy mountain than any beast we had seen before. Its baleful, ferocious eyes were like huge glaring beacons from a vampire's castle heights, while cavernous jaws seemed to lead to the very gates of hell, and from its horrible throat came the sound of hurricanes and volcanoes announcing the approaching apocalypse for miles to come. Its shaggy, grotesque skin hung in great folds like ancient cliffs. Our arrows broke as harmlessly as a wave on the shore; they were merely swept aside by something much more powerful and enduring than anyone had experienced before. Our only hope was to find a weak spot, and I had been chosen from the champions in our land to meet the Goliath. Suddenly—the beast swerved in its advance and found me where I had hidden myself with a small band of loyal followers. We had, under cover of darkness, gained access to the top of a narrow chimney of rock from which we could look directly down into the beast's lair—the dragon howled my name!

"Why do you always waste your time?!" Mr. Sternman glared at me with dragon eyes; the room shook as he scorched his way down the aisle—I was dragon meat!

Sternman's glasses seemed to magnify his burning eyes as they bored into mine—omnipotent, hateful; yet somehow weak and afraid. Frustrated, his hands opened and closed before me. I noticed for the first time that the backs of his hands were covered in a fine mat of black hair like a forest in which purple veinlike roots twitched and pulsed with a life of their own. You could get lost in there, I thought, and a cold shiver ran down my spine. I tried to look busy so I could get back to my daydream. Anything could start it: the tops of tree branches waving in the air; muffled voices from a distant room, sounds in the pipes deep inside the school—they begin. It's like having your own movie—only better! One of his sleeves was frayed and a loose thread hung down; could this be my lifeline to safety? I stared at it until it blurred, but it was no good.

"One sentence! Is that all you have done? Look at the spelling! It's always terrible! You don't know anything!"

Jenny Wise laughed right out loud. Her neat writing and flawless spelling secured her in her position as Sternman's comrade, spy, and self-proclaimed class torturer. I didn't have the heart to tell her about the vampire bat that was inching its way up the back of her chair with all its thirsty attention fixed on her scrawny neck.

"When will you stop dreaming and learn the rules of this class? You have five more minutes to finish your summer vacation story—get to work!"

After all that I couldn't think of anything to write; Sternman, I noticed, was planning another attack as he was tapping his pencil on his desk with a frustrated beat and grimaced at his reflection in the window. I don't think he was dreaming; what would teachers dream about? Besides, this was no time to be idle because there was a rather large bear standing right behind his chair—should I warn him?

"Get to work!"

I put my head down; I really do know the class rules. Rule number one: always keep your head down. The recess bell went off like a buzzer at a hockey game, and when I looked up I was alone in the room; Mr. Sternman had narrowly missed being eaten by a bear—he had been saved by the bell!

As a fellow teacher, I had often heard Sternman complain about his students, but today, he seemed particularly bitter.

"Where am I going wrong? I've tried time and time again to involve Billy, but nothing seems to work! Many times I've stayed late to help him with his spelling, or with something he didn't understand; it just doesn't sink in. I really want to help the kid, but he's too far behind. He doesn't know anything—it's a hopeless case."

He wrung his hands in resignation and then shaking his head he confided, "You know, he sits at the back of the room in his own little world—I just can't get through to him! Sometimes I get so frustrated I could shake him."

"It's almost the end of the year; you've had a difficult class to work with this year," I said.

"You know, that kid can't do anything right. Try to get him to read the simplest work and he gets stuck on the first word. Try to get him to write something, and he can't spell—why don't they put him back in the grade where he belongs?"

Muttering in anguish, he headed for the coffee machine.

I wanted to say that I sympathized with him. In fact, I have shared many of the same feelings he had just expressed; we all have our dragon days. However, I couldn't agree with his pessimistic view of Billy, which I believed was a major source of his frustration. Had he, for example, ever talked to the boy to find out about his interests or talents? I also couldn't accept his view that some students can't do anything, or know nothing. I believe, instead, that all students are capable of learning; they have learned a tremendous amount outside of school. Take, for example, the linguistic sophistication of preschool children, or older students who are self-taught experts in a variety of fields from medieval knights to computers. How can we say these students know nothing or are incapable of learning?

It is precisely this belief that seriously hampers our effectiveness with students who are having "learning difficulties." They become the victims of our negative attitude. Because we believe they are devoid of knowledge we adopt a transmission style of teaching (Barnes, 1976). That is, instead of building on students' prior knowledge and interests we place priority on learning of specific school-based content and regurgitation of "the facts." For a variety of reasons a transmission curriculum is ineffective, particularly for students with learning problems. It fails to consider their interests and attitudes. It allows little room for negotiating what is to be learned. It emphasizes what students don't know, what they can't do, rather than recognizing the value of error for learning. It doesn't allow the classroom to become a supportive environment. It doesn't build on a great deal of current research which indicates that learners must be in control of their own learning (Harste, Burke, and Woodward, 1981; Edelsky, Draper, and Smith, 1983; Graves, 1983). An alternative view sees students involved in a transaction. It sees them having some say about what it is that they will learn and how they will learn it. It also encourages them to talk and write about what they are learning. It focuses on what students can do and sees errors as evidence of the learning process in action.

I was going to have a chance to put my beliefs into practice because I was to inherit Sternman's class of so-called misfits for the coming school year. I knew this class would be a challenge. I wanted to resist the transmission trap to which Sternman had succumbed. I knew I would have to find out about what they knew and about what interested them. I would have to lure these reticent students into taking a lot of risks, which I realized they would be reluctant to take. I was aware that I couldn't expect these sixteen students, ranging in age from nine to thirteen, to move through a predetermined curriculum at the same rate or in the same way.

Instead, I would need to redirect their creative energies, which they used for avoiding school tasks, to helping them engage with learning in a more constructive way. I would have to help them discover themselves as learners, to make them aware of their learning potential, to help them make connections between what they were learning from their participation in the world in general and what they could be learning in the classroom.

I believed I could accomplish these goals by instituting a literacy program in which writing would play a significant role. I believed that helping these students explore writing as a vehicle for understanding rather than emphasizing accurate use of mechanics or conventions would assist their development as learners. A "meaning-centered" writing program would give them a chance to create their own curriculum materials. It would let them have some choice about what they would be learning. The whole process of writing, reading, reworking, and publishing their work in a supportive environment would let them become free of the strategies and attitudes which were blocking their learning and let them experience success. They could prove both to themelves and to others that they were indeed capable learners.

Once again it was time to prepare for battle as summer's drowsy magic drew to a close. We had lived such a short time in bliss. Children once again, we fished and swam and played for hours under the green shade trees only to flop exhausted in the wind-ruffled seas of tall grass. Haircuts were received, new clothes were bought, return we must. As all great heroes, we had to rise again to meet the enemy who stalked silently every year in that most beautiful and yet wicked month of September.

All around the room you could hear the sound of various battle preparations as old traps were set for a new teacher. We were stronger this year; the summer had made us sleek and fast. Older and wiser now, we would be no match for any unseasoned veteran. A hush fell over the room. As before any great battle, there is that moment of calm in which we reflected on memories of summer past: some sorted lovingly through old baseball cards—probably for the last time; others thought wistfully of the family dog at home alone; others merely stared out the windows thinking of times gone by, dreaming of times to come.

Footsteps approached. We tensed in preparation for the onslaught. He stood before us, powerful and confident, a worthy opponent, no doubt. Smiling, he said, "I would like to begin today by just getting to know you."

We were stunned.

"Why don't you start by telling me a little bit about yourselves and the kind of things you like to do."

Something was very different here; could this be a sneak attack designed to lure us into complacency? We had never been permitted to talk so freely, and what was even more surprising was that he really seemed to be interested in what we had to say. By the end of the morning, everyone had talked about something that they believed was important—that is, everyone except me. I wouldn't be brought around that easily.

That afternoon, he read us a story, something about a paper bag princess. We talked about what our favorite parts of that story were. Then we made masks that looked like helmets, for fighting dragons with. There seemed to be kind of a warm glow that settled over the room. The other kids were excited and a busy hum grew louder, and yet there was order; everyone was so interested in what they were doing, we forgot all about our battle plans.

In the weeks that followed, our class really began to change for the better. This time the teacher didn't have all the answers and really seemed to want to hear what we knew about. Why, just the other day we started talking about knights and dragons—my favorite subject— when right out of the blue I heard the teacher say, "Really! I wonder why that happened. It sounds very interesting. Can anyone help us with this question?"

Before I knew it, I was chattering on about jousting, castles, kings, and Black Knights. . . .

"What's a Black Knight?" the teacher said. "I've always wanted to know that."

Beaming with pride, I began: "A Black Knight is someone who likes to travel by himself, kind of a loner. Anyway, most knights had helpers called squires who looked after their suits of armor, kept the knight's sword sharpened, and always slept with one eye opened in case a dragon should try to eat them during the night."

The kids started to laugh, but the teacher said, "Keep on going, Billy; this is really very interesting."

"Well, OK," I said, pleased to have the floor again. I was really getting warmed up. "If you didn't have a squire to polish your armor, it would get rusty. Trying to sneak up on a sleeping dragon in rusty armor is no fun, and not very smart."

Laughter.

"The Black Knight didn't have a squire, and he didn't have time to polish his armor, and he certainly wouldn't go around all rusty and squeaky, so he dipped his armor in kind of a black oil. This oil changed his suit color from silver to black. That's how they got their name—Black Knights."

When I had finished, everyone was quiet and the questions started; I didn't feel so dumb after all. The teacher just stood there with a smile on his face. I grinned back; I guess he wasn't such a bad guy after all.

Time passed quickly. We made things; our teacher read to us and had a collection of fun books that we could all enjoy. He wrote us notes and we had a big message board to tell us about special things or to send us a nice message. We even made a movie about one of our favorite poems. This class was a lot of fun. Everything was going great until . . . one day our teacher brought in some notebooks for writing in. At these words, my knees turned to jelly and I felt that old familiar going-to-the-dentist feeling. I knew I couldn't write—my pencil jumped right out of my hand and slithered through a crack in the floor. I knew things were too good to be true—just as I was beginning to trust him. Oh well, back to the daydreams.

I was a little bit rusty after all this time, so I had trouble conjuring up an escape route. I noticed that the other kids were starting to write; what was must surprising was that our teacher was writing too—I had never seen that before.

"How is your story coming along?" he asked.

"Not too good," I mumbled; "I don't know what to write about." I braced myself for the lecture.

"Tell me some more about medieval days. You know, I think you're the class expert."

He let me draw a picture and then we talked. You know, it was funny, but after we talked for a while I had a much better idea about what I wanted to write about. I got stuck on the spelling, but he told me just to write it the way I thought it should be spelled and that he would be able to read it. Any word I wanted help with I should underline.

When we had finished our stories, we read them to each other to see how they sounded. The other kids told me what their favorite part was, and they asked questions about some of the things that they wanted to hear more about. We had proofreading partners. I always ask Jenny Wise to help me; she's not so bad after all. We published our stories by typing them, drawing pictures to go with the book, and making our own covers. There were a lot of smiling faces when we had finished. I wonder what I will write about next.

On the way out, Billy, with his latest "best-seller" clutched to his chest and a proud, shiny look in his eye, said to me: "Don't look now, but there is this huge bear standing right behind you."

"Huh?"

"Just kidding." He laughed right out loud. "I guess school is not so bad after all. See ya next year?"

"I wouldn't miss it for the world. Hey, watch out for those dragons. They can get nasty, if you don't watch your step."

"The Black Knight shall return," he added with a flourish.

As he walked, I could have sworn I heard the clink, clink of chain mail. I guess you can never tell with these kids, but I know now that there is always more than meets the eye.

Danny

A Case History
of an
Instructionally
Induced Reading
Problem

**Susan Church
and
Judith M. Newman**

A great deal of energy has been expended in an effort to identify underlying causes of reading failure. Most generally these causes have been sought within the child. We have looked for problems with visual or auditory perception, language deficits, or some other sort of learning disability. Emotional problems have also been thought to contribute to difficulties with learning to read. Some researchers have looked outside the child at socioeconomic factors as responsible for determining a child's success as a reader. Only recently, however, has instruction itself been considered a possible cause of reading failure.

In the search to understand the difficulties some students encounter with learning to read in school, we need to look beyond causes per se. We need, in fact, to examine the theoretical models of reading upon which "diagnosis" and instruction have been based.

There are two ways of looking at reading and learning to read. Traditionally, reading instruction has been founded on a model of reading in which the process is seen as linear (Gough, 1972). Reading is thought to begin with the print, which is processed and interpreted within the brain of the reader, resulting finally in meaning. In other words, reading proceeds from part to whole. The reader first discriminates among letters, which are then paired with sounds and synthesized into words. The words are then formed into sentences. Since meaning, in this view, is derived from the text, comprehension is considered to depend on accurate reproduction of what is on the page. Instruction based on what can be called an accuracy model of reading is also linear, with the skills thought to be necessary for reading being taught in an ordered hierarchical sequence. Children are taught to make precise visual and auditory discriminations, to blend word parts, to remember isolated words, and to apply rules. Failure to learn to perform these tasks is often taken to be evidence of an underlying deficit of some sort.

The alternative model of the reading process is seen to begin, instead, with the reader. Readers, it is argued, make hypotheses about the text based on relevant prior knowledge or nonvisual information (Smith, 1978). They sample the graphic display to confirm or alter predictions; they actively construct meaning. Readers bring knowledge of language, experiential knowledge, as well as concepts about how the reading process works, to every reading situation. As they read, readers use information from several different language systems (graphophonic, syntactic, and semantic) in addition to information from the page for predicting, confirming, and integrating. Fluency depends on the efficiency with which the reader uses both the language systems and strategies in a given reading situation. In this model, in which reading is viewed as a constructive process, instruction proceeds from whole to part. Children learn to read with whole, connected text. Literacy is developed through experiences with reading and writing. The teacher demonstrates the process in action and facilitates both the development of strategies and the use of the language systems by interacting with the children as they engage in a variety of language activities. In a constructive model, children are encouraged to use all available language cues. Difficulty handling any one language system is considered relatively unimportant because other sources of information are available to the reader. It is the orchestration of available language cues and specific strategies for constructing and maintaining meaning that is essential. In this constructve view of reading, meaning can be created without identifying every word accurately.

From a constructive view, instruction itself can be an important contributing factor to a student's reading difficulty. The following case study illustrates the relationship between a theoretical model of the reading process and instruction based on that model. It demonstrates the kinds of effect that instruction can have on a child's reading development.

Danny's history is revealing. He had spent nine years in school and was still unable to read fluently despite all the efforts of the school system. This student, from an intact middle-class family, emotionally and socially well adjusted, of average intelligence, received special help from a learning-disabilities teacher, a reading teacher, many classroom teachers, as well as a university reading clinic. Yet, at the beginning of ninth grade his reading level on a standardized reading test was still only 2.6. Let's begin by examining Danny's early reading efforts.

School History

1971–72 Primary

Reading Readiness Checklist: All tasks satisfactory.
Comment from teacher: "Danny requires extra time to complete many tasks because he is inclined to waste his time."
Reading Skills Checklist Level 2 and 3, Ginn 360
(lists all skills taught in each unit at each level): Most tasks satisfactory. Teachers' comments: "Extra drill required on words."

"Slow at saying words." "Extra help on graphemic bases."
"Danny not applying himself to reading carefully."
Level 3 Test
Vocabulary   86%
Word Analysis 91%
Comprehension 63%

1972–73 Grade 1

Level 4 Test
Vocabulary   100%
Word Analysis 91%
Comprehension 75%
Teacher's comment: "Danny must be reminded to apply what he knows."
Level 5 Test (missing)

1973–74 Grade 2

Level 6 Test March 1974
Vocabulary   96%
Word Analysis 93%
Comprehension 45%
Re-teach/Re-test May 1974
Vocabulary   100%
Word Analysis 100%
Comprehension 100%

In his early years, from primary to grade two, Danny was successful with those skills which were considered an essential part of learning to read. He consistently scored high on the Vocabulary and Word Analysis sections of the end-of-unit skills tests. His Comprehension scores were lower, but they still indicate Danny was understanding some of what he was reading. His teachers' comments demonstrate their dissatisfaction, however, with his progress. In primary, his teacher was concerned with his "careless" word identification. His first grade teacher was also concerned that he wasn't applying the phonics and word-identification strategies she was teaching. His second grade teacher unhappy with his end-of-unit test results, retaught and retested Level 6 of the basal reading program. Her strategy seemed to work. By May of that year her reteaching of the unit had helped him substantially improve his Comprehension score.

It is interesting to consider what Danny's test scores show us. The instruction Danny had been receiving and the evaluation of his progress were both based on an accuracy model; that is, his teachers emphasized word analysis (phonics) and word identification (skills) in their teaching. The end-of-unit test results confirm Danny was learning those subskills, but what about his Comprehension scores? According to a linear accuracy model if Danny can analyze words and identify them he should be comprehending. This he clearly was not doing. His teachers, mystified by his poor comprehension performance, were unable to see that his test scores were violating their reading instruction model. Rather than questioning their model, however, they concluded Danny needed more practice with word analysis and word identification.

1974–75 Grade 3

    Level 7 Test
        Vocabulary   90%
        Word Analysis   92%
        Comprehension 67%
    Danny was switched to the Ginn Basic Readers.
    Referral to Resource Program: October 1974
        Assessment:
            Frostig Test of Visual Perception:
                Weakness in Position in Space
            Wepman Test of Auditory Discrimination:
                X-14/30, Y-1/10

Problems:	Program:
Visual perception	Frostig and DLM visual activities
Auditory discrimination	DLM auditory tapes
	DLM Sound Foundation
Auditory Memory	Games

1975–76 Grade 4

    Continued in Resource Program.
    Resource teacher's comment in December, 1975: "Danny showed good improvement in visual perception. His reading, however, has still not improved." Suggested more sight vocabulary games in classroom.
    June 1975: Removed from Resource caseload.
        Suggested reinforcement in sound blending and vowels.
        Recommended referral to the reading teacher.
    Reading Skills Checklist (Ginn Basic Readers)
        105 separate skills assessed, Danny's performance varied, usually about 50–60%
    Switched to Griffin Pirate Series

The following fall, at the beginning of third grade, while Danny's scores on Vocabulary and Word Analysis were still high, his lower Comprehension score, plus the fact that he was now a couple of units behind where he was expected to be, led his teacher to try another program which emphasized the same skills as the basal reader being used in the classroom. This was her way of having him repeat what she felt he hadn't yet learned, without reusing the old material. She referred him, as well, to the Resource teacher for remedial assistance.

In the Resource program, a traditional learning disabilities program, Danny was diagnosed as having "auditory and visual perceptual problems." During third and fourth grade, the Resource teacher worked diligently at remediating these "deficits." She was able to improve his visual/perceptual performance considerably. However, his reading didn't improve, and she recommended he be referred to the reading teacher for help in the fifth grade. She also recommended that the classroom teacher try another reading program (the Griffin

Pirate Series)—one which had a very restricted vocabulary based on words which can be sounded out.

During this two-year period we see little or no improvement in Danny's reading. Once again we see his teachers' model of reading influencing their instructional decisions. The difficulty Danny continues to have comprehending what he reads can, in their view, only stem from an inability to deal with the sound/symbol relationships and his difficulty identifying words. They therefore continue teaching him how to sound out words and how to identify them. Their choice of instructional material reflects those decisions. Switching Danny to a program with a highly controlled vocabulary is based on the belief that what Danny needs is a great deal of practice reading material which is built from a limited number of phonetically "regular" words.

1976–77 Grade 5

Reading Teacher's Assessment: October, 1976
    Slossen Intelligence Test: MA - 10–6; IQ - 96
    Slossen Oral Reading Test: Grade 1.9
    Spache Reading Diagnostic Scales:
        Weak in all phonic areas
        Listening comprehension - 6.5 +
        Oral reading - 1.8
    Diagnostic spelling: 2.0

Teacher's comments: "Suggest that perceptual deficits have affected reading growth. Recommend total remedial reading program including reteaching of basic skills beginning with blends and digraphs, and Dolch sight words."

Reading Teacher's Report: June 1977
    Slossen Oral Reading: 3.8
    Mastered all Dolch words, phonic skills improved.
    Reading slow and laborious above the second grade level.

Placed in Open Highways program in the classroom.

1977–78 Grade 6

Reading Consultant's Assessment: Sept. 1977
    Word Recognition   3.8
      (errors substitutions, i.e., across for along)
    Oral Reading   2.8
    Silent Reading   4.5
    Word Analysis—many problems

Teacher's comments: "Suggest that he be taught digraph 'th,' long/short vowels, then other vowels. Continue Open Highways Basal Program. Recreational reading every day."

In the fifth grade Danny was again given intensive instruction in phonics and sight words. According to the reading teacher he mastered the Dolch list and his phonics skills improved. Yet, his reading was still "slow and laborious above the second grade level." This teacher recommended he be placed in yet another basal reading series—this one having been designated a remedial program. In grade six, it appears Danny was using some meaning-getting strategies when reading silently which he did not use when reading orally. Instead of exploring this strength further, the reading teacher, who was concerned with accurate translation of print, recommended more word analysis instruction.

1978–79 Grade 7

No information

1979–80 Grade 8

Danny referred by his mother to the reading clinic at a local university. Tutor identified the following needs:
1. Using context to help decoding and construction of meaning
2. Focusing attention more on meaning and not on decoding alone
3. Using more effective decoding strategies
4. Organizing reading tasks
5. Developing confidence in his ability to read
6. Developing a more positive attitude
7. Developing a faster rate

1980–81 Grade 9

Resource Screening: October 1980
Woodcock-Johnson Reading Cluster
Letter/word identification 29/51; Grade 2.7–3.5
Word Attack 3/26; Grade 1.5–2.0
Passage Comprehension 13/26; Grade 3.0–4.0
Cluster Score 2.6

At the end of eighth grade Danny was referred to the reading clinic at a local university. Although some attention was given to helping him focus on meaning, the instruction he received still largely emphasized decoding and word recognition. At the beginning of ninth grade Danny's reading level was assessed at 2.6. At this point in his schooling, despite the great deal of instruction in phonics and word analysis, Danny now scored poorly on letter/word identification and word attack. His comprehension was similarly low.

Looking at Danny's school record, we can see that all of the instruction he received was based on a phonics/skills accuracy model of reading; it focused on visual and auditory discrimination, sight word recognition, and word analysis. It wasn't through lack of effort that Danny failed to become a fluent reader. His teachers, concerned with his reading difficulties, tried everything they knew how to do. Their instruction wasn't haphazard: they provided individualized instruction; they did what they could so that learning to read wouldn't be frustrating for him; they tried to prepare him for reading by drilling the vocabulary he would encounter; they taught him word attack skills; they used controlled-vocabulary reading material. Both he and his teachers worked hard. Yet Danny seemed worse off in spite of all of their efforts.

Danny's teachers, firm in their beliefs about the reading process, were unable to see what his test results were repeatedly showing them—Danny was actually learning what he was being taught. The problem resided not in Danny and his "perceptual deficits," as they thought, but with their own beliefs about what's involved in reading and learning to read. His teachers' beliefs about reading were reflected in the choice of materials they were offering Danny to read and in the way they interacted with him while he was reading. The greater the difficulty Danny seemed to have, the more constrained the material they chose to use with him and the more focused on accuracy their instruction became. Danny, therefore, came to view reading in the same way his teachers did. By the time he had reached ninth grade Danny was indeed having serious difficulty.

At the beginning of ninth grade an attempt was made once again to help Danny learn to read. This time, however, evaluation and instruction were based on a constructive model of the reading process. The assessment, an analysis of Danny's oral reading miscues, revealed some interesting strengths in his reading which had gone undetected previously. While he was relying rather heavily on graphophonic cues (he attempted to deal with unfamiliar words by sounding them out, usually producing nonsense words with high graphic and sound similarity), he was also using the other language cue systems. There was evidence of some rereading or reading ahead; he also self-corrected some semantically and/or syntactically unacceptable miscues. His retelling showed a general understanding of the story and he was able to recall additional detail when questioned. His overreliance on graphophonemic cues wasn't unexpected, given his instructional history. That he continued to try to make sense of what he was reading was encouraging. However, when Danny was interviewed he indicated he disliked reading, never read at home, and really did not want any more help.

After some discussion Danny agreed to try some further instruction. The instructional program that was now implemented was also based on a constructive model of reading. It was designed to move Danny away from his overdependence on graphophonemic cues and to encourage the use of syntactic and semantic information; to help him feel more comfortable with strategies such as rereading and reading ahead, skipping and substituting; and to help Danny understand the reader's active role in constructing meaning. The ultimate goal of the instruction was to convince him he was capable of gaining information and enjoyment from reading.

The challenge in teaching Danny was to develop some instructional strategies which not only would increase his written language competence but would also help him pass his academic year. Because Danny was a reluctant participant in the Resource program, it was important that he see its relevance to the classroom program and also see some immediate positive effects on his classroom performance.

Instead of introducing different materials and reading skills activities, as is often done in withdrawal remedial programs, the Resource teacher used Danny's classroom texts, notes, and supplementary materials related to the classroom content for reading material and often provided direct assistance with classroom assignments. However, the approach differed from traditional tutoring situations in two ways. First, the instructional emphasis was on the development of learning strategies rather than the mastery of traditional reading "skills." As he developed more effective strategies, Danny did, in fact, begin to understand and remember content more readily, although that was not the primary objective of instruction. Second, Danny received instruction in a group setting, based on the belief that he would learn much through his interaction with the other students.

Danny (as well as the other students in the group) was encouraged to become an active participant in designing the learning program; he was helped to identify those aspects of the curriculum with which he has having trouble and to seek assistance with particular assignments. Social studies and science were causing him greatest concern. In both of these subjects he was required to read textbooks and lengthy teacher-prepared notes, to complete many written assignments, and to write essay responses to questions on tests. He was making the least sense of British history because he lacked background knowledge and had little interest in the subject. Science presented less of a problem because he was more interested in it and he had some prior knowledge upon which to build.

The Resource teacher proceeded by helping Danny work from whole to part, tackling big chunks of text, developing overall understanding and then tying in details. Danny needed to learn that reading every word was not essential to understanding, that he could understand the meaning of a word without pronouncing it, and that it was useful to reread and read ahead when stuck. In addition, he needed to learn how to read actively, to predict what might come next, to confirm or disconfirm those predictions through reading, and to relate new information to what he already knew.

The strategy which proved most useful for helping Danny deal with classroom tasks utilized mapping or diagramming the information from the text. There are five organizational patterns generally used in expository text: general statement and elaboration, cause and effect, comparison and contrast, question and answer, sequence of events. Learning to recognize these text organizational patterns plus diagramming the information showing the relationships among ideas after reading greatly facilitated Danny's understanding of what he was reading, particularly when he summarized (either orally or in writing) what he had read, using the diagram as a guide.

The text organizational structures were introduced through short articles, each of which illustrated a particular organizational pattern. Initially, the Resource teacher provided assistance constructing outlines or diagrams by asking questions to elicit information from Danny and the other students. They then wrote brief summaries from the diagrams.

Once Danny understood the process and was comfortable with it, he began to analyze sections of his textbooks, following the same procedures. He learned to use textual aids such as headings and margin notes, and he was encouraged to rearrange the author's organization if it did not make sense to him. He also began reorganizing his class notes in diagram form. The Resource teacher played a fairly active role by proposing questions to direct discussion and providing background information when necessary. She also consulted regularly with classroom teachers so that she would be aware of their instructional objectives and expectations.

The textbooks were obviously very difficult for Danny to read. Both Danny and his teachers believed he could not read them. However, he was able to construct an understanding of the whole when encouraged to use a variety of meaning-getting strategies and when given appropriate support by the Resource teacher. The diagramming and summarizing which he did fostered an understanding of the content because he was able to see the relationships among the concepts. He became particularly adept at categorizing, seeing both superordinate and subordinate relationships. Danny's writing became more coherent as well. He could see a purpose for creating written summaries which he could use for completing homework assignments and for writing essay answers on tests.

At the end of that school year Danny's reading score on the Woodcock-Johnson test rose to 4.6 (as compared with 2.6 at the beginning of the year). This score is interesting because the test is based on an accuracy model of reading, whereas the instruction Danny was receiving, based on a constructive model, was aimed at helping him focus on and maintain meaning instead of being overly concerned with accurate word identification. Danny's two-year gain on this standardized reading test reflected, in this instance, an improvement in "reading skills" which were not being taught in any formal way during this instruction.

There were other changes in Danny's reading as well. In addition to this improved ability to deal with word identification and analysis (an incidental by-product of the meaning-focused instruction he was receiving), he had become more willing to take risks as a reader. He was more comfortable skipping words or substituting something that made sense when he encountered something he was unsure about. Most important, Danny was able to pass all his courses at the end of the year. When interviewed he indicated he felt more confident dealing with classroom work. Time spent on recreational reading had increased somewhat. His mother reported she no longer had to coerce him quite so often. It seemed reading was beginning to make sense to Danny and he was beginning to enjoy it.

Danny's case is not atypical. Like many children having difficulty reading in school, Danny struggled with instruction that took him further and further from what reading actually is. He worked hard to learn sight word lists, phonics rules, and word analysis, and he mastered those skills, as his test scores and teachers' comments show. At the end of each instructional unit, at the end of each school year, he demonstrated he had learned what had been taught, but his reading didn't improve much. Despite his ability to do the "skills," his teachers, confused by his lack of progress, prescribed more of the same—more phonics, more word analysis, more sight word drills—and all to little avail.

Danny's difficulties with reading actually began when he started school. The theoretical model underlying his teachers' instructional decisions led them to use reading materials (basal readers and workbooks) which direct the reader's attention to the surface features of text and away from meaning. The other children, perhaps more sure of their own learning strategies, disregarded to a great extent the instruction they were receiving, using instead their intuitions of how language operates to guide them in their attempts to make sense of print. Danny, on the other hand, was led to accept the instructional model being used. His reading problems became more pronounced when his teachers demonstrated to him how much difficulty, in their estimation, he was having. All of the extra assistance he received focused on words and parts of words. The drills, exercises, accurate oral reading all served to direct his attention away from the important business of reading—that of making sense. What is surprising is that Danny still persisted in trying to make sense of print. The miscue analysis done at the beginning of grade nine showed he was still trying to understand what he was reading; he was still trying to use what he knew about language to help him read.

Danny's case history is important because it helps us see the relationship between theory and instruction, between instruction and learning. Danny's teachers had a specific view of what was important for learning to read, and the instruction they implemented was consistently directed at helping him deal with the bits and pieces they thought he needed in order to become a fluent reader. If Danny was unable to answer comprehension questions, or if his oral reading was labored and inaccurate, the only explanation available to account for his nonfluent reading was to surmise he hadn't learned the "skills" despite evidence to the contrary. That Danny was led to accept his teachers' interpretation of the situation was inevitable. From his earliest experiences with print and reading he was made aware that he was not performing as they would have liked. Every time he had to read or do some reading workbook exercise he found himself in difficulty.

By the time he reached ninth grade Danny was pretty sure he would never be able to read very well and avoided reading whenever he possibly could. The instruction he received, however, at this point was focused on understanding. There was consistency here, too, between what the reading teacher believed about the reading process and the instruction she offered. As a result of that instruction Danny began feeling comfortable with the strategies he had been trying to use all along. This instruction let him function as a language user; it let him control the process for himself. His two-year gain in "skills" as well as the fact that he passed all of his classes at the end of ninth grade suggest the importance of considering reading and learning to read from a constructive perspective.

While all of Danny's teachers were consistent in implementing their theoretical beliefs, the instructional practices which focused Danny's attention on graphophonic relationships and on words as independent of context were preventing him from seeing meaning as central to the reading process. On the other hand, the instruction based on a constructive model of reading was consistent with what Danny knew intuitively about how language, both written and spoken, should operate. This instruction which focused on making sense from print (at the same time deemphasizing accurate word identification) was augmenting Danny's strengths as a language user.

Over the last two decades, as we've learned a great deal about language and reading, it has become clear that reading instruction must reflect how real readers engage in the process. In order for instruction to be effective, not only must the activities and materials we use allow learners to function as real readers, but also the way we respond to children when they are having difficulty reading must provide them with some insight into what they are doing right. Despite the best of intentions, instruction can actually be the cause of children's reading difficulty, if it directs their attention away from what reading actually involves.

18

Yes, That's an Interesting Idea, But . . .

On Developing Whole Language Curriculum

Judith M. Newman

Whenever I talk with educators, I find the participants in the audience attentive, but as the presentation draws to a close, their expressions become perplexed and questions begin to flow. "Yes, your ideas are interesting, but . . ." It is the very nature of that "Yes, but . . ." I wish to deal with. I want to argue that every "Yes, but . . ." has theory behind it, whether we recognize it or not, and that if we want to build curriculum successfully, we need to examine and understand the theoretical issues which underlie each "Yes, but . . ." we raise.

Two basic sorts of "Yes, but . . ."s get raised. There are those that deal with how theory might be translated into practice, with instructional implications. But there are also "Yes, but . . ."s that focus on the obstacles to change. The "Yes, but . . ."s raised by some teachers, principals, and administrators are the barriers they erect to avoid looking at current practice. Their "Yes, but . . ."s are their way of dismissing uncomfortable theoretical questions. They say, "Yes, that's an interesting idea, but. . . ." Such "Yes, but . . ."s function, most often, as an excuse for doing nothing. Their "Yes, but . . ."s tend to be those which reflect the underlying belief that they have little or no responsibility for decision making. Their "Yes, but . . ."s dismiss contemplation of any new ideas because:

"It's too expensive."
"It sounds like a great deal of work."
"It would take too much of my time."
"I don't have that kind of energy."
"It's only another bandwagon."
"It's only for a certain kind of teacher."
"It won't work with my children!"

For these teachers, principals, and administrators, the "Yes, but . . ."s freeze the existing constraints; their "Yes, but . . ."s are an acceptance of the situation as it is. These educators seem unwilling (or unable) to recognize that we created that world out there in the

181

first place and therefore have the responsibility as well as the right to examine and even change it. By refusing to look beyond practice to the theoretical constructs underlying it, these educators build practice on practice. Without first looking to see whether the assumptions of one activity are compatible with those of the second, they end up with a curriculum lacking theoretical coherence.

The promise I see for the future lies with those other teachers, principals, and administrators, whose "Yes, but ..."s function in a different way. For these individuals the "Yes, but ..." is an expression of real concern. They are interested in the implications of what they've been hearing about and are genuinely interested in considering how they might change what they're currently doing. For them, the "Yes, but ..."s represent the first steps toward building a closer relationship between theory and classroom practice. Their hesitation is generated by the problems they can foresee developing along the way, a concern with the practical "how to"s. "Yes, but ...":

"How do I incorporate reading/writing with science, social studies, and math?"

"How can I evaluate the children's progress?"

"When do I introduce writing?"

"How can I get enough books and other materials?"

These "Yes, but ..."s fall into several categories. There are those which deal with classroom practice directly. Some "Yes, but ..."s are concerned with how to maximize the time available for learning when milk money and lunch money need to be collected, attendance has to be taken, when specialist teachers require out-of-classroom time for phys. ed., music, art, and French, and recess interrupts what's going on. Other questions deal with the limited availability of funds for books and other materials, particularly when the school has allocated what money there is to a single basal program.

There are questions about curriculum: "How do I manage all of this reading/writing when I have social studies, math, and science to teach?" There is the realization that there isn't enough time during a day to handle the range of subjects to be covered if they are to be taught separately. There are worries about evaluating what the children are learning, especially when learning and teaching goals are in the process of being changed or developed.

There are "Yes, but ..."s which deal with the teacher's role: with how we shift from our emphasis on the teacher as "the only one in the classroom who knows anything" to creating an environment in which the children's resources are recognized and used. There are the "Yes, but ..."s which focus on the children and how they learn. There are questions about discipline when children are permitted to work more independently.

Other "Yes, but ..."s are concerned with the classroom in the larger context of school and community. Teachers are worried about how parents will view what they are doing. There is the belief that if they change what goes on in the classroom, parents might object. Teachers are also worried about how other teachers in their school see them. These colleagues, they fear, will judge them on the children's performance next year. If the children don't print neatly and spell correctly, don't know and use "the phonics rules," what will next year's teacher think of their teaching ability? What about the principal who insists on the basal readers being used, wants the results from the end-of-unit tests, insists that the children's spelling be corrected, even in their journals, and checks to see if it is being done?

"Yes, your ideas are interesting, but what about the core curriculum, behavioral objectives, and minimum competency which are being imposed from above?"

Underlying all of these "Yes, but . . ."s is the recognition of a lack of knowledge. Each one is an expression of the frightening realization "Yes, but I don't know enough" and the implicit plea "Help! What do I do?"

The beginning of change in Nova Scotia started with a group of teachers asking these very questions. Their questions arose out of a class in which reading and language development were examined. The research undergirding the ideas of a whole language curriculum was studied by exploring the reading and writing of children. The number of teachers involved was small to begin with. Many of these teachers became interested in how theory would translate into practice for children just starting school; others were intrigued with the implications for older children and special-education students.

A number of years ago, we formed two study groups. One group focused on young children, the other on older elementary and junior high students. We had several reasons for forming those first groups. First, we needed to get together fairly often to share classroom ideas. While we were working from a common theoretical understanding, we were uncertain about its translation into practice. Each teacher had ideas about what we should try with the children and needed to talk about them. At first the study groups functioned as a "show and tell" forum, but with each "show and tell" the group would discuss ways of improving the activities. Through this sharing of ideas we were able to explore the ways in which we were violating the theoretical model we wanted to implement. For example, the research and the theoretical model suggest that children could be reading and writing from the first day they enter primary (kindergarten). One teacher had an idea for involving the children in a class news story to begin the day. She would write on the blackboard, "Today is Tuesday, September 12," then turn to the children and invite them to help her read what was written. Then she would add some news: "Today we will go outside to collect some leaves" or "Yesterday, Crystal brought her hamster to school." Again the children would be invited to read with her. Next she would ask the children if they had some news to share and would write, with their help, "Kenny has lost a tooth." The exchange would take from five to ten minutes; it was paced quickly so that the children would attend to what she was doing. She found that the children were reading along with her within a few days, and when she transferred the news stories to chart paper, some of the children would reread them.

While we were pleased with the children's interest in reading, the other study group teachers wondered if there wasn't some way this activity could lead the children to writing. We explored copying and/or tracing of the news story. However, we soon observed that the children weren't enthusiastic about doing that. We wondered why that was so. Our discussions focused on what the copying activity might be saying to the children. We decided it was intended, basically, to serve as practice for forming letters, writing on lines, and learning how to space words, etc. Besides, we realized, the information in the copied story was no longer interesting; it had already been discussed. By asking them to copy we were, in effect, telling the children they had neither the ideas nor the means to do "real writing" themselves. We realized that such a practice contradicted our theoretical beliefs and decided to provide the children, instead, with notebooks having a few blank unlined pages and covers on which was printed "My News." The children were invited to write their own news each day. We were excited when the children thought these journals were a good idea and began writing their own news items. The study group, then, was allowing us to explore ways of putting theory to use.

The study groups also served a second function. Because each of the teachers involved was often the only person in his or her school trying to develop whole language curriculum, each of them had experienced some confrontation with either other teachers, principals, or consultants. They had not known how to handle the questions and challenges they were encountering. They both needed and wanted more theoretical knowledge as well as an opportunity to discuss the problems with which they were faced.

We did both. We talked about those sticky situations. We pooled our ideas and came to the conclusion that we would deal with challenges by allowing the children to be our advocates whenever we could. That meant, for example, that when the principal expressed reservations about the children's spelling we would show the writing samples we had been saving on a regular basis. We believed it would be possible for us, as well as others, to see the children's progess through their written work.

One actual incident involved a reading consultant who was skeptical about the children's reading ability. He arrived to observe in one primary classroom two days after I had brought a new big book for the children to read. He had no sooner entered the room when he was besieged by several children wanting to read to him, a number of them with this new book in their hands. One particularly fluent six-year-old reader began reading to him, not from the new book itself, but from the teachers' manual accompanying it. The consultant was, nevertheless, still reluctant to admit the children were "really reading." The study group provided a forum for expressing our exaspera- tion when others were unwilling either to see or acknowledge the children's accomplishments.

In addition, we were constantly aware of a need to know more to present our arguments better. So we prepared for each meeting by reading research reports, books, and relevant journal articles. Articles by Goodman, Graves, and others, books by Smith, Britton, and Holdaway provided the focus for our theoretical discussions. We were convinced that the better we understood the theoretical underpinnings of whole language the more secure we would feel each time those "Yes, but . . ."s were raised. The study group often took on the character of a debating society; in fact, sometimes the arguments became quite heated. But we learned that conflict was an essential component of learning. It was through such conflict that our under-standing of both theory and practice grew.

The study group served another important function as well. The teachers visited one another's classrooms to see how someone else's whole language curriculum was developing. These class visits were extremely valuable; they both confirmed established activities and suggested new ones. Each teacher went away with fresh enthusiasm.

In addition, I am often asked if it is possible to see a whole language classroom in action. The teachers in the study group were eager to have visitors to their classes. This gave us an opportunity to share the children and their work. We formulated one rule for such occasions: every visitor had to participate with the children. This created some interesting problems. Sometimes, our visitors weren't as well versed in whole language as we might have liked. On one occasion, a superintendent corrected a child's functional spelling. Next day, to the teacher's supportive "Do the best you can, pretend you know how, I can read it," the child replied, "but Mr. —— said I can't spell." It was several days before that child was comfortable with functional writing again. That was when we realized the need to brief visitors before having them interact with the children.

As interest in whole language curriculum grew, requests for visits and in-services increased. The study group teachers now found themselves being asked to share their ideas. This led to a number of summer workshops. The sessions were given by the study group teachers, who began experimenting with applying whole language ideas to the teaching of teachers.

What did we gain from our experiences? We now know that developing whole language curriculum takes time. Some of us tried to change with "graceful gazelle-like leaps" only to learn it had to be done in small increments. We discovered that trying whole language means (to quote Jerry Harste) "Getting into trouble"—with other teachers, with principals, with parents, and sometimes even with the children. One third grade teacher found, for example, that her students were telling her how they expected her to be teaching them: "We used workbooks last year," they keep reminding her.

We have also learned that trying whole language requires lots of support from others: from academics who can share their knowledge of the research and theoretical literature; from principals and other administrators prepared to trust their teachers, allowing them to be professionals who know how to help children learn; and, most of all, from other teachers with whom we need to share. Being a whole language teacher can be scary at times; those "Yes, but . . ."s keep appearing when we least expect them. We've learned it's essential to talk with other people who are able to listen and willing to help.

The most valuable thing we've learned has been the importance of understanding theory. The more we have learned about language, about how children learn, about how children function as language users, the better able we have been to develop and implement a curriculum which supports the children's learning efforts. We've learned that by watching and trying to understand what it is the children are trying to do, we can come to know how best to help them learn.

Introduction

Barnes, D. *From Communication to Curriculum.* Harmondsworth: Penguin, 1976.

Eisner, E. *Cognition and Curriculum: A Basis for Deciding What to Teach.* New York: Longman, 1982.

Fish, S. *Is There a Text in This Class?* Cambridge, Mass: Harvard University Press, 1980, 303–321.

Goodman, Y. "Kid Watching: An Alternative to Teaching." In Farr, B. P., and D. J. Strickler (eds.), *Reading Comprehension: Resource Guide.* Bloomington, Ind.: Indiana University Reading Programs, 1980.

Harste, J., and Burke, C. "Examining Instructional Assumptions: The Child as Informant." In DeFord, Diane (ed.), "Learning to Write: An Expression of Language." *Theory into Practice,* 1980, *19(3),* 170–178.

Harste, J., and Stevens, D. "Toward a Practical Theory of Literacy Development." Draft manuscript, 1984.

Smith, F. "Demonstrations, Engagement and Sensitivity: The Choice Between People and Programs." *Language Arts,* 1981, *58,* 634–642.

———. "The Myths of Writing." Language Arts, 1981, *57,* 792–798.

Wells, G. *Learning Through Interaction.* Cambridge: Cambridge University Press, 1981.

1 *Insights from Recent Reading and Writing Research and Their Implications for Developing Whole Language Curriculum*

Bissex, G. L. *GNYS AT WORK: A Child Learns to Read and Write.* Cambridge, Mass.: Harvard University Press, 1980.

Bloom, L. M. *Language Development: Form and Function in Emerging Grammars.* Cambridge, Mass.: MIT Press, 1970.

Britton, J., Burgess, T., Martin, N., McLeod, A., and Rosen, H. *The Development of Writing Abilities (11–18).* Urbana, Ill.: NCTE, 1975.

Chafe, W. L. *Meaning and the Structure of Language.* Chicago: University of Chicago Press, 1970.

Chomsky, N. *Syntactic Structures.* The Hague: Mouton Publishers, 1959.

Clark, E. V. "What's in a Word? On the Child's Acquisition of Semantics in His First Language." In Moore, T. E. (ed.), *Cognitive Development and the Acquisition of Language.* New York: Academic Press, 1973.

Clark, M. M. *Young Fluent Readers.* London: Heinemann, 1976.

Clay, M. *What Did I Write?* London: Heinemann, 1975.

Doake, D. "Book Experience and Emergent Reading Behavior." Paper presented at the annual meeting of the International Reading Association, Atlanta, 1979.

Durkin D. *Children Who Read Early.* New York: Teachers College Press, 1966.

Emig, J. *The Composing Process of Twelfth Graders.* Urbana, Ill.: NCTE, 1971.

Fillmore, C. J. "The Case for Case." In Bach, E. and Harms, R. T. (eds.), *Universals in Linguistic Theory.* New York: Holt, Rinehart, and Winston, 1973.

Ferriero, E. "The Relationships between Oral and Written Language: The Children's Viewpoints." In Goodman, Y., Haussler, M., and Strickland, D. (eds.), *Oral and Written Language Development Research: Impact on the Schools.* Urbana, Ill.: NCTE, 1981.

Goodman, K. "Reading: A Psycholinguistic Guessing Game." *Journal of the Reading Specialist,* 1967, *6,* 126–135.

———. *Miscue Analysis: Application to Reading Instruction.* Urbana, Ill.: NCTE, 1973.

Goodman, K., and Goodman, Y. "Learning about Psycholinguistic Processes by Analyzing Oral Reading." *Harvard Educational Review,* 1977, *47,* 317–333.

Gollasch, F. (ed.). *Language & Literacy: The Selected Writings of Kenneth S. Goodman.* Boston: Routledge & Kegan Paul, 1982.

Graves, D. H. *Writing: Teachers & Children at Work.* Portsmouth, N.H.: Heinemann Educational Books, 1983.

———. *A Researcher Learns to Write.* Portsmouth, N.H.: Heinemann Educational Books, 1984.

Halliday, M. A. K. *Learning How to Mean.* New York: Elsevier North-Holland, Inc., 1975.

———. *Language as Social Semiotic: The Social Interpretation of Language and Meaning.* Baltimore: University Park Press, 1978.

Harste, J., Burke, C., and Woodward, V. *Children, Their Language and World: Initial Encounters with Print.* Final Report, NIE Project No. NIE-G-79-0132. Bloomington, Ind.: Language Education Departments, 1981.

———. *The Young Child as Writer-Reader and Informant.* Final Report, NIE Project No. NIE-G-80-0121. Bloomington, Ind.: Language Education Departments, 1983.

Harste J., Woodward, V., and Burke, C. *Language Stories and Literacy Lessons.* Portsmouth, N.H.: Heinemann Educational Books, 1984.

King, D. "Interrelationships and Transactions: The Education of a Language User." Paper presented at IRA Impact Conference: Child Language Development, Columbia, Mo., 1982.

Lindfors, J. W. *Children's Language and Learning.* Englewood Cliffs, N.J.: Prentice-Hall, 1980.

Macnamara, J. "Cognitive Basis of Language Learning in Infants. *Psychological Review,* 1972, *79,* 1–13.

Read, C. "Pre-school Children's Knowledge of English Phonology." *Harvard Educational Review,* 1971, *41,* 1–14.

Smith F. *Understanding Reading.* New York: Holt, Rinehart and Winston, 1971.

———. *Understanding Reading,* 3rd ed. New York: Holt, Rinehart and Winston, 1982.

———. *Writing and the Writer.* New York: Holt, Rinehart and Winston, 1982.

———. *Essays into Literacy.* Portsmouth, N.H.: Heinemann Educational Books, 1983.

Wells, G. *Learning through Interaction.* Cambridge: Cambridge University Press, 1980.

Wilkinson, A., Barnsley, G., Hanna, P., and Swan, M. *Assessing Language Development.* Oxford: Oxford University Press, 1980.

Ylisto, I. "Early Reading Responses of Young Finnish Children." *The Reading Teacher,* 1977, *31,* 167–172.

2   *What Teachers Are Demonstrating*

Calkins, L. "The Craft of Writing," *Teacher,* 1980, Nov/Dec., 41–44.

Goodman, Y. "Kidwatching: Evaluating Written Language." Unpublished manuscript, 1982.

Graves, D. "Andrea Learns to Make Writing Hard." *Language Arts,* 1979, *56,* 569–576.

Graves, D., and Giacobbe, M. E. "Research Update Questions for Teachers Who Wonder If Their Writers Change." *Language Arts,* 1982, *59,* 495–503.

Harste, J. "Research in Context: Where Theory and Practice Meet." Unpublished manuscript, 1982.

Smith, F. "Research Update Demonstrations, Engagement and Sensitivity: A Revised Approach to Language Learning." *Language Arts,* 1981, *58,* 103–112.

———. *Writing and the Writer.* New York: Holt, Rinehart and Winston, 1982.

3   *Andrew and Molly: Writers and Context in Concert*

Deford, D., and Harste, J. "Child Language Research and Curriculum." *Language Arts,* 1982, *59,* 590–601.

Harste, J., Burke, C., and Woodward, V. *Children, Their Language and World: Initial Encounters with Print.* Final Report, NIE Project, No. NIE-G-79-0132. Bloomington, Ind.: Language Education Departments, 1981.

Smith, F. *Writing and the Writer.* New York: Holt, Rinehart and Winston, 1982.

4 Using Children's Books to Teach Reading

Brown, R. *A First Language: The Early Stages.* Cambridge, Mass.: Harvard University Press, 1973.

Clark, M. M. *Young Fluent Readers.* London: Heinemann, 1976.

Forester, A. "Learning the Language of Reading: An Exploratory Study." *Alberta Journal of Educational Research,* 1975, *21,* 56–62.

Holdaway, D. *Foundations of Literacy.* Auckland: Ashton-Scholastic, 1979.

Smith, F. *Reading without Nonsense.* New York: Teachers College Press, 1979.

7 Learning to Spell

Beers, J. W., and Henderson, E. H. "A Study of Developing Orthographic Concepts among First Graders." *Research in the Teaching of English,* 1977, *11,* 133–148.

Beers, J. W., Beers, C. S., and Grant, K. "The Logic behind Children's Spelling." *The Elementary School Journal* 1977, *77,* 238–242.

Nova Scotia Department of Education. *Spelling 2–8* (Halifax, N.S., 1979), p. 16.

Read, C. "Pre-school Children's Knowledge of English Phonology." *Harvard Educational Review,* 1971, *41,* 1–34.

———. *Children's Categorization of Speech Sounds in English.* Urbana, Ill.: NCTE, 1975.

9 What about Reading?

Fisher, A. "The Living Sea." *International Wildlife,* 1977, *7(3),* 4–10.

Goodman, Y., and Burke, C. *Reading Strategies: Focus on Comprehension.* New York: Holt, Rinehart and Winston, 1980.

Kolers, P. "Reading Is Only Incidentally Visual." In Goodman, K. S., and Flemming, J. T. (eds.), *Psycholinguistics and the Teaching of Reading.* Newark, Del.: International Reading Association, 1969.

Piston, W. *Harmony,* 3rd ed. New York: W. W. Norton and Co., 1962.

Smith, F. *Understanding Reading.* New York: Holt, Rinehart and Winston, 1971.

Tait, G. E., and Mould, V. *One Dominion,* 2nd ed. Toronto: McGraw-Hill Ryerson Ltd., 1973.

10 *Text Organization: Its Value for Literacy Development*

Alvermann, C. "Reconstructing Text Facilitates Written Recall of Main Ideas." *The Reading Teacher,* 1982, *25,* 754–758.

Baker, L., and Stein, N. "The Development of Prose Comprehension Skills." In Santa, C., and Hayes, B. *Children's Prose Comprehension.* Newark, Del.: International Reading Association, 1981.

Beck, I., and McKeown, C. "Developing Questions That Promote Comprehension: The Story Map." *Language Arts,* 1981, *58,* 913–918.

Cleland, C. J. "Highlighting Issues in Children's Literature through Semantic Webbing." *The Reading Teacher,* 1981, *34,* 642–646.

Dreher, M. J., and Singer, H. "Story Grammar Instruction Unnecessary for Intermediate Grade Students." *The Reading Teacher,* 1980, *34,* 261–268.

Freeman, G., and Reynolds, E. G. "Enriching Basal Reader Lessons with Semantic Webbing." *The Reading Teacher,* 1980, *33,* 677–684.

Hanf, M. B. "Mapping: A Technique for Translating Reading into Thinking." *Journal of Reading,* 1971, *14,* 225–230, 270.

King, M. L., and Rentel, V. M. "Conveying Meaning in Written Texts." *Language Arts,* 1981, *58,* 721–728.

Lindsay, P. H., and Norman, D. A. *Human Information Processing,* 2nd ed. New York: Academic Press, 1977.

McConaughty, S. H. "Using Story Structure in the Classroom." *Language Arts,* 1980, *57,* 157–165.

Meyer, B. J. "Identification of the Structure of Prose and Its Implication for the Study of Reading and Memory." *Journal of Reading Behavior,* 1975, *7,* 7–47.

Meyer, B. J., Brandt, D. M., and Bluth, G. J. "Use of Top-Level Structure in Text: Key for Reading Comprehension of Ninth-Grade Students." *Reading Research Quarterly,* 1980, *16,* 72–103.

Norton, D. E. "A Web of Interest." *Language Arts,* 1977, *54,* 928–932.

———. "Using a Webbing Process to Develop Children's Literature Units." *Language Arts,* 1982, *59,* 348–356.

Smith, F. *Understanding Reading,* 3rd ed. New York: Holt, Rinehart and Winston, 1982.

Taylor, B. M. "Children's Memory for Expository Text after Reading." *Reading Research Quarterly,* 1980, *15,* 399–411.

Thelen, J. "Preparing Students for Content Reading Assignments." *Journal of Reading,* 1982, *25,* 544–549.

Tierney, R. J., Bridge, C., and Cera, M. J. "The Discourse Processing Operations of Children." *Reading Research Quarterly,* 1979, *14,* 539–573.

Tierney, R. J., and Mosenthal, J. "Discourse Comprehension and Production: Analyzing Text Structure and Cohension." In Langer, J. A., and Smith-Burke, T. (eds.), *Reader Meets Author: Bridging the Gap.* Newark, Del.: International Reading Association, 1982.

Vaughn, J. L. "Use the CONSTRUCT Procedure to Foster Active Reading and Learning." *Journal of Reading,* 1982, *25,* 412–432.

Whaley, J. F. "Story Grammars and Reading Instruction." *The Reading Teacher,* 1981, *34,* 762–771.

11 *Conferencing: Writing as a Collaborative Activity*

Calkins, L. *Lessons from a Child.* Portsmouth, N.H.: Heinemann Educational Books, 1983.
Elbow, P. *Writing without Teachers.* New York: Oxford University Press, 1973.
Graves, D. *Writing: Teachers and Children at Work.* Portsmouth, N.H.: Heinemann Educational Books, 1983.

14 *Mealworms: Learning about Written Language through Science Activities*

Smith, F. "The Language Arts and the Learner's Mind." *Language Arts,* 1959, *56 (2),* 118–125.

15 *The War of the Words*

Barnes, D. *From Communication to Curriculum.* Harmondsworth: Penguin, 1976.

16 *Yes They Can Learn*

Barnes, D. *From Communication to Curriculum.* Harmondsworth: Penguin Books, 1976.
Edelsky, C., Draper, K., and Smith, K. "Hookin' 'Em in at the Start of School in a 'Whole Language' Classroom." *Anthropology and Education Quarterly,* 1983, *14,* 257–281.
Graves, D. *Writers: Teachers & Children at Work.* Portsmouth, N.H.: Heinemann Educational Books, 1983.
Harste, J., Burke, C., and Woodward, V. *Children, Their Language and World: Initial Encounters with Print.* Final Report, NIE Project No. NIE-G-79-0132. Bloomington, Ind.: Language Education Departments, 1981.

17 *Danny: A Case History of an Instructionally Induced Reading Problem*

Gough, P. "One Second of Reading." In J. F. Kavanaugh and I. G. Mattingly (eds.), *Language by Ear and by Eye.* Cambridge, Mass.: M.I.T. Press, 1972, pp. 331–358.
Smith, F. *Understanding Reading,* 2nd ed. New York: Holt, Rinehart and Winston, 1978.

The questions raised most frequently by teachers interested in learning more about whole language and wanting to explore whole language curriculum in their classrooms center around the practical "how to"s. One of the problems with "messing around" with alternative curriculum is that, having set aside the basal program, teachers are suddenly faced with the responsibility for creating a curriculum themselves. For most teachers creating a curriculum from scratch requires some kind of support and assistance. At present there are still few books which describe classroom application of these theoretical ideas. And unlike basal reading programs, the kinds of materials which would be used in a whole language classroom are not accompanied by a teacher's manual offering detailed suggestions for classroom activities. Teachers interested in whole language find themselves pretty much on their own when it comes to using theory. This bibliography has been compiled in response to teachers' requests for more information about and suggestions for theoretically based classroom practice. The articles were chosen because they make the theoretical arguments clearer and because they offer insights into how some people are exploring the whole langauge theory–practice relationship.

I *Language and Literacy—Some Issues*

Froese, V. "How to Create Word-by-Word Reading." *The Reading Teacher,* 1977, *30,* 611–615.

Goodman, K. S. "The Know-More and the Know-Nothing Movements in Reading: A Personal Response." *Language Arts,* 1979, *56,* 657–663

Gourley, J. W. "This Basal Is Easy to Read—or Is It?" *The Reading Teacher,* 1973, *32,* 174–182.

Jackson, L. A. "Whose Skills? Mine or Penny's?" *The Reading Teacher,* 1981, *35,* 260–262.

Lange, B. "Readability Formulas: Second Looks, Second Thoughts." *The Reading Teacher,* 1982, *35,* 858–861.

Lapp, D., and Tierney, R. J. "Reading Scores of American Nine Year Olds: NAEP's Tests." *The Reading Teacher,* 1977, *30,* 756–760.

Petrosky, H. "A Little Learning: A Parent's Introduction to Reading." *The Reading Teacher,* 1981, *34,* 628–632.

Rigg, P. "Getting the Message, Decoding the Message." *The Reading Teacher,* 1977, *30,* 745–749.

Riley, J. D. "Teachers' Responses Are as Important as the Questions They Ask." *The Reading Teacher,* 1979, *32,* 543–537.

Schickedanz, J. A., and Sullivan, M. "Mom, What Does U-F-F Spell?" *Language Arts,* 1984, *61,* 7–17.

Shantz, M. "Read-Ability." *Language Arts,* 1981, *58,* 943–944.

Smith, F. "Language Arts and the Learner's Mind." *Language Arts,* 1979, *56,* 118–125.

———. "Demonstrations, Engagement and Sensitivity: A Revised Approach to Language Learning." *Language Arts,* 1981, *58,* 103–112.

———. "Demonstrations, Engagement and Sensitivity: The Choice between People and Programs." *Language Arts,* 1981, *58,* 636–642.

———. "The Unspeakable Habit." *Language Arts,* 1982, *59,* 550–554.

Tovey, D. R. "Children's Grasp of Phonics Terms vs. Sound-Symbol Relationships." *The Reading Teacher,* 1980, *33,* 431–437.

Weaver, C. "Using Context: Before or After?" *Language Arts,* 1977, *54,* 880–886.

II *Language Development*

Burke, C. L. "Making Connections." *Language Arts,* 1982, *59,* 115–118.

Carey, R. F. "Making Connections." *Language Arts,* 1982, *59,* 323–327.

Fox, S. E. "Research Update: Oral Language Development, Past Studies and Current Directions." *Language Arts,* 1983, *60,* 234–243.

Geller, L. G. "Linguistic Consciousness-Raising: Child's Play." *Language Arts,* 1982, *59,* 120–125.

Goodman, Y. "Making Connections." *Language Arts,* 1982, *59,* 433–437.

Hoffman, S., and McCully, B. "Oral Language Functions in Transaction with Children's Writing." *Language Arts,* 1984, *61,* 41–50.

Hill, M. W. "Making Connections." *Language Arts,* 1982, *59,* 201–222.

McDonnell, G. M. "Relating Language to Early Reading Experiences." *The Reading Teacher,* 1975, *29,* 438–444.

Read, C. "What Children Know about Language: Three Examples." *Language Arts,* 1980, *57,* 144–148.

Taylor, D. "Children's Social Use of Print." *The Reading Teacher,* 1982, *36,* 144–149.

III *Reading Development*

Adams, M. J., Anderson, R. C., and Durkin, D. "Beginning Reading: Theory and Practice." *Language Arts,* 1978, *55,* 19–25.

Atwell, M. A., and Rhodes, L. K. "Strategy Lessons as Alternatives to Skills Lessons in Reading." *Journal of Reading,* 1984, *27,* 700–704.

Cholewinski, M., and Holliday, S. "Learning to Read: What's Right at Home is Right at School." *Language Arts,* 1979, *56,* 671–674.

Cohn, M. "Observations of Learning to Read and Write Naturally." *Language Arts,* 1981, *58,* 549–556.

Crafton, L. K. "Comprehension before, during and after Reading." *The Reading Teacher,* 1982, *36,* 293–297.

———. "Learning from Reading: What Happens When Students Generate Their Own Background Information?" *Journal of Reading,* 1983, *26,* 586–593.

Forester, A. D. "What Teachers Can Learn from 'Natural Readers.'" *The Reading Teacher,* 1977, *31,* 150–155.

Hoge, S. "A Comprehension-centered Reading Program using Reader Selected Miscues." *Journal of Reading,* 1983, *27,* 52–55.

Hoskisson, K. "Learning to Read Naturally." *Language Arts,* 1979, *56,* 489–496.

Kavale, K., and Schreiner, R. "Psycholinguistic Implications for Beginning Reading Instruction." *Language Arts,* 1978, *55,* 34–40.

King, E. M. "Prereading Programs: Direct versus Incidental Teaching." *The Reading Teacher,* 1978, *31,* 504–510.

Lass, B. "Portrait of My Son as an Early Reader." *The Reading Teacher,* 1982, *36,* 20–28.

Manna, A. L. "Making Language Come Alive through Reading Plays." *The Reading Teacher,* 1984, *37,* 712–717.

Menosky, D. "Making Connections." *Language Arts,* 1981, *58,* 899–900.

Morris, R. D. "Some Aspects of the Instructional Environment and Learning to Read." *Language Arts,* 1979, *56,* 479–502.

Teale, W. H. "Positive Environments for Learning to Read: What Studies of Early Readers Tell Us." *Language Arts,* 1978, *55,* 922–932.

IV *Understanding Oral Reading*

Au, K. L. "Analyzing Oral Reading Errors to Improve Instruction." *The Reading Teacher,* 1977, *31,* 46–49.

Black, J. K. "Those 'Mistakes' Tell Us a Lot." *Language Arts,* 1980, *57,* 505–513.

Dysan, A. H. "Reading, Writing, and Language: Young Children Solving the Written Language Puzzle." *Language Arts,* 1982, *59,* 829–839.

Irwin, P. A., and Mitchell, J. N. "A Procedure for Assessing the Richness of Retellings." *Journal of Reading,* 1983, *26,* 391–396.

Rupley, W. H. "Miscue Analysis Research: Implications for Teacher and Researcher." *The Reading Teacher,* 1977, *30,* 580–583.

V *The Development of Writing*

Bissex, G. L. "Growing Writers in Classrooms." *Language Arts,* 1981, *58,* 785–791.

Calkins, L. M. "Heads up: Write What You See." *Language Arts,* 1978, *55,* 355–357.

———. "Writers Need Readers, not Robins." *Language Arts,* 1978, *55,* 704–707.

———. "Children Write—and Their Writing Becomes Their Textbook." *Language Arts,* 1978, *55,* 804–810.

———. "When Children Want to Punctuate: Basic Skills Belong in Context." *Language Arts,* 1980, *57,* 567–573.

Catroppa, B. D. "Working with Writing Is like Working with Clay." *Language Arts,* 1982, *59,* 687–695.

Cordeiro, P., Giacobbe, M. E., and Cazden, C. "Apostrophes, Quotation Marks, and Periods: Learning Punctuation in the First Grade." *Language Arts,* 1983, *60,* 323–332.

Clay, M. M. "Learning and Teaching Writing: A Developmental Perspective." *Language Arts,* 1982, *59,* 65–70.

Donnelly, C., and Stevens, G. "Streams and Puddles: A Comparison of Two Young Writers." *Language Arts,* 1980, *57,* 735–741.

Dyson, A. H. "Oral Language: The Rooting System for Learning to Write." *Language Arts,* 1981, *58,* 776–784.

Dyson, H. A., and Genishi, C. " 'Whatta Ya Tryin' to Write?': Writing as an Interactive Process." *Language Arts,* 1982, *59,* 126–132.

Edelsky, C., and Smith, K. "Is That Writing—or are Those Marks Just a Figment of Your Curriculum?" *Language Arts,* 1984, *61,* 24–32.

Flowers, B. S. "Madman, Architect, Carpenter, Judge: Roles and the Writing Process." *Language Arts,* 1981, *58,* 834–836.

Golden, J. M. "The Writer's Side: Writing for a Purpose and an Audience." *Language Arts,* 1980, *57,* 756–762.

Graves, D. H. "Handwriting Is for Writing." *Language Arts,* 1979, *55,* 393–399.

———. "We Don't Let Them Write." *Language Arts,* 1978, *55,* 635–640.

———. "How Do Writers Develop?" *Language Arts,* 1982, *59,* 173–179.

Graves, D. H., and Giacobbe, M. E. "Questions for Teachers Who Wonder If Their Writers Change." *Language Arts,* 1982, *59,* 495–503.

Graves, D., and Hansen, J. "The Author's Chair." *Language Arts,* 1983, *60,* 176–183.

Haley-James, S. M. "When Are Children Ready to Write?" *Language Arts,* 1982, *59,* 458–463.

Hauser, C. M. "Encouraging Beginning Writers." *Language Arts,* 1982, *59,* 681–686.

Jett-Simpson, M. "Writing Stories Using Model Structures: The Circle Story." *Language Arts,* 1981, *58,* 293–300.

Klein, A. and Schickedanz, J. "Preschoolers Write Messages and Receive Their Favorite Books." *Language Arts,* 1980, *57,* 742–749.

Lancaster, W., Nelson, L., and Morris, D. "Invented Spellings in Room 112: A Writing Program for Low-Reading Second Graders." *The Reading Teacher,* 1982, *35,* 906–911.

Moss, R. K., and Stansell, J. C. "Wof Stew: A Recipe for Writing and Enjoyment." *Language Arts,* 1983, *60,* 346–349.

Newkirk T. "Archimedes' Dream." *Language Arts,* 1984, *61,* 341–350.

Newman, J. M. "On Becoming A Writer: Child and Teacher." *Language Arts,* 1983, *60,* 860–870.

Pradl, G. M. "Learning How to Begin and End a Story." *Language Arts,* 1979, *56,* 21–25.

Sager, C. "Improving the Quality of Written Composition in the Middle Grades." *Language Arts,* 1977, *54,* 760–762.

Schwartz, M. "Rewriting or Recopying: What Are We Teaching?" *Language Arts,* 1977, *54,* 756–759.

Searle, D., and Dillon, D. "Responding to Student Writing: What Is Said or How It Is Said." *Language Arts,* 1980, *57,* 773–786.

Smith, F. "Myths of Writing." *Language Arts,* 1981, *58,* 792–798.

Staton, J. "Writing and Counseling: Using a Dialog Journal." *Language Arts,* 1980, *57,* 514–518.

Thomas, S. "Making Connections." *Language Arts,* 1982, *59,* 3–7.

Tway, E. "Teacher Responses to Children's Writing." *Language Arts,* 1980, *57,* 763–772.

————. "Six Bland Methods and the Writing Elephant." *Language Arts,* 1983, *60,* 343–345.

Weaver, C. "Welcoming Errors as Signs of Growth." *Language Arts,* 1982, *59,* 438–444.

Wilde, J., and Newkirk, T. "Writing Detective Stories." *Language Arts,* 1981, *58,* 292–296.

Wiseman, D., and Watson, D. "The Good News about Becoming a Writer." *Language Arts,* 1980, *57,* 750–755.

Zarnowski, M. "A Child's Composition: How Does It Hold Together?" *Language Arts,* 1981, *58,* 316–319.

VI *Conferencing*

Calkins, L. M. "Andrea Learns to Make Writing Hard." *Language Arts,* 1979, *56,* 569–576.

————. "Children Learn the Writer's Craft." *Language Arts,* 1980, *57,* 207–213.

Estabrook, I. W. "Talking about Writing—Developing Independent Writers." *Language Arts,* 1982, *59,* 696–706.

Graves, D. H. "What Children Show Us about Revision." *Language Arts,* 1979, *56,* 312–319.

Hansen, J. "Authors Respond to Authors." *Language Arts,* 1983, *60,* 970–976.

Russell, C. "Putting Research into Practice: Conferencing with Young Writers." *Language Arts,* 1983, *60,* 333–340.

VII *The Relationship between Reading and Writing*

Atwell, N. "Writing and Reading Literature from the Inside Out." *Language Arts,* 1984, *61,* 240–252.

Beaver, J. M. *"Say It!* Over and Over." *Language Arts,* 1982, *59,* 143–148.

Blackburn, E. "Common Ground: Developing Relationships between Reading and Writing." *Language Arts,* 1984, *61,* 367–375.

Boutwell, M. A. "Reading and Writing Process: A Reciprocal Agreement." *Language Arts,* 1983, *60,* 723–730.

DeFord, D. E. "Literacy: Reading, Writing and Other Essentials." *Language Arts,* 1981, *58,* 652–658.

DeFord, D., and Harste, J. C. "Child Language Research and Curriculum." *Language Arts,* 1982, *59,* 590–601.

Goodman, K., and Goodman, Y. "Reading and Writing Relationships: Pragmatic Function." *Language Arts,* 1983, *60,* 590–599.

Holt, S. L., and Vacca, J. L. "Reading with a Sense of Writer: Writing with a Sense of Reader." *Language Arts,* 1981, *58,* 937–941.

Hoskisson, K. "Writing Is Fundamental." *Language Arts,* 1979, *56,* 892–896.

Morris, D. "Concept of Word: A Developmental Phenomenon in the Beginning Reading and Writing Processes." *Language Arts,* 1981, *58,* 659–668.

Moss, J. F. "Reading and Discussing Fairy Tales—Old and New." *The Reading Teacher,* 1982, *35,* 656–660.

Smith, F. "Reading like a Writer." *Language Arts,* 1983, *60,* 558–567.

Teale, W. "Toward a Theory of How Children Learn to Read and Write Naturally." *Language Arts,* 1982, *59,* 555–570.

Tierney, R. J., and LaZansky, J. "The Rights and Responsibilities of Readers and Writers: A Contractual Agreement." *Language Arts,* 1980, *57,* 606–613.

Wilson, M. J. "A Review of Recent Research on the Integration of Reading and Writing." *The Reading Teacher,* 1981, *34,* 896–901.

Wiseman, D. L. "Helping Children Take Early Steps toward Reading and Writing." *The Reading Teacher,* 1984, *37,* 340–345.

VIII *The Development of Spelling*

Beers, J. W., and Beers, C. S. "Vowel Spelling Strategies among First and Second Graders: A Growing Awareness of Written Words." *Language Arts,* 1980, *57,* 166–172.

Beers, C. S., and Beers, J. W. "Three Assumptions about Learning to Spell." *Language Arts,* 1981, *58,* 573–580.

Beers, J. W., Beers, C. S., and Grant, K. "The Logic Behind Children's Spelling." *The Elementary School Journal,* 1977, *19,* 238–242.

Gentry, J. R. "Learning to Spell Developmentally." *The Reading Teacher*, 1978, *31*, 632–637.

———. "An Analysis of Developmental Spelling in *GYNS AT WRK*." *The Reading Teacher*, 1982, *36*, 192–201.

Johnson, T. D., Langford, K. G., and Quorn, K. C. "Characteristics of an Effective Spelling Program." *Language Arts*, 1981, *58*, 581–590.

Marino, J. L. "What Makes a Good Speller?" *Language Arts*, 1980, *57*, 173–177.

———. "Spelling Errors: From Analysis to Instruction." *Language Arts*, 1981, *58*, 567–572.

Rule, R. "The Spelling Process: A Look at Strategies." *Language Arts*, 1982, *59*, 379–384.

Templeton, S. "Young Children Invent Words: Developing Concepts of 'Word-ness.'" *The Reading Teacher*, 1980, *33*, 454–459.

Zutell, J. "Some Psycholinguistic Perspectives on Children's Spelling." *Language Arts*, 1978, *55*, 844–851.

 Predictable Books

Abrahamson, R. F. "An Analysis of Children's Favorite Picture Story-books." *The Reading Teacher*, 1980, *34*, 167–170.

———. "An Update of Wordless Picture Books with an Annotated Bibliography." *The Reading Teacher*, 1981, *34*, 417–421.

Armstrong, M. K. "Petunia and Beyond: Literature for the Kindergarten Crowd." *The Reading Teacher*, 1981, *35*, 192–195.

Bridge, C. "Predictable Materials for Beginning Readers." *Language Arts*, 1978, *55*, 593–597.

Bridge, C. A., Winograd, P. N., and Haley, D. "Using Predictable Materials vs. Preprimers to Teach Beginning Sight Words." *The Reading Teacher*, 1983, *36*, 884–891.

Emans, R. "Children's Rhymes and Learning to Read." *Language Arts*, 1978, *55*, 937–940.

Kantor, K. J. "'A Camel in the Harbor': Poetry and Prediction." *Language Arts*, 1978, *55*, 933–963.

Lauritzen, C. "Oral Literature and the Teaching of Reading." *The Reading Teacher*, 1980, *33*, 787–790.

Rhodes, L. K. "I Can Read! Predictable Books as Resources for Reading and Writing Instruction."*The Reading Teacher*, 1981, *38*, 511–518.

Tompkins, G. E., and Webeler, M. B. "What Will Happen Next? Using Predictable Books with Young Children." *The Reading Teacher*, 1983, *36*, 498–503.

 Shared Reading Experiences

Carbo, M. "Teaching Reading with Talking Books." *The Reading Teacher*, 1978, *32*, 267–273.

———. "Making Books Talk to Children." *The Reading Teacher*, 1981, *35*, 186–189.

Chomsky, C. "After Decoding: What?" *Language Arts,* 1976, *53,* 288–296, 314.

Hoskisson, K. "The Many Facets of Assisted Reading." *Elementary English,* 1975, *52,* 312–315.

Lauritzen, D. "A Modification of Repeated Readings for Group Instruction." *The Reading Teacher,* 1982, *35,* 456–458.

Slaughter, J. P. "Big Books for Little Kids: Another Fad or a New Approach for Teaching Beginning Reading?" *The Reading Teacher,* 1983, *36,* 758–763.

XI *Language Experience*

Hall, M. "Language-centered Reading: Premises and Recommendations." *Language Arts,* 1979, *56,* 664–670.

Johnson, T. D. "Language Experience: We Can't All Write What We Can Say." *The Reading Teacher,* 1977, *31,* 297–299.

Pienaar, P. T. "Breakthrough in Beginning Reading: Language Experience Approach." *The Reading Teacher,* 1977, *30,* 489–496.

Sulzby, E. "Using Children's Dictated Stories to Aid Comprehension." *The Reading Teacher,* 1980, *33,* 772–778.

XII *Sustained Silent Reading*

Farrell, E. "SSR as the Core of a Junior High Reading Program." *Journal of Reading,* 1982, *26,* 484–51.

Gambrell, L. B. "Getting Started with Sustained Silent Reading and Keeping It Going." *The Reading Teacher,* 1978, *32,* 328–331.

Hong, L. K. "Modifying SSR for Beginning Readers." *The Reading Teacher,* 1981, *34,* 888–891.

Levine, S. G. "USSR—A Necessary Component in Teaching Reading," *Journal of Reading,* 1984, *27,* 394–399.

Mork, T. A. "Sustained Silent Reading in the Classroom." *The Reading Teacher,* 1972, *26,* 438–441.

McCracken, R. A., and McCracken, M. J. "Modeling Is the Key to Sustained Silent Reading." *The Reading Teacher,* 1978, *31,* 406–408.

XIII *Text Structure*

Applebee, A. N. "A Sense of Story." *Theory into Practice,* 1977, *16,* 342–347.

———. "Children's Narratives: New Directions." *The Reading Teacher,* 1980, *34,* 137–142.

Beck, I. L., and McKeown, M. G. "Developing Questions That Promote Comprehension: The Story Map." *Language Arts,* 1981, *58,* 913–918.

Bruce, E. "What Makes a Good Story?" *Language Arts*, 1978, *55*, 460–466.

———. "Stories within Stories. *Language Arts*, 1981, *58*, 931–936.

Cleland, C. G. "Highlighting Issues in Children's Literature through Semantic Webbing." *The Reading Teacher*, 1981, *34*, 643–646.

Davidson, J. L. "The Group Mapping Activity for Instruction in Reading and Thinking." *Journal of Reading*, 1982, *26*, 52–56.

Guthrie, J. T. "Story Comprehension." *The Reading Teacher*, 1977, *30*, 574–576.

Hanf, M. B. "Mapping: A Technique for Translating Reading into Thinking." *Journal of Reading*, 1971, *14*, 225–230, 270.

Hennings, D. G. "A Writing Approach to Reading Comprehension: Schema Theory in Action." *Language Arts*, 1978, *59*, 8–17.

King, M. L., and Rentel, V. M. Conveying Meaning in Written Texts." *Language Arts*, 1981, *58*, 721–728.

McConaughty, S. H. "Using Story Structure in the Classroom." *Language Arts*, 1980, *57*, 157–165.

———. "Developmental Changes in Story Comprehension and Levels of Questioning." *Language Arts*, 1982, *59*, 580–589.

Norton, D. E. "A Web of Interest." *Language Arts*, 1977, *54*, 928–932.

———. "Using a Webbing Process to Develop Children's Literature Units." *Language Arts*, 1982, *59*, 348–356.

Olson, M. W. "A Dash of Story Grammar and . . . Presto! A Book Report." *The Reading Teacher*, 1984, *37*, 458–461.

Sadow, M. W. "The Use of Story Grammar in the Design of Questions." *The Reading Teacher*, 1982, *30*, 518–521.

Thelen, J. "Preparing Students for Content Reading Assignments." *Journal of Reading*, 1982, *25*, 544–549.

Tuinman, J. J. "The Schema Schemers." *Journal of Reading*, 1980, *23*, 414–419.

Vaughn, J. L. "Use the ConStruct Procedure to Foster Active Reading and Learning." *Journal of Reading*, 1982, *25*, 412–423.

Whaley, J. F. "Story Grammars and Reading Instruction." *The Reading Teacher*, 1981, *34*, 762–771.

XIV *Literacy and Curriculum*

Billig, E. "Children's Literature as a Springboard to Content Areas." *The Reading Teacher*, 1977, *30*, 855–859.

Hennings, D. G. "Reading Picture Storybooks in the Social Studies." *The Reading Teacher*, 1982, *36*, 284–289.

McClure, A. A. "Integrating Children's Fiction and Informational Literature in a Primary Reading Curriculum."*The Reading Teacher*, 1982, *35*, 784–788.

Mikkelsen, N. "Celebrating Children's Books throughout the Year." *The Reading Teacher*, 1982, *35*, 790–795.

Olson, M., and Hatcher, B. A. "Cultural Journalism: A Bridge to the Past." *Language Arts*, 1982, *59*, 46–51.

Smarco, F. A. "Using Children's Literature to Clarify Science Concepts in Early Childhood Programs." *The Reading Teacher,* 1982, *36,* 267–273.

XV *Helping Nonfluent Readers*

Cunningham, P. M. "Teaching Were, With, What, and Other 'Four-Letter' Words." *The Reading Teacher,* 1980, *33,* 160–163.

Cunningham, P. "Horizontal Reading." *The Reading Teacher,* 1980, *33,* 222–224.

Eeds, M. "What to Do When They Don't Understand What They Read: Research-based Strategies for Teaching Reading Comprehension." *The Reading Teacher,* 1981, *34,* 565–571.

Gaskin, I. W. "A Writing Program for Poor Readers and Writers and the Rest of the Class, Too." *Language Arts,* 1982, *59,* 854–863.

Harman, S. "Are Reversals a Symptom of Dyslexia?" *The Reading Teacher,* 1982, *35,* 424–428.

Manzo, A. V. "The ReQuest Procedure." *Journal of Reading,* 1969, *12,* 123–126.

Maring, G. H. "Matching Remediation to Miscues." *The Reading Teacher,* 1978, *31,* 887–891.

Rice, E. M. "Tutor and Child, Partners in Learning." *Language Arts,* 1984, *61,* 18–23.

Singer, H. "Active Comprehension: From Answering to Asking Questions." *The Reading Teacher,* 1978, *31,* 901–907.

Smith, J. P. "Writing in a Remedial Reading Program: A Case Study." *Language Arts,* 1982, *59,* 245–253.

Stansell, J. C., and DeFord, D. E. "When Is a Reading Problem Not a Reading Problem?" *Journal of Reading,* 1981, *24,* 14–20.

Watson, D. J. "In College and in Trouble—with Reading." *Journal of Reading,* 1982, *25,* 640–645.

XVI *Peer Tutoring*

Ellis, D. W., and Preston, F. W. "Enhancing Beginning Reading Using Wordless Picture Books in a Cross-Age Tutoring Program." *The Reading Teacher,* 1984, *37,* 692–699.

King, R. T. "Learning from a PAL." *The Reading Teacher,* 1982, *35,* 682–685.

Lehr, F. "ETIC/RCS: Peer Teaching." *The Reading Teacher,* 1984, *37,* 636–641.

XVII *Parents and Reading*

Bingham, A. "Writing Newletters for Parents." *Language Arts,* 1982, *59,* 445–450.

Hoskisson, K., Sherman, T. M., and Smith, L. L. "Assisted Reading and Parent Involvement." *The Reading Teacher,* 1974, *27,* 710–714.

Nicholson, T. "Why We Need to Talk to Parents about Reading." *The Reading Teacher*, 1980, *34*, 19–21.

Teale, W. H. "Parents Reading to their Children: What We Know and Need to Know." *Language Arts*, 1981, *58*, 902–912.

Vukelich, C. "Parents' Role in the Reading Process: A Review of Practical Suggestions and Ways to Communicate with Parents." *The Reading Teacher*, 1984, *37*, 472–477.

XVIII *Teachers as Researchers*

Bayer, A. S. "Teachers Talking to Learn." *Language Arts*, 1984, *61*, 131–140.

Brause, R. S., and Mayher, J. S. "Learning through Teaching: The Classroom Teacher as Researcher." *Language Arts*, 1983, *60*, 758–765.

Brice-Heath, S. "Research Currents: A Lot of Talk about Nothing." *Language Arts, 1983, 60*, 999–1007.

Rich, S. "On Becoming Teacher Experts: Teacher-Researchers." *Language Arts*, 1983, *60*, 892–894.

XIX *Books about Literacy Development*

Barnes, D. *From Communication to Curriculum*. Harmondsworth: Penguin, 1976.

Beers, J., and Henderson, E. *Developmental and Cognitive Aspects of Learning to Spell: A Reflection of Word Knowledge*. Newark, Del.: International Reading Association, 1980.

Bissex, G. *GNYS AT WRK: A Child Learns to Write and Read*. Cambridge, Mass.: Harvard University Press, 1980.

Clay, M. M. *What Did I Write?* Portsmouth, N.H.: Heinemann Educational Books, 1975.

Calkins, L. M. *Lessons from a Child*. Portsmouth, N.H.: Heinemann Educational Books, 1983.

DeFord D. E. (ed.) *Learning to Write: An Expression of Language (Theory into Practice)*. Columbus, Ohio: College of Education, The Ohio State University, 1980.

Donaldson, M. *Chidren's Minds*. New York: W.W. Norton & Co., 1978.

Goodman, K. S. *Miscue Analysis: Application to Reading Instruction*. Urbana, Ill.: NCTE, 1973.

Goodman, Y., and Burke, C. *Reading Strategies: Focus on Comprehension*. New York: Holt, Rinehart and Winston, 1980.

Graves, D. *Writing: Teachers & Children at Work*. Portsmouth, N.H.: Heinemann Educational Books, 1983.

Harste, J., Woodward, V., and Burke, C. *Language Stories and Literacy Lessons*. Portsmouth, N.H.: Heinemann Educational Books, 1984.

Holdaway, D. *The Foundations of Literacy*. Sydney, Australia: Ashton Scholastic, 1979.

Newkirk, T., and Atwell, N. *Understanding Writing: Ways of Observing, Learning and Teaching.* Chelmsford, Mass.: The Northeast Regional Exchange, Inc., 1982.

Newman, J. M. *The Craft of Children's Writing.* Toronto: Scholastic, 1984.

Smith, E. B., Goodman, K. S., and Meredith, R. *Language and Thinking in School.* New York: Holt, Rinehart and Winston, 1975.

Smith, F. *Understanding Reading,* 3rd ed. New York: Holt, Rinehart and Winston, 1982.

————. *Writing and the Writer.* New York: Holt, Rinehart and Winston, 1982.

————. *Essays into Literacy.* Portsmouth, N.H.: Heinemann Educational Books, 1983.

Taylor, D. *Family Literacy: Young Children Learning to Read and Write.* Portsmouth, N.H.: Heinemann Educational Books, 1983.

Wells, G. *Learning through Interaction: The Study of Language Development.* Cambridge: Cambridge University Press, 1981.

Wilkinson, A., Barnsely, G., Hanna, P., and Swan, M. *Assessing Language Development.* Oxford: Oxford University Press, 1980.